T0329971

Industrial Concentration
and Economic Inequality

Industrial Concentration and Economic Inequality

Essays in Honour of Peter Hart

Edited by

Mark Casson

University of Reading, UK

and

John Creedy

University of Melbourne, Australia

Edward Elgar

Published by
Edward Elgar Publishing Limited
Gower House
Croft Road
Aldershot
Hants   GU11 3HR
England

Edward Elgar Publishing Company
Old Post Road
Brookfield
Vermont 05036
USA

A CIP catalogue record for this book
is available from the British Library

ISBN 978 1 85278 648 9

Printed and bound by CPI Group (UK) Ltd, Croydon, CR0 4YY

Contents

Contributors

Tony Atkinson is Professor of Political Economy, University of Cambridge, and Fellow of Churchill College. He was previously Thomas Tooke Professor of Economic Science and Statistics at the London School of Economics, and Chairman of STICERD (Suntory-Toyota International Centre for Economics and Related Disciplines). He is the author of numerous books, including *Economics of Inequality* (Oxford: Oxford University Press, 1975), *Lectures on Public Economics* (with Joseph Stiglitz) (London: McGraw Hill, 1980), *Poverty and Social Security* (London: Harvester, 1989) and *Economic Transformation in Eastern Europe and the Distribution of Income* (with John Micklewright) (Cambridge: Cambridge University Press, 1993).

John Cantwell is Reader in International Economics at the University of Reading. He was appointed Lecturer in Economics in 1984, and became Reader in 1991. He has been a Visiting Professor of Economics at the University of Rome 'La Sapienza' (in 1988 and 1990) and the University of the Social Sciences, Toulouse (in 1990). His main research areas are the economics of technological change and international production. He is the author of *Technological Innovation and Multinational Corporations* (Oxford: Basil Blackwell, 1989). He has especially worked on international aspects of technological change and is currently directing an Economic and Social Research Council funded project into the historical structure of innovative activity in the UK, Europe and the USA since 1890. He is also known for his writings on the theory and statistics of international production. Dr Cantwell is the co-ordinator of a network of economists from six European countries working on multinational company activity and the completion of the EC's single market, supported under the EC Stimulation Plan for Economic Science. He is President of the European International Business Association and was the convener of its Annual Meeting in Reading in December 1992.

Mark Casson is Professor of Economics at the University of Reading. He was one of Peter Hart's undergraduate tutees at Bristol University and joined Reading University as a lecturer two years after Peter Hart was appointed Professor of Economics there. His recent publications include

Enterprise and Competitiveness (Oxford: Oxford University Press, 1990) and *Economics of Business Culture* (Oxford: Oxford University Press, 1991). He has also recently edited volumes on *Entrepreneurship* (Aldershot: Edward Elgar, 1991), *Multinational Corporations* (Aldershot: Edward Elgar, 1991), *International Business and Global Integration* (London: Macmillan, 1992) and related topics, including a *festschrift* for another Reading colleague, John Dunning.

Roger Clarke is Professor of Economics at the University of Wales, College of Cardiff, having previously held appointments at the National Institute of Economic and Social Research, Reading University, Sheffield University, Tulane University (New Orleans) and George Washington University (Washington, D.C.). His main areas of research activity are in microeconomics, industrial economics, and the theory of the firm, and he has published a number of books and articles in these fields including *Concentration in British Industry* (with Peter Hart) (Cambridge: Cambridge University Press, 1980), *Industrial Economics* (Oxford: Basil Blackwell, 1985) and *Economics of the Firm* (with Tony McGuinness) (Oxford: Basil Blackwell, 1987). He is a joint co-ordinator of the ESRC Industrial Economics Study Group and an associate editor of the *Journal of Industrial Economics*.

John Creedy is the Truby Williams Professor of Economics at the University of Melbourne, and a Fellow of the Academy of Social Sciences in Australia. He was educated at Bristol and Oxford Universities and has previously taught at the universities of Reading, Durham and The Pennsylvania State University. Books include: *State Pensions in Britain* (Cambridge: Cambridge University Press, 1982), *Economics: An Integrated Approach* (with others) (Englewood Cliffs, N.J.: Prentice-Hall, 1984), *Dynamics of Income Distribution* (Oxford: Basil Blackwell, 1985), *Edgeworth and the Development of Neoclassical Economics* (Oxford: Basil Blackwell, 1986), *Social Insurance in Transition: An Economic Analysis* (with Richard Disney) (Oxford: Oxford University Press, 1985), *Demand and Exchange in Economics: A History from Cournot to Marshall* (Aldershot: Edward Elgar, 1992), *Income, Inequality and the Life Cycle* (Aldershot: Edward Elgar, 1992). Edited books include: *The Economics of Unemployment in Britain* (London: Butterworths, 1984), *Economic Analysis in Historical Perspective* (with D.P. O'Brien) (London: Butterworths, 1984), *Foundations of Economic Thought* (Oxford: Basil Blackwell, 1990), *Recent Developments in Game Theory* (with J. Borland and J. Eichberger) (Aldershot: Edward Elgar,

1992), *Chaos and Non-linear Models in Economics* (with V. Martin) (Aldershot: Edward Elgar, 1993).

Richard Disney is Professor of Economics at the University of Kent at Canterbury, and Research Fellow, Institute for Fiscal Studies, London. He has also held teaching and research appointments at Reading University, Strathclyde University and the National University of Ethiopia. He has written books and numerous articles on labour economics and the economics of social security, with current interests focusing on the economics of pensions, and models of trade union behaviour and impact. Books include *Social Insurance in Transition: An Economic Analysis* (with John Creedy) (Oxford: Oxford University Press, 1985) and *Helping the Unemployed* (with Alan Carruth, Richard Layard and others) (London: Anglo-German Foundation, 1992).

Patrick Francois is currently completing a doctorate at the University of British Columbia, Canada. He has BComm and MA degrees from the University of Melbourne. Research interests include public choice, industrial organization and development economics. He has published several papers on financing higher education and voting over tax schedules.

N. Anders Klevmarken is Professor of Econometrics at the Swedish Council for the Humanities and Social Sciences and located at the Department of Economics, Göteborg University, Sweden. He received his PhD in statistics from the University of Stockholm in 1972 and was appointed Docent in Statistics in 1972 (University of Stockholm) and in Economics in 1983 (Göteborg University). Among his previous positions were Professor of Statistics at Göteborg University, Head of the Department for Evaluation and Research at the National Swedish Insurance Board, senior reseach associate at the Industrial Institute for Economic and Social Research (IUI) and Associate Research Professor of Empirical Econometrics at the Swedish Council for Social Science Research. He has also been Visiting Professor at the University of Michigan and the University of Georgia. He is the 1992 President of the European Society for Population Economics, member of the co-ordinating committee of the European Science Foundation Network on Household Panel Studies, member of the Swedish Council for Social Research, the Tore Browaldh Scientific Foundation, the Gothenburg School of Economics Research Funds, the Scientific Council of Statistics, Sweden, and of the Supervisory Committee for the Consumer Price Index of Sweden. His research covers topics in labour economics (pay-setting, the structure of earnings), population economics (fertility), demand analysis (complete systems of demand functions) and econometric methods. He is presently directing the HUS panel study of Swedish households.

John Micklewright is Reader in Economics at Queen Mary and Westfield College, University of London, and Associate Professor of Economics at the European University Institute, Florence. He graduated from Exeter University, gained his PhD from the London School of Economics in 1984, and was subsequently Prize Research Fellow at Nuffield College, Oxford. He specialises in research on public economics and the distribution of income.

Eleanor J. Morgan is a Senior Lecturer in Industrial Economics at the School of Management, University of Bath, and Director of the full time MBA. She graduated in Economics from University College London and the University of Massachusetts, Amherst. She spent three years at Reading University where she collaborated with Peter Hart on research into structure–performance relationships in UK manufacturing. Since moving to Bath in 1975, her research and publications have been mainly concerned with economic aspects of decision-making within the firm, especially investment behaviour, and the interactions between regulation, the competitive environment and business performance.

Anthony Shorrocks is Professor of Economics at the University of Essex and Director of Economic Research for the British Household Panel Study. He has also held teaching positions at the London School of Economics, Queen's University in Ontario and Southern Methodist University in Dallas. He has published widely on topics concerned with economic welfare, income inequality, poverty and wealth distribution, with particular emphasis on measurement issues and the construction of indices. Publications include *Personal Income Distribution* (editor, with W.Krelle) (Amsterdam: North Holland, 1978).

Satwinder Singh is Senior Research Fellow in Economics at the University of Reading. He has worked in the areas of technology management in multinational enterprises and the competitive behaviour of firms. He is currently working on western multinationals in developing countries and, with Mark Casson, on the economics of human resource management in multinational enterprises. He has taught in the areas of industrial economics and international business. His publications include *Globalising Research and Development* (with Robert Pearce) (London:

Macmillan, 1992), *Multinational Corporations and the Indian Drug Industry* (Delhi: Criterion Publications, 1985), and several papers and chapters in edited volumes on international business.

Michael Utton is Professor of Economics at the University of Reading where he was formerly Lecturer and Reader. For a number of years he was a consultant at the National Institute of Economic and Social Research where he worked with Peter Hart on a project which led to the publication of *Mergers and Concentration in British Industry* (Cambridge: Cambridge University Press, 1973). Other books have included *Diversification and Competition* (Cambridge: Cambridge University Press, 1979), *The Political Economy of Big Business* (Oxford: Basil Blackwell, 1982), *The Profits and Stability of Monopoly* (Cambridge: Cambridge University Press, 1986) and *The Economics of Regulating Industry* (Oxford: Basil Blackwell, 1986). He has recently been working on an empirical study of strategic behaviour by UK firms as well as on a book on market dominance and antitrust policy.

Michael Waterson is Professor of Economics at the University of Warwick. He has taught previously at the University of Reading and the University of Newcastle upon Tyne and, as a visitor, at the University of Sydney. He is the author of two books: *Economic Theory of the Industry* (Cambridge: Cambridge University Press, 1984) and *Regulation of the Firm and Natural Monopoly* (Oxford: Basil Blackwell, 1988). He has published over 30 papers in scholarly journals and has made a number of other contributions to the literature. His academic interests lie mainly in the area of industrial economics.

Edward Whitehouse read PPE at Jesus College, Oxford, and joined the Institute of Fiscal Studies, London, as Research Officer in 1989. His research focuses on wage determination, retirement behaviour and pensions, some of it being carried out jointly with Richard Disney and Costas Meghir.

Bibliography of Peter Hart's Publications on Industrial Concentration and Income Inequality

1956   The analysis of business concentration: a statistical approach (with S.J. Prais), *Journal of the Royal Statistical Society*, Series A, **119**, 150–91.

1957   On measuring business concentration, *Bulletin of the Oxford Institute of Statistics*, **19**, 225–48.

1958   Concentration in selected industries, *Scottish Journal of Political Economy*, **5**, 185–201.

1960   Business concentration in the United Kingdom, *Journal of the Royal Statistical Society*, Series A, **123**, 50–88.

Concentration and its measurement in the UK, in *Die Konzentration in der Wirtschaft*, vol. 1, ed. H. Arndt (Berlin: Duncker & Humblot) 653–74.

1961   Statistical measures of concentration v. concentration ratios, *Review of Economics and Statistics*, **43**, 85–6.

The use of moments and moment distributions to measure concentration, *Papers and Proceedings* [of] *Verein für Socialpolitik Conference*, Bad Kissingen, 1960.

1962   Size and growth of the firm, *Economica*, N.S. **29**, 29–39.

1965   *Studies in Profits, Business Saving and Investment in the UK, 1920–1960*, vol. I (London: Allen & Unwin).

1968   (editor) *Studies in Profits, Business Saving and Investment in the UK*, 1920–60, vol. II (London: Allen Unwin).

1971   Entropy and other measures of concentration, *Journal of the Royal Statistical Society*, Series A, **134**, 108–25.

1973   *Mergers and Concentration in British Industry* (with M.A. Utton and G. Walshe) (Cambridge: Cambridge University Press).

1975   Moment distributions in economics: an exposition, *Journal of the Royal Statistical Society*, Series A, **138**, 423–34.

1976   The comparative statics and dynamics of income distributions, *Journal of the Royal Statistical Society*, Series A, **139**, 108–25.

The dynamics of earnings, 1963–1973, *Economic Journal*, **86**, 551–65.

1977   Market structure and economic performance in the United Kingdom (with Eleanor Morgan), *Journal of Industrial Economics*, **25**, 177–93.

1979   On bias and concentration, *Journal of Industrial Economics*, **27**, 211–26.

Age and the distribution of earnings (with John Creedy), *Economic Journal*, **89**, 280–93.

1980   *Concentration in British Industry 1935–75* (with Roger Clarke) (Cambridge: Cambridge University Press).

Lognormality and the principle of transfers, *Oxford Bulletin of Economics and Statistics*, **42**, 263–7.

1981   The effects of mergers on industrial concentration, *Journal of Industrial Economics*, **29**, 315–20.

The statics and dynamics of income distributions: a survey, in N.A. Klevmarken and J.A. Lybeck (eds), *The Statics and Dynamics of Income* (Clevedon: Tieto) 1–20.

The distribution of cohort incomes in Sweden 1960–73: a comparative static analysis (with John Creedy, A. Jonsson and N.A. Klevmarken), in Klevmarken and Lybeck, op. cit. 55–80.

Income mobility in Great Britain and Sweden (with John Creedy and N.A. Klevmarken), in Klevmarken and Lybeck, op. cit., 195–211.

1982   Entropy, moments and aggregate business concentration, *Oxford Bulletin of Economics and Statistics*, **44**, 113–26.

1983   The size mobility of earnings, *Oxford Bulletin of Economics and Statistics*, **45**, 181–93.

1986   Growth patterns of the world's largest firms (with R.D. Pearce), *Weltwirtschaftliches Archiv*, **122**, 65–79.

1987   The lognormal distribution, in *The New Palgrave: A Dictionary of Economic Theory and Doctrine* (London: Macmillan) 156.

Introduction

This volume of specially contributed chapters, on a range of topics within the general areas of industrial concentration and economic inequality, is presented as a tribute to Peter Hart, who has himself made many significant contributions to these closely related subjects. Many authors of the following chapters have benefited directly from Peter Hart's generous advice and friendship as a colleague, particularly at the University of Reading, as well as indirectly from his writings. A list of his publications in these areas precedes this Introduction, but it should be stressed that this represents just a proportion of his total work. However, the list demonstrates the range of contributions: from theoretical examinations of the properties of measures of industrial concentration and income inequality, to the detailed empirical explorations of changes in concentration over time and the factors associated with those changes.

Many alternative measures of inequality and concentration have been proposed in the literature. Peter Hart has contributed to the understanding of the properties of many such measures. In using particular measures he has always stressed the importance of ascertaining the form of the relevant distributions, since such information immediately allows results about the behaviour of a wide range of measures to be used. In adopting specific functional forms for describing the size distribution of firms, trade unions or personal incomes, his work is also notable for the enthusiastic (though of course qualified) use of the lognormal distribution, with its associated and highly tractable moment distributions which play such a central role in inequality measurement; see, for example, the surveys in Hart (1975, 1987). An example of the use of the lognormal and its moment distributions within wider economic models is provided in Chapter 4.

A valuable lesson to be obtained from much of Peter Hart's work is that considerable attention should be given to the dynamics as well as to the statics of concentration and income inequality. He often stressed that a static view or 'snapshot' of an economy at a particular point in time does not provide sufficient information on which to pass judgements or formulate appropriate policies. What is required is detailed information about the dynamic processes involved, such as the way concentration is influenced by the relative growth of firms and the way in which income inequality is influenced by individuals' mobility within the income distribution over time.

For example, he has argued that 'the traditional link between incentives and inequality is misleading: it is mobility and the prospect of going up, or down, the distribution of incomes which provides incentives' (1983, p. 190). However, incentives are not directly related to mobility in a simple linear way. Thus he argued that both extreme immobility (as in a caste society) and extreme mobility (reflecting considerable uncertainty about income prospects) are harmful to incentives. This leads to the argument that there is some optimal value of mobility in society; see Hart (1983, p. 191; 1976, p. 112). The argument that incentives are not simply related to static inequality suggests importantly that a concern to provide incentives is 'not inconsistent with a desire to help the poor' (1976, p. 112).

A further implication of the need to consider dynamics is that a cross-sectional view of, say, the distribution of individuals in different age groups may give quite misleading information about the experience of particular cohorts over their life-cycles. This kind of emphasis led to pioneering longitudinal studies, often involving a great deal of effort in order to obtain unpublished data. Early studies of income dynamics used samples specially selected from records used for the administration of the National Insurance system in the UK.

It is appropriate here to pay tribute to his exemplary behaviour in encouraging other researchers to use in their own work the data which he had taken so much trouble to obtain, even before he had published his own findings. He also generously gave much time and energy in advising others how to make the best use of their data, when there was no prospect of obtaining the data for his own use. With the more recent availability of several large data sets giving longitudinal information, it is perhaps easy for the modern researcher to forget just how scarce such data were and how much effort was required to persuade those in authority to collect and make available the required data. Those using such data sets in the UK are much indebted to Peter Hart's efforts and to his own demonstrations that much can be learnt from careful analysis of them.

An example of the use of longitudinal earnings data to examine mobility is provided in Chapter 3. Economists are, of course, seldom able to obtain the precise data required and must learn how to make the best use, and understand the limitations, of available data. Chapter 2 illustrates this problem and explores the available data on income distribution in Eastern Europe

In examining the dynamics of distributions Peter Hart has long been an enthusiastic advocate of the use of regression methods, using the sense of the word 'regression' as originally intended in the pioneering work of Francis Galton (in his studies of inherited characteristics). This contrasts, for example, with the extensive use of measures of mobility based on empirical transition matrices. The basic Galtonian model, of firm size or earnings mobility, involves a modification of Gibrat's famous 'law of proportionate effect' in which successive proportional changes (in the ratio of income to geometric mean income) are independent and apparently random. The Galtonian model allows for 'regression' either towards or away from the (geometric) mean, permitting those with relatively lower incomes to experience, on average, either larger or smaller percentage increases. The regression coefficient measures this tendency, while the reciprocal of the correlation coefficient measures the degree of mobility. The basic model can be written simply as:

$$Y_{i,t} = \beta \, Y_{i,t-1} + u_{it}$$

where Y is the logarithm of the ratio of an individual's income (or firm size, say) to the geometric mean. If ρ denotes the correlation between Y_t and Y_{t-1}, and the variance of u is σ_u^2, then the ratio of the standard deviation of Y_t to Y_{t-1} is the ratio of the regression to the correlation coefficent. Thus it is possible for inequality (as measured by the variance of logarithms) to increase over time even if there is significant 'regression towards the mean' (reflected in a value of β less than unity). A combination of systematic 'equalizing' changes with a high degree of relative earnings mobility may therefore lead to increasing inequality, so that a simple judgement based only on observed changes in inequality may not be appropriate. Alternative situations are discussed in detail in Hart (1976, p. 113). In the simple Galton model, the variance of growth rates can be shown to be equal to $\sigma_u^2 + (1-\beta)^2 \, \text{var} \, (Y_{t-1})$, and therefore depends on the regression coefficent as well as the variance of the us, and the initial dispersion of the Ys. Instead of using the variance of growth rates as a measure of mobility, the reciprocal of the correlation coefficient is therefore used.

This approach was used in the influential pioneering work of Hart and Prais (1956) on the growth of firms and was later applied to earnings dynamics. The basic model can also be modified to allow for successive proportional changes to be serially correlated; this allows for the hypothesis that 'success breeds success' to be tested, if sufficient data are available, since at least three time periods are required. A later study of the world's largest firms along these lines was reported in Hart and Pearce (1986), and the approach was used in a number of studies of earnings dynamics, including Hart (1976) and Creedy and Hart (1979).

It is therefore fitting that Chapter 1 examines in detail the properties of the 'Hart' mobility measure, and compares it with other measures that have been proposed. Extensive use of the approach is also made in Chapter 11.

Peter Hart fully recognized that, since the Galtonian process can only be applied to a constant sample of firms or individuals, attention must also be given to 'births and deaths'. In the context of industrial concentration, this also means that appropriate allowance must be made for mergers. In order to judge the relative importance of mergers in the process of industrial concentration, Hart and Prais (1956) used a decomposition of the variance of logarithms of firm size. The approach has, of course, had its critics, but has been defended in Hart (1979, 1980). It is appropriate that mergers, and particularly merger policy, are discussed in the present volume, and this forms the subject of Chapters 8 and 9.

The work on industrial concentration is in the tradition of the structure–conduct–performance debate, in which information about the structure of an industry is regarded as giving information about the conduct of participants, therefore providing a guide to policy-makers. Chapter 7 is within this tradition, while Chapter 6 discusses the neglect of this type of work arising from the recent emphasis within the field of industrial organization of game theory.

In discussing the relevance of earnings dynamics to economic policy formulation, Peter Hart referred briefly to the proposed UK government pension scheme, in which the pension was based on the individual's best 20 years of earnings. He argued that 'since the best twenty years for an individual depend not only on this time path [of average earnings], but also on irregular movements around it, any forecast of the cost of pensions based merely on the average path, or even worse, merely on the average income in a cross-section, is likely severely to underestimate the future pensions burden' (1976, p. 561). Despite this warning, official estimates neglected these important dynamic aspects, and changes in the pension scheme were subsequently made. The use of extensive information about earnings dynamics to examine pensions schemes is illustrated in Chapter 5.

While at the University of Reading, Peter Hart has influenced not only research on topics in which he has specialized but also research on rather different topics carried out by other groups in the department. For example, Cantwell and Pearce have focused their research on international business issues, and Casson and Singh also fit into this category. For them Peter Hart has been first and foremost a role model, demonstrating the value of scholarly empiricism in researching policy issues. Chapter 10 on research and development strategies exemplifies the wide range of research at Reading which has been indirectly influenced by Peter Hart.

Like any academic profession, economics contains many different people with different personalities, ranging from the quiet scholar on the one hand to the entrepreneur and publicist on the other. There is, perhaps, a tendency for the latter type to attract too much attention to themselves. Credit does not always go to those to whom it is really due. This volume will have succeeded in its purpose if it helps to correct this imbalance, by bringing to the attention of more people a substantial body of research pioneered by Peter Hart himself and carried out under his influence by an enthusiastic and appreciative group of younger colleagues.

PART I

Income Inequality

1. On the Hart Measure of Income Mobility

Anthony F. Shorrocks[1]

1.1 INTRODUCTION

Peter Hart has been a pioneer of research on income mobility. In his view, the 'snapshots' provided by income distributions in a single year are valuable sources of information on living standards, inequality and poverty. But their significance can only be fully appreciated in the context of a 'movie' which reveals how the cross-section pattern evolves over time and, more importantly, how individuals shift around within the overall distribution. The more complete picture provided by income dynamics may well modify the conclusions drawn on the basis of cross section evidence regarding the relative desirability of the alternative social processes that generate these data (Hart, 1981).

The framework employed most often by Hart is the Galtonian model

$$\ln x_{t+1} = \alpha_t + \beta_t \ln x_t + \varepsilon_{t+1} , \qquad (1.1)$$

where ε_{t+1} is identically and independently distributed across individuals and has expected value zero. This simple specification of income dynamics can be used to address issues concerned with both individual income fluctuations over time and the impact of mobility on the distribution as a whole. At the level of individual profiles, the value of β_t captures the extent to which incomes regress towards the (geometric) mean income. This is evident if m_t is used to represent the geometric mean income at time t, and equation (1.1) is written in the form

$$\ln (x_{t+1}/m_{t+1}) = \beta_t \ln (x_t/m_t) + \varepsilon_{t+1} . \qquad (1.2)$$

If $\beta_t \in (0,1)$, as normally assumed, those with incomes above the geometric mean at time t can expect a relative decline in their incomes over the next period, while $\beta_t = 1$ corresponds to Gibrat's 'law of proportional effect', where changes in relative income are independent of current income (i.e., a simple random walk). The value of ε_{t+1} represents influences which, while perhaps explicable in terms of personal characteristics and experiences, may be viewed as random shocks from the perspective of the population as a whole. Serial correlation in ε indicates whether those who have done unexpectedly well (from the aggregate perspective) are more likely to be fortunate in subsequent periods. Evidence of positive serial correlation ('success breeds success') or negative serial correlation can prompt speculation on the causes of these phenomena.[2]

As regards the impact of income mobility on the overall distribution, equations (1.1) and (1.2) yield

$$\sigma^2(\ln x_{t+1}) = \beta_t^2 \sigma^2(\ln x_t) + \sigma^2(\varepsilon_{t+1}) . \tag{1.3}$$

This suggests that Galtonian regression ($\beta_t < 1$) tends to reduce inequality, while the random fluctuations captured by ε_{t+1} work in the opposite direction. For a measure of mobility, Hart proposes an index inversely related to the correlation coefficient between $\ln x_t$ and $\ln x_{t+1}$. The Hart index of mobility may therefore be defined as[3]

$$H(x_t, x_{t+1}) = 1 - r(\ln x_t, \ln x_{t+1}), \tag{1.4}$$

where $r(\cdot)$ denotes the sample correlation coefficient. Assuming that $\text{cov}(\ln x_t, \varepsilon_{t+1}) = 0$ in equation (1.1), this can be rewritten

$$H(x_t, x_{t+1}) = 1 - \hat{\beta}_t \frac{s(\ln x_t)}{s(\ln x_{t+1})} , \tag{1.5}$$

where $\hat{\beta}_t$ is the OLS estimate of β_t and $s(\cdot)$ denotes the sample standard deviation. Thus, given the marginal distributions x_t and x_{t+1}, the degree of mobility depends only on the value of the Galtonian coefficient β_t, although this is linked to the value of $\sigma^2(\varepsilon)$ via equation (1.3).

The principal objective of this chapter is to evaluate the performance of the Hart index as a measure of income mobility. Of course, if the Galtonian equation (1.1) accurately describes income dynamics in the real world, the values of β_t, together with the cross section log variances $s^2(\ln x_t)$, summarize everything that needs to be known in the most parsimonious manner, and the Hart index could not be seriously challenged (although the implications of different values of β may need to be explored). On the other hand, if there are doubts concerning the validity of the Galtonian model or, indeed, reservations concerning any specification of income dynamics, the Hart index H may still have a useful role to play as a measure of mobility. The degree of support for this view will depend on whether the properties of H are deemed appropriate and desirable.

Section 1.3 of this chapter examines a number of candidates for desirable index properties, and assesses the performance of the Hart index under each of the criteria. To a large extent, the discussion is driven by a desire to find suitable analogues of the requirements commonly imposed on inequality indices. Section 1.4 summarizes the features of the Hart index and compares its performance with a number of alternative indices. Before addressing these issues, some general points on the concept and measurement of mobility are discussed.

1.2 SUMMARIZING INFORMATION ON INCOME MOBILITY

Suppose that a researcher is faced with an $n \times T$ matrix X of income observations whose typical element x_{it} denotes the income of person i ($i = 1, \ldots, n$) in period t ($t = 1, \ldots, T$). Regard X as an *income structure* and, to avoid unnecessary complications, assume that incomes are always positive. Then

$$\mathscr{X}_{nT} = \{X \mid \dim X = n \times T; \ x_{it} > 0\} \qquad (1.6)$$

denotes the feasible set of n-person, T-period income structures. The periods do not necessarily have to represent consecutive time intervals, although it will be assumed throughout that time periods are numbered chronologically. The marginal (cross-section) distribution in period t will be indicated by the ($n \times 1$) vector x_t, and the arithmetic and geometric mean income in period t by μ_t and m_t, respectively.

One common method of summarizing data on mobility involves a partition of the income range at each time t into a set of income intervals, and the construction of (forward) transition matrices $P(s, t)$, whose typical element $p_{jk}(s, t)$ denotes the proportion of those with incomes in class j at time s who are later found in class k at time t.[4] It is often assumed that the proportions $p_{jk}(s, t)$ can also be interpreted as the transition probabilities of a Markov chain, in which case the sequence of one period transition matrices $P(t, t + 1)$, $t = 1, \ldots, T - 1$, completely characterize the evolution of incomes given the initial distribution $\pi(1)$. In addition, transition matrices over intervals longer than one period satisfy[5]

$$P(s, u) = P(s, t) \, P(t, u) \quad \text{for } s < t < u. \qquad (1.7)$$

An extensive literature has developed on mobility indices derived from transition matrices. No attempt is made to review this literature here, but several ideas and definitions are worth noting. A forward transition matrix P (s, t) is said to be *perfectly mobile* if $p_{jk}(s, t)$ is independent of j or, in other words, if all individuals at time s have the same probability $\pi_k(t)$ of occupying income class k at time t. A perfectly mobile society, in the sense just described, is one that is unlikely to be approximated in practice. It does, however, correspond to a situation that is easily comprehended, and for this reason it provides a useful benchmark in the later analysis.

The other benchmark case occurs when $P(s, t)$ is an identity matrix (and can only therefore arise when P is square). This situation, in which no one changes income class between time s and time t, is called *complete immobility*. If $P(s, t)$ is completely immobile, the distribution $\pi(t)$ across income classes at time t must be identical to $\pi(s)$. It therefore follows that a transition matrix cannot be completely immobile if the original and final distributions are dissimilar: in other words, a change in the cross-section distributions between time s and time t necessarily induces some degree of mobility.[6] Sociologists have referred to these 'distribution-induced' transitions as *structural mobility*, and distinguished them from the *exchange mobility* changes in income rank positions over time.[7] In the context of transition matrices, the notion of exchange mobility can be captured by constructing the income classes in each period so that the intervals all contain a fixed proportion $^1/_k$ of the population. The $k \times k$ transition matrix is then bi-stochastic, with both rows and columns summing to unity, and the perfectly mobile society corresponds to a matrix in which all the elements are equal to $^1/_k$ (Atkinson and Bourguignon, 1982).

The distinction between structural and exchange mobility is important, because it raises a fundamental question about mobility: should it be viewed as a characteristic that is independent of the marginal distributions? An analogy with inequality measurement is useful here. Inequality indices are usually first conceived in terms of distributions with a given mean income, and the subclass of indices that are 'mean independent' (or 'scale invariant') are then identified. A similar procedure applied to income dynamics suggests that mobility measures might first be constructed for a given sequence of cross-section distributions. The subset of measures which are 'distribution independent' may then be distinguished. However, requiring inequality indices to be invariant to changes in a single variable – mean income – is far less demanding than requiring mobility measures to be invariant to all possible changes in the cross-section distributions. So it is not clear that there exists a measure of pure exchange mobility which also satisfies other desirable properties.

Can the Hart index be regarded as a measure of exchange mobility? Apparently not, since the formulae given in equations (1.4) and (1.5) contain characteristics of the marginal distributions. However, (1.5) suggests that we may be able to decompose $1 - H$ into the product of two terms, one indicating exchange mobility (β_t) and the other reflecting the structural mobility caused by a change in the marginal distributions ($s(\ln x_t)/s(\ln x_{t+1})$). The following argument cautions against accepting either of these claims, at least if the distributions of x_t and x_{t+1} have a similar functional form.

Suppose that x_t and x_{t+1} are both lognormally distributed. To compute the degree of exchange mobility, imagine that the distribution x_{t+1} is transformed in such a way that all individuals maintain their same final income *position*, while the overall distribution becomes identical to that of x_t. This can be achieved by defining the 'new' final incomes x'_{t+1} according to the rule

$$\ln x'_{i,t+1} = \ln m_t + \frac{s(\ln x_t)}{s(\ln x_{t+1})} [\ln x_{i,t+1} - \ln m_{t+1}]. \qquad (1.8)$$

It is now reasonable to argue that the exchange component of mobility corresponds to the relationship between x_t and x'_{t+1} (since the marginal distributions are identical), while the structural component corresponds to the change from x'_{t+1} to x_{t+1}. However, it follows from (1.8) that $r(\ln x_t, \ln x'_{t+1}) = r(\ln x_t, \ln x_{t+1})$ and hence

$$H(x_t, x'_{t+1}) = H(x_t, x_{t+1}). \qquad (1.9)$$

Thus, in the circumstances described, H appears to satisfy the requirements of an index of exchange mobility, an unexpected, and perhaps even bizarre, conclusion.

1.3 PROPERTIES OF MOBILITY MEASURES

This section examines the features of the Hart index (1.4) in more detail, and attempts to identify a number of general properties that may be desirable in a measure of mobility. In many cases, the proposed properties are natural analogues of the axioms imposed on inequality indices.[8] The desirability of some of the properties may be sufficiently evident that they can be viewed as requirements of any satisfactory measure of mobility. The desirability of others may be less obvious or compelling, and these can, if necessary, be sacrificed. As will become evident, the initial list of proposed properties is not consistent, so one or more will have to be discarded.

While the term 'mobility index' normally indicates a function that takes a single numerical value, the term 'mobility measure' admits a wider interpretation. Foster (1985), for example, suggests that the Lorenz curve can be regarded as a measure of inequality, despite the fact that its 'value' is a function, and that it provides only a partial ordering of distributions. While this idea is not pursued here, an attempt is made throughout to state the properties in ways that accommodate the possibility of more broadly interpreted mobility measures.

The first point to consider is the domain of income structures X over which the measure is well defined. The most obvious candidate is the union of the sets $\mathcal{X}_{nT}$ given in (1.6), for any integers $n, T \geqslant 2$. However, there is at least one type of income structure that may be difficult to relate to the notion of mobility: situations in which, in every period t, all individuals receive the same income μ_t. Eliminating these structures from consideration yields the sets

$$\mathcal{X}^0_{nT} = \mathcal{X}_{nT} \setminus \{X \in \mathcal{X}_{nT} | x_{it} = \mu_t \text{ for all } i, t\} \tag{1.10}$$

$$\mathcal{X} = \bigcup_{n=2}^{\infty} \bigcup_{T=2}^{\infty} \mathcal{X}^0_{nT} \tag{1.11}$$

and suggests the property:

(A1) *Universal domain*: A mobility measure should be well defined for all $X \in \mathcal{X}$.

The Hart index (1.4) violates this condition for two reasons. First, it is defined at present for just two time observations, although this might be rectified by using a multiple correlation coefficient in (1.4) when $T > 2$. Secondly, even when $T = 2$, the index is not defined when either $s(\ln x_1)$ or $s(\ln x_2)$ is zero. It may be argued that this is not a serious limitation in practice, but there seems no reason *a priori* why the notion of mobility cannot be applied to an income structure in which individuals begin with different incomes, and yet all have the same income one period later. This would probably be regarded as a rather mobile society.

Inequality indices are typically assumed to be continuous, so that marginal changes in incomes have a marginal impact on the index value. A similar property is also appropriate for mobility measures.

(A2) *Continuity*: The degree of mobility varies continuously with the incomes in X.

This formulation is a little vague, although its implications should be evident in any specific application. The Hart index $H(X)$ is, of course, continuous over its support.

The Hart index also has the property that it treats individuals anonymously, so that it does not matter how they are numbered. This property corresponds to the symmetry condition imposed on inequality measures, and is unlikely to be controversial. It may be stated as:

(A3) *Population symmetry*: X and X' are equally mobile whenever $X' = \Pi X$ for some permutation matrix Π.

The term 'population symmetry' is used here because the analysis of mobility, unlike inequality, allows permutations of the time period distributions (the columns of X) to be considered, as well as permutations of the individual income profiles (the rows of X). It is therefore possible to formulate the analogous property of time symmetry:

Definition: A mobility measure is *time symmetric* if X and X' are equally mobile whenever $X' = X\Pi$ for some permutation matrix Π.

Broadly speaking, time symmetry suggests that, in the analysis of mobility, the distribution of a person's income receipts may matter, but not the time sequence of those receipts. This is rather more than time symmetry actually implies, since a permutation Π swaps *all* the incomes in period s, say, with the corresponding incomes in period t, not just x_{is} with x_{it} for a single person i. However, even the weaker idea of time symmetry captured in the above definition is questionable on the grounds that the time sequence of incomes may be important. For instance, it might be thought desirable to distinguish between the situation where incomes are originally different and then become equal, and the time symmetric equivalent structure in which incomes are initially equal and then become different. So it is not immediately clear whether the time symmetry property, which the Hart index satisfies, is a good or bad feature.

The rows and columns of X can be replicated, as well as permuted. Specifically, $X' \in \mathscr{X}_{rn,T}$ will be said to be a *population replication* of $X \in \mathscr{X}_{nT}$ if r is a positive integer and $x'_{jt} = x_{it}$ whenever $j = kn + i$ for some integer $k \geq 0$. This is a somewhat convoluted way of capturing the idea that X' is the aggregate income structure for r sub-populations each having the income structure X. Similarly, $X' \in \mathscr{X}_{n,rT}$ will be said to be a *time replication* of $X \in \mathcal{X}_{nT}$ if r is a positive integer and $X' = [X, X, \ldots, X]$. Invariance with respect to population replication is the assumption typically used in inequality measurement to compare income distributions for different sized populations. The analogue here is:

(A4) *Population replication invariance*: X and X' are equally mobile whenever X' is a population replication of X.

Replication invariance with respect to time may be defined in a similar manner:

Definition: A mobility measure is *time replication invariant* if X and X' are equally mobile whenever X' is a time replication of X.

The Hart index $H(X)$ exhibits replication invariance with respect to the population. It does not immediately satisfy time replication invariance since it has not been defined for $T > 2$ periods. However, replication invariance with respect to time is objectionable, for much the same reason that time symmetry is suspect. It implies that the degree of mobility is unchanged if the pattern of incomes received in the first T periods is exactly repeated for all individuals in the next T periods. But this does not take into account the fact that the distribution of income in period T may be radically different from that in period 1, so moving from period T to period $T+1$ (and hence back to period 1 incomes again) may be quite a jolt. The desirability of time replication invariance is therefore less than transparent.

Now consider the benchmark income structures associated with complete immobility and perfect mobility. Since mobility is concerned with income changes, no serious objection could be made to the argument that a structure is completely immobile if the incomes of all individuals are constant over time. More generally, the notion of complete immobility may be extended to cases in which relative incomes are constant over time:

Definition: A structure X is completely immobile if and only if $x_{is}/\mu_s = x_{it}/\mu_t$ for all i, s, t.

This definition carries with it the implicit assumption that the concept of mobility refers to changes in relative incomes. So those who find it disagreeable may be satisfied with a statement to the effect that attention has been confined to measures of *relative* income mobility.

Completely immobile income structures perform a role similar to that played by completely equal distributions in inequality measurement. The normalization condition in inequality analysis therefore suggests the analogous property:

(A5) *Normalization*: Mobility is a minimum whenever X is completely immobile.

The Hart index $H(X)$ attains its minimum value of 0 when X is completely immobile, so the normalization property (A5) holds. It does not, however, satisfy the stricter requirement:

(A6) *Strong normalization*: Mobility is a minimum if and only if X is completely immobile,

since $H(X)$ also takes the value 0 if $\ln x_2 = \alpha + \beta \ln x_1$ and $\beta \neq 1$. In other words, for the Hart index, mobility is zero in the Galtonian model (1.1) whenever $\beta > 0$ and $\sigma^2(\varepsilon) = 0$. Such situations include cases (corresponding to $\beta \approx 0$) in which incomes are initially unequal, and then become almost equal in period 2. As already noted, most people would probably view these as mobile structures, not immobile ones as the Hart index suggests.

The other benchmark case, discussed in the last section, corresponds to a perfectly mobile society, in which the probability of achieving an income level y_{t+1} in period $t+1$ is independent of the income y_t received in period t. The concept of perfect mobility is difficult to formulate in terms of observed income structures X: essentially the preconditions require not only x_s and x_t to be uncorrelated, but also any arbitrarily transformed vectors $\varphi_s(x_s)$ and $\varphi_t(x_t)$, where $\phi_t(x_t) \equiv (\varphi_t(x_{1t})$, $\varphi_t(x_{2t}), \ldots, \varphi_t(x_{nT}))$ for some real valued function φ_t. The best solution is to define a perfectly mobile structure indirectly, in terms of these requirements.

Definition: An income structure $X = [x_1, \ldots, x_T]$ is *perfectly mobile* if and only if $\varphi_s(x_s)$ and $\varphi_t(x_t)$ are uncorrelated for all s, t and all real functions φ_s, ϕ_t.

Those who may wonder whether nontrivial perfectly mobile structures exist will be reassured by the following example. Suppose there are J income levels $y_{11}, y_{21}, \ldots, y_{J1}$ at time 1 and K income levels $y_{12}, y_{22}, \ldots, y_{K2}$ at time 2, and let X consist of the JK income profiles (y_{j1}, y_{k2}) for $j=1, \ldots, J$ and $k=1, \ldots, K$. Then, writing

$$\bar{\phi}_1 = \frac{1}{J} \sum_{j=1}^{J} \phi_1(y_{j1}); \quad \bar{\phi}_2 = \frac{1}{K} \sum_{k=1}^{K} \phi_2(y_{k2}), \qquad (1.12)$$

it follows that

$$\text{cov}(\phi_1(x_1), \phi_2(x_2)) = \frac{1}{JK} \sum_{j=1}^{J} \sum_{k=1}^{K} [\phi_1(y_{j1}) - \bar{\phi}_1][\phi_2(y_{k2}) - \bar{\phi}_2]$$

$$= \frac{1}{J} \sum_{j=1}^{J} [\phi_1(y_{j1}) - \bar{\phi}_1] \frac{1}{K} \sum_{k=1}^{K} [\phi_2(y_{k2}) - \bar{\phi}_2]$$

$$= 0. \tag{1.13}$$

More generally, if there are K_t income levels at time t (not necessarily distinct), it is possible to construct a perfectly mobile structure consisting of $n = K_1 K_2 \ldots K_T$ income profiles in which each of the incomes $y_{1t}, y_{2t}, \ldots, y_{k,t}$ at time t occurs exactly n/K_t times.

If perfect mobility is associated with the greatest possible degree of mobility, as the term suggests, it is reasonable to require

(A7) *Perfect mobility*: Mobility is a maximum whenever X is perfectly mobile.

For a mobility index, this property may be split into two parts: the requirement that all perfectly mobile structures yield the same index value; and the requirement that this common value is the maximum that can be achieved. The Hart mobility index $H(X)$ satisfies the first condition but not the second, since the common value of 1 is not a maximum. Higher degrees of mobility are recorded if $\ln x_1$ and $\ln x_2$ are negatively correlated. However, it may be argued that 'more than perfect' mobility, while theoretically possible, is unlikely to be observed in practice, so that the perfect mobility value of 1 represents a likely upper bound. This argument has some merit, and leads to a reassessment of the Universal Domain condition (A1). For example, should further restrictions be placed on the set of feasible income structures?[9]

As with the normalization condition, a stricter version of the perfect mobility assumption (A7) can be formulated by requiring:

(A8) *Strong perfect mobility*: Mobility is a maximum if and only if X is perfectly mobile.

Even if one accepts that $H(X)$ is likely to be bounded above by 1, property (A8) is violated because $H(x_1, x_2) = 1$ whenever $\ln x_1$ and $\ln x_2$ are uncorrelated, and this does not imply that $\phi_1(x_1)$ and $\phi_2(x_2)$ are uncorrelated for all ϕ_1 and ϕ_2.

The discussion of benchmark income structures leads on to the question of the range of possible index values. It is often thought desirable that an index value should be confined to the unit interval, with the minimum value 0 and maximum value 1 achieved in particular polar cases. This suggests the normalization condition:

(A9) *Unit interval range*: The range of a mobility index should be [0,1].

Although the Hart index technically violates (A9) for $X \in \mathcal{X}$, since its range is [0,2], the requirement is easily accommodated either by renormalizing the mobility index as $H(X)/2$, or else by arguing, as before, that the range of $H(X)$ will be limited in practice to the unit interval.

The next issue to be considered is the effect of multiplying all incomes by the same factor. In inequality measurement, the scale invariance condition requires that inequality does not change if all incomes are multiplied by the factor $\lambda > 0$. This property almost always holds for the inequality indices used in empirical studies, although counterarguments can be made (Kolm, 1976). The simplest analogue for measures of mobility is:

(A10) *Scale invariance*: X and X' are equally mobile whenever $X' = \lambda X$ for some scalar $\lambda > 0$.

However, the situation here differs from inequality measurement since the scale factors $\lambda_1, \ldots, \lambda_{IT}$ can be applied separately to each of the time periods. A stronger version of (A10) is therefore given by:

(A11) *Intertemporal scale invariance*: X and X' are equally mobile whenever $X' = X\Lambda$ for some positive diagonal matrix Λ.

It is easy to confirm that the Hart index H is both scale invariant and intertemporally scale invariant.

The justification for imposing (A10) would presumably be similar to the rationale for scale invariant inequality indices: for example, that they avoid the problem of converting currencies to a common base when making intercountry comparisons. Such arguments have less force when attempting to justify the stronger condition (A11), unless the currency unit changes over time (from pounds sterling to ECU, perhaps?). So the desirability of intertemporal scale invariance is less compelling. However, if scale invariance does not hold independently in each period, it will be necessary to decide whether incomes over time should be adjusted for inflation and, if so, whether the retail price index or some other deflator should be used. So practical considerations may still argue in favour of (A11). Furthermore, the definition of a completely immobile structure was justified earlier in terms of an interest in changes in *relative* incomes. So the definition of complete immobility provides additional grounds for accepting (A11).[10]

The last question to be addressed is perhaps the most important: under what circumstances is an income structure X' more mobile than some alternative structure X? This question has already been answered in part by presuming that perfectly mobile structures exhibit more mobility than completely immobile structures. But this provides little assistance. What is required here is an analogue of the Pigou–Dalton condition in inequality analysis, which says that a progressive transfer reduces the level of inequality. What type of transformation applied to an income structure X would permit a similar kind of statement to be made in the context of mobility measurement?

Several possible candidates come to mind. Consider, for example, the argument that mobility is concerned with variations in income over time, so a change which redistributes the income of person i from high-income periods to low-income periods necessarily reduces mobility. This may be formalized by defining the $(n \times T)$ *transfer matrix* $\delta(i; s, t)$ by the rule

$$\delta_{is}(i; s, t) = 1; \; \delta_{it}(i; s, t) = -1;$$
$$\delta_{ju}(i; s, t) = 0 \text{ for all } u \text{ and all } j \neq i \qquad (1.14)$$
$$\delta_{ju}(i; s, t) = 0 \text{ for all } j \text{ and all } u \neq s, t.$$

In other words, $\delta(i; s, t)$ is a matrix which has its (i, s) element equal to 1, its (i, t) element equal to -1 and zeros everywhere else. Now define a 'progressive' redistribution of the income profile of person i as follows:

Definition: The income structure X' is obtained from X by a (mean preserving) *smoothing transfer* if $X' = X + \delta(i; s, t)\Delta$ for some i, s, t and $\Delta > 0$; and $x'_{is} \leq x'_{it}$.

The above argument then suggests that X' is less mobile than X whenever X' is obtained from X by a smoothing transfer.

The main problem with this proposal is that it conflicts with the normalization condition (A5). For if $x_{it} = \lambda_i \mu_t$ for all i and t, then X is completely immobile, and mobility is a minimum, by (A5). But if $\mu_s < \mu_t$, say, a smoothing transfer can be constructed which raises the income of person i in period s, and reduces it in period t; and this smoothing transfer cannot reduce mobility if it is already at its minimum. Another problem is that a smoothing transfer changes the mean income, and hence the relative incomes of all individuals, in the periods affected by the transfer. So it may not be self-evident that the overall impact is a reduction in mobility.

Both of these problems are avoided if mean income in each period is preserved by a *pair* of smoothing transfers, suitably constructed.

Definition: The income structure X' is obtained from X by a *compensated smoothing* if $X' = X + \delta(i; s, t)\Delta - \delta(j; s, t)\Delta$ for some i, j, s, t and $\Delta > 0$; and if $x'_{is} \leqslant x'_{it}$ and $x'_{js} \geqslant x'_{jt}$.

A compensated smoothing involves two individuals, labelled i and j, and two time periods, labelled s and t, where person i has a higher income in period t than in period s, while person j has a higher income in period s than in period t. The profiles of person i and person j can then be smoothed simultaneously, while maintaining the same mean income in each period. Note that, if X is completely immobile and $x_{it} > x_{is}$, then $x_{jt} > x_{js}$ for all j, and it is impossible to construct a compensated smoothing. A requirement that X is more mobile than X' whenever X' is obtained from X by a compensated smoothing would not, therefore, immediately conflict with the normalization condition (A5). Nor does a compensated smoothing alter relative incomes, apart from those of the two individuals involved in the two periods affected.

As already observed, $H(X)$ can take its minimum value of zero when X is not completely immobile, for instance when $\ln x_2 = \alpha + \beta \ln x_1$ and $\beta \neq 1$. For these structures, a compensated smoothing can be constructed. Since the value of $H(X)$ cannot fall below zero, it follows that the Hart index will not satisfy the requirement that a compensated smoothing reduces mobility.

While a compensated smoothing does not alter the time means μ_t, it does change the cross section distributions in the periods affected by the pair of transfers. There is one further simple type of operation which preserves the marginal distributions at all times – a permutation of the incomes of two of the individuals in one period. In the case $T=2$, a simple permutation of this kind applied to the incomes of persons i and j may be regarded as mobility enhancing if the incomes of these individuals initially satisfy $x_{i1} > x_{j1}$ and $x_{i2} > x_{j2}$, say, and end up being negatively rank correlated. To take a simple illustration, this argument would claim that if

$$X = \begin{bmatrix} 1 & 3 \\ 2 & 5 \end{bmatrix} \text{ and } X' = \begin{bmatrix} 1 & 5 \\ 2 & 3 \end{bmatrix}, \tag{1.15}$$

then X' is more mobile than X. Atkinson and Bourguignon (1982) have emphasized the significance of these simple permutations or 'switches'.[11] It is therefore appropriate to propose

(A12) *Atkinson–Bourguignon condition*: The income structure X' is more mobile than $X \in \mathcal{X}_{n2}$ whenever X' is obtained from X by a simple switch, where

Definition: The income structure X' is obtained from $X \in \mathcal{X}_{n2}$ by a simple switch if, for some i, j and t such that $(x_{i1}-x_{j1})(x_{i2}-x_{j2})>0$,

$$x'_{it} = x_{jt}; \; x'_{jt} = x_{it};$$
$$x'_{ks} = x_{ks} \text{ for } s \neq t \text{ and all } k$$
$$x'_{ks} = x_{ks} \text{ for all } s \text{ and all } k \neq i, j.$$

The Atkinson–Bourguignon condition (A12) implies that, if the income profiles of person i and person j are initially rank correlated, then a swap of incomes in either period increases the level of mobility. It follows that mobility is a maximum if and only if the vectors x_1 and x_2 are perfectly negatively rank correlated, and a minimum if and only if x_1 and x_2 have a rank correlation coefficient of 1. Unfortunately, the condition does not generalize easily to $T > 2$ periods. Attempting to apply it to pairs of adjacent periods, for example, would imply that if

$$X = \begin{bmatrix} 1 & 1 & 2 \\ 2 & 2 & 1 \end{bmatrix} \text{ and } X' = \begin{bmatrix} 1 & 2 & 2 \\ 2 & 1 & 1 \end{bmatrix}, \tag{1.16}$$

then X' is more mobile than X, by a switch of the x_2 incomes in the structure (x_1, x_2), and X is more mobile than X', by a switch of the x_2 incomes in the structure (x_2, x_3).

To investigate whether the Hart index satisfies (A12), suppose, without loss of generality, that X' is obtained from X by a simple switch that affects the period 2 incomes of persons 1 and 2. Since the simple switch does not alter the distributions in either period, nor the incomes of individuals $j \neq 1,2$, the sign of the change in the Hart index depends on the sign of

$$- \ln x'_{11} \ln x'_{12} - \ln x'_{21} \ln x'_{22} + \ln x_{11} \ln x_{12} + \ln x_{21} \ln x_{22}$$
$$= - \ln x_{11} \ln x_{22} - \ln x_{21} \ln x_{12} + \ln x_{11} \ln x_{12} + \ln x_{21} \ln x_{22}$$
$$= \ln (x_{11}/x_{21}) \ln (x_{12}/x_{22}) > 0,$$

since initially $(x_{11} - x_{21})(x_{12} - x_{22}) > 0$. So the Hart index rises when X' is obtained from X by a simple switch, as required by the Atkinson–Bourguignon condition.

1.4 COMPARISONS OF MOBILITY INDICES

The Hart index $H(X)$ has been shown to have many of the properties that might be desirable in an index of mobility. The summary provided in Table 1.1 suggests that, if 'more than perfectly mobile' income structures are disregarded, the Hart index satisfies 9 of the 12 properties listed as (A1)–(A12), plus the additional feature of time symmetry. The principal,

Table 1.1 Summary of mobility index properties

Equation		Hart index (1.4)	Shorrocks index (1.17)	Maasoumi–Zandvakili index (1.15)	'Ideal' index (1.20)
(A1)	Universal domain	0	1	1	1
(A2)	Continuity	1	1	1	1
(A3)	Population symmetry	1	1	1	1
(A4)	Population replication invariance	1	1	1	1
(A5)	Normalization	1	1	1	1
(A6)	Strong normalization	0	1	1	1
(A7)	Perfect mobility	1?	0	0	1?
(A8)	Strong perfect mobility	0	0	0	0
(A9)	Unit interval range	1?	1	1	1
(A10)	Scale invariance	1	1	1	1
(A11)	Intertemporal scale invariance	1	0	1	1
(A12)	Atkinson–Bourguignon condition	1	1	1	1
Total Score		9	9	10	11
	Time symmetry	1	1	1	1
	Time replication invariance	?	1	1	1

and perhaps only serious, deficiency of $H(X)$ is its inability to decide whether a structure in which incomes are initially unequal and then become equal one period later should be assigned the mobility value 0 or 1. In essence, the Hart index wants to regard it as both completely mobile and completely immobile simultaneously. That is the reason why the index fails to register a value for such structures (and why it would violate the continuity assumption (A2) if a value was arbitrarily allocated).

No great significance should be attached to the Hart index performance score of 75 per cent. The properties listed are not equally desirable, and different people will place different weights on the individual features. Furthermore, the set of properties as stated are not independent: for instance, strong normalization (A6) implies the normalization condition (A5), and strong perfect mobility (A8) implies the perfect mobility property (A7). Nor is the list of properties consistent at present. A two-period perfectly mobile income structure (x_1, x_2) is not one for which x_1 and x_2 are perfectly negatively rank correlated, so the Atkinson–Bourguignon condition will not allow it to be assigned the maximum degree of mobility (unless 'more than perfectly mobile' structures are dismissed, which implies a restatement of (A1)).

It is also the case that (A1)–(A12) omit properties that may be thought highly desirable. There is no analogue of the subgroup consistency condition for inequality and poverty indices (Shorrocks, 1988; Foster and Shorrocks, 1991). Nor is the mobility index required to admit a welfare interpretation, or to have any normative content. It is, for instance, commonly assumed that greater mobility is desirable. Yet it is not self-evident that higher values of the Hart index are preferred; indeed, Hart himself rejects this claim, since he states that 'very low and very high values of [H] may yield similar values of social welfare' (Hart, 1983, p. 190).

An alternative index that does have normative content is the 'rigidity' measure

$$R(X) = \frac{I(\Sigma_t x_t)}{\Sigma_t \mu_t I(x_t) / \Sigma_t \mu_t} \,, \tag{1.17}$$

proposed in Shorrocks (1978a), where $I(\cdot)$ is any (scale invariant) inequality index that can be expressed as a strictly convex function of relative incomes. This index can be interpreted as the extent to which mobility tends to reduce inequality as the accounting period is extended. Assuming that $I(\cdot)$ is chosen to be continuous and replication invariant, and taking $1 - R(X)$ to be the mobility index corresponding to the rigidity index $R(X)$, it turns out that $R(X)$ satisfies 9 of the 12 properties (A1)–

(A12), and is, in addition, time symmetric and time replication invariant.[12] The Shorrocks index is defined for any number of time periods, and allows inequality to be zero in some (but not all) of the marginal distributions, so it performs better on the domain requirement (A1). It also associates a zero mobility value only with completely immobile income structures, and hence satisfies the strong normalization condition (A6). However, it is not invariant to scalar multiplication of the incomes in one period alone, nor does it associate the maximum mobility value with perfectly mobile structures. In essence, it agrees with the conclusion of the Atkinson–Bourguignon condition that, *given* the distributions in period 1 and period 2, mobility is maximized when the rank correlation between x_1 and x_2 is -1. The fact that the Hart index H and the Shorrocks index R achieve the same 'score' of 75 per cent is, of course, proof positive that this comparison has been done in an even-handed manner!

Can the score of 75 per cent be improved? The answer is yes, if the suggestion of Maasoumi and Zandvakili (1986) is adopted, to allow generalizations of $R(X)$ of the form

$$\frac{I(\Sigma_t w_t x_t)}{\Sigma_t w_t \mu_t I(x_t) / \Sigma_t w_t \mu_t} \tag{1.18}$$

where w_t denotes an arbitrary set of weights.[13] For if w_t is chosen to be $1/\mu_t$, then (1.18) reduces to the rigidity index

$$M(X) = \frac{I(\Sigma_t x_t/\mu_t)}{\frac{1}{T}\Sigma_t I(x_t)}, \tag{1.19}$$

which inherits all of the properties of the Shorrocks index, and also satisfies intertemporal scale invariance.

To proceed one step further, suppose that the square of the coefficient of variation, $\sigma^2\mu$, is used for the inequality index in (1.19). Then $M(X)$ becomes

$$S(X) = \frac{\sigma^2(\Sigma_t x_t/\mu_t)}{T\Sigma_t \sigma^2(x_t/\mu_t)}. \tag{1.20}$$

If X is perfectly mobile, so that $\text{cov}(x_s, x_t) = 0$ for all s and t, it follows that

$$S(X) = \frac{\Sigma_t \sigma^2(x_t/\mu_t)}{T\Sigma_t \sigma^2(x_t/\mu_t)} = \frac{1}{T}. \tag{1.21}$$

Thus, given the number of time periods T, the index $S(X)$ assigns the same value to all perfectly mobile structures. This number is not the maximum value that the index can attain, for reasons already cited. So the perfect mobility property (A7) is not technically satisfied. But it certainly captures the spirit of condition (A7), and will give a mobility value $1-S(X)$ near the upper bound of 1 as $T \to \infty$. It is probably as close to an ideal measure of mobility as one is likely to get.

NOTES

1   I am grateful to Andrew Clark, Stephen Jenkins, Dan Slottje and, most especially, Essie Maasoumi for valuable comments and suggestions.
2   See Hart (1976a, 1976b, 1981, 1983) and Creedy *et al.* (1981) for examples of applications of the Galtonian model. A more complete survey is contained in Creedy (1985).
3   Hart's discussion of mobility is typically framed in terms of $r(\ln x_t, \ln x_{t+1})$, which may be regarded as an index of income stability. The precise form that an index of mobility should take is not clear, although Hart appears to favour $1/r$. (See, for example, Hart, 1976b, p. 557; Hart, 1983, p. 184.) The specification given in (1.4) is better from the perspective of the criteria discussed in section 1.3 below. On other occasions, Hart appears to use the R^2 value obtained from OLS estimation of equation (1.3). (See, for example, Creedy *et al.*, 1981.) This is monotonically related to H when $\beta \geqslant 0$.
4   The rows of $P(s, t)$ always sum to one.
5   In practice, this implication of the Markov assumption is usually violated: see, for example, Shorrocks (1978a).
6   Assuming that mobility is a minimum if and only if $P(s, t)$ is completely immobile.
7   See, for example, Goldthorpe (1980). Markandya (1984) applies these ideas to income mobility.
8   For details of these axioms, see Shorrocks (1988).
9   This suggestion is explored in Shorrocks (1978a).
10 It may be thought that the normalization assumptions (A5) and (A6) together with scale invariance (A10) would necessarily imply (A11). This is not the case, as the index R given below in equation (1.17) demonstrates.
11 See also Atkinson *et al.* (1990). The Atkinson–Bourguignon analysis is framed in terms of multidimensional comparisons, of which income mobility can be viewed as the special case occurring when the different dimensions correspond to income in separate time periods. All of the axioms discussed in this section have analogues in the context of multidimensional comparisons, although their desirability may not be as evident.
12 Confirmation of the properties is straightforward. For the Atkinson–Bourguignon condition, observe that a simple switch maintains the value of $I(x_t)$ in each period, so the sign of the change in $R(X)$ depends on the sign of the change in $I(x_1 + x_2)$. But the impact of a simple switch on the vector $(x_1 + x_2)$ has the same effect as a mean preserving progressive transfer, reducing the aggregate income of the person whose income is initially higher in both periods, and raising the aggregate income of the person whose income is initially lower. So a simple switch must decrease the value of $I(x_1 + x_2)$, and the mobility level $1-R(X)$ rises as a consequence. Computed values of $R(X)$ for several inequality indices $I(\cdot)$ are reported in Shorrocks (1981).
13 See also Maasoumi and Zandvakili (1989, 1990).

REFERENCES

Atkinson, A.B. and F. Bourguignon (1982): 'The comparison of multi-dimensional distributions of economic status', *Review of Economic Studies*, **49**, 183–201.

Atkinson, A.B., F. Bourguignon and C. Morrisson (1990): 'Empirical studies of earnings mobility', London School of Economics, mimeograph.

Creedy, J. (1985): *Dynamics of Income Distribution* (Oxford: Basil Blackwell).

Creedy, J., P.E. Hart and N.A. Klevmarken (1981): 'Income mobility in Great Britain and Sweden', in Klevmarken and Lybeck (1981).

Foster, J.E. (1985): 'Inequality measurement', in H.P. Young (ed.), *Fair Allocation* (Providence, R. Is.: American Mathematical Society).

Foster, J.E. and A.F. Shorrocks (1991): 'Subgroup consistent poverty indices', *Econometrica*, **59**, 687–709.

Goldthorpe, J.M. (1980): *Social Mobility and Class Structure in Modern Britain* (Oxford: Oxford University Press).

Hart, P.E. (1976a): 'The comparative statics and dynamics of income distribution', *Journal of the Royal Statistical Society*, Series A, **139**, 108–25.

—— (1976b): 'The dynamics of earnings, 1963–1973', *Economic Journal*, **86**, 551–65.

—— (1981): 'The statics and dynamics of income distributions: a survey', in Klevmarken and Lybeck (1981).

—— (1983): 'The size mobility of earnings', *Oxford Bulletin of Economics and Statistics*, **45**, 181–93.

Klevmarken, N.A. and J.A. Lybeck (eds) (1981): *The Statics and Dynamics of Income* (Clevedon: Tieto).

Kolm, S.-Ch. (1976): 'Unequal inequalities II', *Journal of Economic Theory*, **13**, 82–111.

Maasoumi, E. and S. Zandvakili (1986): 'A class of generalized measures of mobility with applications', *Economics Letters*, **22**, 97–102.

—— (1989): 'Mobility profiles and time aggregates of individual incomes', *Research on Economic Inequality*, **1**, 195–218.

—— (1990): 'Generalized entropy measures of mobility for different sexes and income levels', *Journal of Econometrics*, **43**, 121–33.

Markandya, A. (1984): 'The welfare measurement of changes in economic mobility', *Economica*, **51**, 457–71.

Shorrocks, A.F. (1976): 'Income mobility and the Markov assumption', *Economic Journal*, **86**, 566–77.

—— (1978a): 'The measurement of mobility', *Econometrica*, **46**, 1013–24.

—— (1978b): 'Income inequality and income mobility', *Journal of Economic Theory*, **19**, 376–93.

—— (1981): 'Income stability in the United States', in Klevmarken and Lybeck (1981).

—— (1988): 'Aggregation issues in inequality measurement', in W. Eichhorn (ed.), *Measurement in Economics* (Heidelberg: Physica-Verlag).

2. The Distribution of Income in Eastern Europe

A.B. Atkinson and John Micklewright[1]

2.1 INTRODUCTION

This chapter contains an empirical study of the distribution of income, a subject which has been a long-standing concern of Peter Hart, and to which he has made notable contributions. This study examines the distribution of household incomes in Eastern Europe before the economic transformation that began in 1990. Was there less inequality in these countries under communism than in Western economies? If so, how large was the difference? If the cost of improved economic performance is that inequality can be expected to rise to Western levels, how large an increase in average income is necessary to compensate the bottom income groups?

In the literature on Eastern Europe one finds two distinctly different opinions about the communist record. The first is that there was in fact no less inequality under communism. For example, Lydall (1979) set the distribution of income in the United Kingdom alongside that in Czechoslovakia, Hungary and Poland. Comparing the percentiles of the distribution and the Gini coefficient he found for the early 1970s 'little difference between the United Kingdom and this group of countries' (Lydall, 1979, p. 33).

A similar conclusion was reached by Morrisson (1984) in a comparison encompassing a wider range of socialist countries, bringing in the former USSR, Bulgaria and Yugoslavia. Morrisson paid particular attention to the non-monetary advantages accruing to the privileged elite in Eastern Europe; included in his estimates are approximate adjustments. It is these adjustments in part which lead him to the finding that the income shares of the top deciles were relatively similar in, for example, Czechoslovakia and the United Kingdom (UK). Even though the relative incomes of the lowest deciles (the bottom four deciles) are higher in Eastern Europe, Morrisson concluded that:

Czechoslovakia excepted, East European countries have *not* a more egali-
tarian income distribution . . . all the other East European countries belong in
the same range of income distribution as the most advanced of the Western
countries. (Morrisson, 1984, pp. 126–7)

The Gini coefficients for the individual distribution of household per
capita incomes (that is, taking individuals ranked according to the per
capita income of their household) were 22 per cent for Czechoslovakia
and 24 per cent for Hungary, compared with 25 per cent in Sweden and
the UK. The Gini was 31 per cent for Poland and the former USSR,
compared with 30 per cent in Canada and 34 per cent in the US. (The data
used by Morrisson relate mainly to the early or mid-1970s.) This
assessment of income inequality in the former USSR accords with the
findings of Bergson that 'Soviet income inequality probably has been
found to be greater than often supposed. It is very possibly as great or
greater than that in Sweden, and not much less than that in some other
Western countries' (Bergson, 1984, p. 1073).

On the other hand, there are those who find that income inequality was
significantly less in Eastern Europe under communism than it was in the
West. McAuley (1979), on whose research Bergson drew, reached a
rather different conclusion about the former USSR:

These estimates . . . yield a value of 3.14–3.21 for the decile coefficient [ratio
of the top to bottom decile], which implies that there is a moderately unequal
distribution of incomes in the USSR. . . . inequality in the USSR was less than
in the United Kingdom and substantially less than in either the USA or Italy.
(McAuley, 1979, p. 66)

The estimates by Wiles (1978) of the per capita income distribution in the
communist countries of Bulgaria, Czechoslovakia, Hungary, Poland and
the former USSR show less inequality in Eastern Europe. His findings
were summarized by the commentator on his paper as showing that
'during the period considered, the USA and Canada had the most
unequal distribution, followed by Italy, Sweden and the UK, with the
socialist countries displaying the lowest inequality of this kind' (Michal,
discussion of Wiles, 1978, p. 193).

This conclusion is in line with that of Pryor, who had earlier estimated
that 'the Gini coefficient of total income inequality is at least [ten
percentage points] less in the East than in the West, other things
remaining equal' (Pryor, 1973, p. 88). The cross-section study by
Chenery *et al.*, which allowed for the influence of per capita GNP and
other variables, found that for socialist countries

the share of the lowest 40 per cent and the middle 40 per cent is significantly higher than would be accounted for by the influence of other variables. Note that the size of the coefficients is very large, indicating substantially higher equality. (Chenery *et al.*, 1974, p. 30)

In this chapter, we present empirical evidence for four Eastern European countries: Czechoslovakia, Hungary, Poland and the former USSR. (For convenience we refer usually to 'Eastern Europe' and take this to include the USSR; on occasion, we refer to the first three countries as 'Central European'.) The choice of these countries is to a degree arbitrary, but the first three are fairly obvious choices, being the countries which are most advanced in terms of economic and political reform. The former USSR is too big to be ignored; and it is the country where the communist experiment had the longest trial.

The sources of evidence used in this chapter on the distribution of income in Eastern Europe are described in section 2.2. Many people appear to believe that no data exist on the distribution of income in Eastern Europe. Such common impressions are, however, largely based on the situation in the former Soviet Union, where the distribution of income appeared with alcoholism and drug addiction in the censor's list of prohibited subjects, but the position in the Central European countries has been quite different. There have been regular household surveys, and a considerable volume of distributional information has been published.

The evidence about the distribution of income in Eastern Europe in the mid-1980s is presented in section 2.3. This period is chosen as one for which data are available, including information for the USSR, and which is at the same time less affected by the changes which took place towards the end of the decade (such as the wage reform initiated by Gorbachev). The degree of income inequality in Eastern Europe is compared with that in the UK. It would be desirable to make comparisons with a wider range of Western countries, including those at a similar stage of development, but for the present we confine the comparison to the Western country we know best. (For a recent comparison involving the Netherlands, rather than the UK, see Bruinooge *et al.*, 1990.)

In drawing attention to the availability of evidence on income inequality in Eastern Europe, we are not suggesting that such data are perfect. The household surveys, particularly that in the former USSR, are subject to a number of qualifications. The limitations of the evidence are the subject of section 2.4. The main conclusions are summarized in section 2.5.

2.2 DESCRIPTION OF THE DATA

Many people believe that under the communist regimes of Eastern

Europe little information about the distribution of income was made available. According to this view, the claims of socialism to have reduced income differentials or to have abolished poverty could not be assessed because of the absence of statistical data. Summarizing the situation in his 1984 survey article, Bergson concluded that 'the Soviet government apparently prefers to withhold rather than to release information' (Bergson, 1984, p. 1091). It would, however, be wrong to suppose that the situation in the USSR was representative of Eastern Europe as a whole. In Czechoslovakia, Hungary and Poland there has been a long tradition of collecting and publishing data on the distribution of income. In a number of respects the availability of data in these countries before 1990 compares favourably with that in Britain. And the situation has changed dramatically with *glasnost'* in the Soviet Union, where information is now available about the distribution of household incomes in the 1980s (see, for example, Ellman, 1990).

The second common belief about data on the distribution of income in Eastern Europe is that they are of poor quality. It is thought that the low priority attached to distributional issues led to inadequate resources being allocated to statistical activities. It is alleged that the relation between communist governments and individual enterprises, and that between the state and its citizens, was not such as to induce accurate reporting. But it is important to judge the quality of data, not by some ideal standard, but by the standard of what can realistically be achieved. All data are imperfect to some degree. Even the best-designed survey has problems of incomplete coverage, of non-response or partial response, and of ambiguity in the interpretation of definitions. There are, even with best-practice statistical techniques, difficulties in grossing-up survey data to be representative of the population as a whole and of reconciling the findings with aggregate statistics.

The main features of the statistical sources on income distribution used in this chapter are summarized in Table 2.1. (More details are given in Atkinson and Micklewright, 1992.) As is made clear in the final column, published information relating to the distribution of household income in the communist period may be found in the annual statistical yearbooks. For example, a quinquennial household income survey was first held in Hungary in 1963, with some limited results published in the 1964 yearbook. A special English-language publication was produced giving results of the 1973 survey (Hungarian Central Statistical Office, 1975).

Turning to the UK, we may note that, in contrast with Hungary, Britain has not to date had a regular purpose-built household survey specifically designed to produce information on the distribution of income in the population as a whole. Evidence about the distribution of

Table 2.1   *Sources of data on the distribution of income used in this
chapter*

	Type of source (latest year prior to 1990)	Response in latest year prior to 1990 and achieved sample size	Income concept	Presentation of results in statistical yearbook
Czechoslovakia	Period microcensus on non-institutional population (1988)	96.6% in 1989 (1988 incomes); about 100,000 households	Annual net per capita income excluding agricultural income in kind	Summary table in yearbook (e.g. *Statisticka Rocenka*, 1990, p. 558)
Hungary	Five-yearly income survey of non-institutional population (1987)	83.1% in 1988 (1987 incomes); about 20,000 households	Annual net income (total household, per capita, or equivalized) including agricultural income in kind	Summary table in yearbook (e.g. *Statistical Yearbook*, 1988, pp. 433–5)
Poland	Annual budget survey of non-institutional population (excluding households of non-agricultural private sector workers) (1989)	58.4% in 1989 among households selected for first participation (substitution of non-respondents); about 30,000 households	Annual net per capita income including income in kind	Summary table in yearbook for 4 household types (e.g. *Rocznik Statystyczny*, 1989, Table 19(233))
USSR	Annual budget survey of households of workers in socialized sector (1989)	Response unknown; about 92,000 families in 1989	Annual net per capita income including agricultural income in kind	Summary table in yearbook (e.g. *Narodnoe Khoziaistvo*, 1989, p. 89)
United Kingdom	Annual budget survey of non-institutional population (FES) (1989)	73% in 1989; about 7,500 households	Gross and net income collected for a variety of periods	No summary table of FES distribution in *Annual Abstract of Statistics*

household income has been obtained from sources whose main purpose is
different. The first of these is the income tax records, which are the basis

for the Survey of Personal Income (SPI) carried out each year by the Inland Revenue. This, however, excludes a substantial part of the non-tax-paying population – several million pensioners and others not at work – and does not cover non-taxable income, particularly certain social security benefits such as child benefit. It is not, therefore, on its own a satisfactory source. For this reason, the official estimates of the overall distribution have been based on a combination of information from the SPI and the annual Family Expenditure Survey (FES). These estimates are referred to as the Blue Book estimates, since they used to be published in the National Income Blue Book. However, the methods by which these estimates are constructed means that they cannot be put in a form comparable with the Eastern European data. In particular, they cannot be used to derive a distribution by *households*, rather than tax units, and they cannot be expressed on a per capita basis. For this reason, we rely on the information on the distribution of income provided by the Family Expenditure Survey, using the basic micro-data tapes.

Survey Design

In terms of survey design, the odd one out in Table 2.1 is the former USSR. In contrast to standard household survey methodology in the West, which samples on a geographic basis, the point of departure for household income data collection in the Soviet Family Budget Survey (FBS) has been the enterprise: the sampling unit has been employees at their place of work. The survey has been a quota sample of families of persons working in state enterprises and on collective farms. This meant that households without employed members were not normally included, although some 'pure' pensioner households have in fact been covered in recent years. Moreover, the quotas in the sampling process have meant that employees in heavy industry, and hence the urban population, appear to be over-represented. The survey is a panel, respondents being pressured to co-operate indefinitely, and this has further implications for the representativeness of the data. The sampling design is one important reason why the FBS has attracted substantial criticism both inside and outside the Soviet Union. Shenfield argues that Soviet planners and academic researchers where possible avoid the FBS and concludes that 'the sample is subject to a great many different biases, often severe and cumulative in effect, and that the survey is highly unrepresentative of the population as a whole' (Shenfield, 1984, p. 3). McAuley (1979, p. 51) argues that 'statistics from this source have been rejected by many, perhaps a majority, of Soviet economists and statisticians as worthless', but goes on to note that it represents the only source of information on a number of questions. It is in this spirit that we use the Soviet FBS here, returning to the deficiencies in section 2.4.

The position is quite different in the other Eastern European countries. In contrast to the methodology described in the USSR, the household surveys used here for Czechoslovakia, Hungary and Poland were all conducted on a geographic basis: in these countries the dwelling, not the worker, was the sampling unit. For example, the sampling frame for the Czechoslovak Microcensus in 1988 was a centralized administrative register used to record addresses of all dwellings so as to collect a combined payment for gas, electricity and other utilities. This seems broadly comparable to the postcode address file used since 1986 in the UK FES.

The planned coverage of the population by these surveys was reasonably complete, but certain categories of households were specifically excluded from the household surveys. This applied in Czechoslovakia and Poland to households with members in the army or the police. Our understanding is that households of members of the government or senior Communist Party officials were not in general excluded deliberately. In Poland a significant exclusion was of all households in which the main employment was the private non-agricultural sector, about 10 per cent of the labour force. All the surveys, including the FES in the UK, exclude persons living in institutions.

Response Rates

The achieved samples in the household surveys have been large: about 20 000 households in Hungary, 30 000 in Poland, 60 000 in the USSR (90 000 from 1988) and 100 000 in Czechoslovakia. These may be compared with a sample size in the UK of only some 7 500 households in the FES. It is true that the other main source of data used to give information in the UK on the distribution of income, the Survey of Personal Incomes, has a sample size of about 125 000 but this is based on a sample of tax records and is not a household survey.

The response rate to the survey by sampled households is also critical. To put the Eastern European surveys in perspective, it is useful to note that the overall level of response in Britain to the FES typically has been around 70 per cent of the effective sample. By this yardstick, the success of the periodic Czechoslovak Microcensus and the quinquennial Hungarian income survey was excellent: response to the former in 1988 was 97 per cent and to the latter was 91 per cent in 1982 and 83 per cent in 1987. In contrast, response in the 1980s by households first selected for the Polish budget survey (the survey has a rotating panel design) was at or below the level of the British FES, averaging 65 per cent during 1982–9, but with more variability, ranging from 71 per cent in 1983 to only 58 per cent in 1989. We have been unable to establish the extent of non-response to the Soviet family budget survey. Soviet statistical service (*Goskomstat*) officials denied to us that non-response was a problem, but Boldyreva (1989, p. 91) argues that it is difficult to get 'deviant' families to participate.

Verification of Data

Considerable effort in Eastern European surveys went into the collection of income data. In all four countries, earnings data provided by respondents were verified with their employers. A great deal of care appears to have been taken: for instance, in the Hungarian Income Survey where job changes had taken place during the year, the information was requested from each employer. In the Czechoslovak Microcensus, information on pensions was collected from post offices.

In the UK, the FES relies solely on information supplied by the respondents themselves. The survey officers do not ask respondents to give the names of their employers so that earnings data can be verified, nor does the survey have access to administrative records on social security payments. In the case of earnings, respondents are asked to verify their replies from wage slips and 70–80 per cent of them do so.

Second Economy

A significant amount of income from second-economy jobs and other activities, legal or otherwise, may be missing from household surveys, and this may be much more important in Eastern Europe than in the UK. The growth of the second economy in Hungary has been referred to by many authors (for example, Éltetö and Vita, 1989). There are reports of large increases in the USSR (Alexeev and Gaddy, 1991, p. 20). In Poland, an important source of income for many households appears to have been transfers of hard currency from relatives working abroad.

The coverage in household surveys of income from outside the official economy is a contentious subject. Writers on Eastern Europe often express concern that the recorded incomes refer only to 'official' income and that 'black economy income' does not enter the data considered. However, the notion that black economy income is *by definition* missing from Eastern European household surveys is in our view incorrect. Our interpretation of the relevant questionnaires, based on discussions with the statistical offices concerned, indicates that a respondent wishing to report all income, legally or illegally obtained, in general had the opportunity to do so without penalty. Of course, the *success* achieved in soliciting information about second-economy income, legal or illegal, is a matter for real debate. In pointing to attempts by statistical offices to collect data on 'illegal' income, we are not arguing that this was carried out in full. In the case of the USSR, a former member of the Soviet statistical service reported that

> people with considerable concealed income refuse to take part in the survey. They are afraid that the rule of confidentiality will not be respected, and justifiably so, because survey staff are not in a position to guarantee confidentiality. If, say, the KGB asks then for information, TsSU [the name of the Soviet statistical service at that time, forerunner to *Goskomstat*] has no right to refuse. (Quoted in Shenfield and Hanson, 1986, p. 64)

Official estimates put aggregate illegal income in the USSR at some 9 per cent of GDP, about 40 per cent of this being derived from the illicit production of alcohol but almost none coming from unlicensed work, which seems hardly credible (*Vestnik statistiki*, 1990, no. 6). Other estimates are significantly higher. Estimates based on a sample of Soviet émigrés suggest that up to a third of the urban population's income came from illegal sources (Grossman, 1987).

The under-reporting of second-economy income is a serious qualification of the distributional estimates for Eastern Europe. In section 2.4 we refer to some of the attempts which have been made to allow for its effect. It should, however, be noted that the problem of under-reporting is not absent in the UK, where there is, for example, concern about the accuracy of recorded self-employment income.

Time Period

The data in Eastern Europe refer to *annual* income, whereas those in the UK refer to a variety of periods depending on source. The UK data presented here are probably best interpreted as *current* income and as such may be expected to be more variable owing to changes in family status, wages and employment over the year. On the other hand, an important source of income variability in Britain, that stemming from unemployment, was largely missing in the pre-reform period in Eastern Europe. This means in turn that, if we were to seek to standardize the time period, it would make a difference whether we took the week/month or the year as the common basis. If there were less monthly variation in Eastern Europe, then the move to a monthly assessment period would not greatly change the measured inequality; but standardization on a year could significantly reduce the measured inequality in the UK.

Presentation of Results

The data for Eastern Europe relate to the distribution of income by *households*, and this is the unit of analysis adopted here. This leads in turn to the question of how each unit's income is adjusted to take account of differences in unit size. The standard practice in Eastern Europe, and that followed here, is to calculate *income per capita*. This practice is easy to carry out and to explain. It is, however, different from that in the UK, where no official statistics have been published on a per capita basis. Indeed, the main official figures, the Blue Book estimates, make no adjustment at all for the size of the income unit.

2.3   DISTRIBUTION OF HOUSEHOLD INCOMES

This section considers the evidence about the distribution of net household income in the five countries in the mid-1980s. Table 2.2 shows data for 1985 in Czechoslovakia, Poland and the USSR, and for 1982 in Hungary. The estimates all relate to the *individual distribution of household per capita income*. In each case, the official data come in tabulated form and we have typically had to interpolate within ranges to arrive at estimates of the quantiles, quantile shares and summary statistics of the distribution. (Details of the interpolation methods are given in Atkinson and Micklewright, 1992, 'Sources and Methods'.) The official statistics do not present data in Britain in per capita terms; for this reason we have given our own calculations for the per capita distribution in the UK based on the original micro-data. The Czechoslovak data exclude the value of income in kind, including that from agriculture, whereas an estimate of the latter is included in the data for the other countries.

If we look first at the percentiles, we find that Czechoslovakia has the least inequality. The bottom decile in Czechoslovakia has an income which is 66 per cent of the median, compared with 62 per cent in Hungary, 58 per cent in Poland, 54 per cent in USSR and 52 per cent in the UK. The lower quartile follows the same ranking, with Czechoslovakia and Hungary relatively close: 81 and 80 per cent, respectively, compared with 72 per cent in the UK. Above the median, Czechoslovakia and Hungary appear to be grouped together in exhibiting the least inequality. Poland and the USSR appear to form a second group, with a marked difference in the upper part of the distribution between these countries and the UK. The top decile in Poland is 175 per cent of the median, in USSR it is 178 per cent, but in the UK it is 201 per cent. Overall, the position is

Table 2.2   Summary of income distribution in 1982–5

Individual distribution of household per capita income					
P_{10}	P_{25}	P_{75}	P_{90}	P_{95}	P_{90}/P_{10}
Czechoslovakia 1985	66.4	81.4	127.1	160.3	182.9	2.41
Hungary 1982	62.0	79.5	128.6	162.1	187.8	2.61
Poland 1985	57.6	75.0	134.2	175.1	209.2	3.04
USSR 1985	53.7	74.3	135.3	177.3	206.9	3.30
United Kingdom 1985	52.0	71.8	144.5	200.9	248.7	3.86

	Cumulative decile shares									
	S_{10}	S_{20}	S_{30}	S_{40}	S_{50}	S_{60}	S_{70}	S_{80}	S_{90}	S_{91}
Czechoslovakia 1985	4.9	11.6	19.2	27.4	36.3	46.0	56.6	68.4	82.1	90.0
Hungary 1982	4.9	11.3	18.6	26.7	35.6	45.3	56.0	67.9	81.4	89.4
Poland 1985	4.2	9.9	16.6	24.2	32.7	42.1	52.7	64.7	78.8	87.4
USSR 1985	3.9	9.4	16.1	23.7	32.2	41.8	52.6	64.9	79.4	88.0
United Kingdom 1985	3.5	8.6	14.7	21.7	29.7	38.8	49.2	61.5	76.5	85.9

Sources: Atkinson and Micklewright (1992), Statistical Appendix Tables CSI1(continued), CSI2, HI1, HI2, PI1, PI2, UI1, UI2, BI3. Interpolation using INEQ program written by F.A. Cowell.

summarized clearly by the ratio of the top to bottom decile, referred to as the decile ratio (and rounded to one decimal place): Czechoslovakia, 2.4; Hungary, 2.6; Poland, 3.0; USSR, 3.3; UK, 3.9.

The distribution of income is more commonly presented in terms of *shares of total income*, which are the ingredients for drawing the Lorenz curves. The lower part of Table 2.2 shows the cumulative income shares, with S_x denoting the share in total income of the people who make up the bottom *x* per cent. The share of the bottom 10 per cent is estimated to be 4.9 per cent in Czechoslovakia and Hungary, compared with 3.5 per cent in the UK (Poland and the USSR hold an intermediate position).

From the point of view of the bottom 10 per cent in the UK, this means that a switch to a 'Czech/Hungarian' *distribution* of income would yield the same cash advantage as a 40 per cent increase in *average* income with the distribution remaining unchanged. Moving up the cumulative distribution, the share of the bottom fifth is 11–12 per cent in Czechoslovakia and Hungary, compared with 8.6 per cent in the UK. The 'advantage' of the more equal Czech distribution is in this case equivalent to a difference of about 35 per cent in average income. This is shown graphically in Figure 2.1. The vertical axis shows the increase in average income which would be necessary to compensate the bottom *x* per cent for a move to a UK distribution of income, for different values of *x* from 10 to 50. In the case of the bottom 30 per cent in Poland, for example, a rise of 13 per cent in average would be necessary to compensate for a move to the UK distribution.

The fact that the shares S_x are in each case higher, or no lower, for Czechoslovakia than for Hungary means that the Lorenz curve lies nearer to the line of equal incomes. (We do not actually draw the Lorenz curves, since the differences can be seen clearly from Table 2.2.) This applies right up the income scale: the share S_{90} is 82.1 per cent in Czechoslovakia, compared with 81.4 per cent in Hungary, which means that the top 10 per cent in Czechoslovakia have a share of 17.9 per cent, compared with a share of 18.6 per cent in Hungary. (Whether or not this, or other, differences are statistically significant is a question that requires information about the standard errors surrounding these figures.)

The Lorenz curves may be used to compare other countries. The curve for Hungary lies inside those for Poland and the USSR, as well as the UK. The curves for Poland and the USSR in turn lie inside that for the UK. With a sole exception, we have a situation of 'Lorenz dominance' where, when comparing two countries, we can say for one of the two countries that the bottom *x* per cent have a larger (or no smaller) share whatever value of *x* we choose. The exception – where the Lorenz curves cross – concerns Poland and the USSR. For shares up to S_{70}, Poland does better, but S_{80} and above are higher in the USSR.

Measures of Inequality

A quantitative indication of the extent of differences in the income

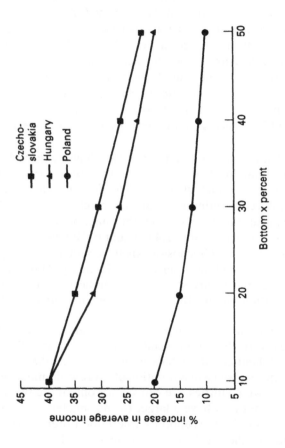

Note: The diagram shows % increase in mean income necessary to compensate for rise in inequality.
Source: Table 2.2

Figure 2.1 Distributional 'advantage' in Czechoslovakia, Hungary and Poland relative to UK

distribution can be provided by a measure of income inequality. The use of such measures does however involve, explicitly or implicitly, judgements about the weight to be placed on different parts of the distribution. It is interesting, therefore, to note the differences in the measures used in different countries.

Table 2.3   Measures of income inquality

	Gini	RHI[a]	HIM[b]	Estimated variance of logarithms[c]
Czechoslovakia 1985	19.9	13.9	1.76	0.113
Hungary 1982	20.9	15.0	1.82	0.132
Poland 1985	25.3	17.8	2.06	0.185
USSR 1985	25.6	18.2	2.08	0.210
United Kingdom 1985	29.7	21.2	2.74	0.268

Notes:
(a) RHI is the 'Robin Hood Index' and measures the amount of the income of those above the mean, expressed as a proportion of total income, that would have to be redistributed to those below the mean to bring about equal income.
(b) HIM is the 'Hungarian Inequality Measure' and is the ratio of the average income of those above the mean to the average income of those below the mean.
(c) See text for description of method used to estimate variance of logarithms.

Source: See Table 2.2.

A favourite in many countries is the Gini coefficient. Table 2.3 shows that the Gini coefficient is 20 per cent in Czechoslovakia and 30 per cent in the UK. Between these two countries there is indeed the ten percentage point difference found by Pryor (1973, p. 88). Nor is Czechoslovakia exceptional, as some writers have suggested. The Gini coefficient for Hungary is nine percentage points less than that in the UK. It is only for Poland and the USSR that the difference from the UK is reduced to four percentage points.

Statisticians in Eastern Europe have tended to emphasize other measures of inequality. The 'maximum equalization percentage' made popular by the UN Economic Commission for Europe (1967, c. 6) has been used extensively in Poland. It involves taking those decile groups whose share exceeds 10 per cent and adding the excess of these shares over that level. For 1985, Table 2.2 gives Table 2.4, so that the total value of the index is 17.8. The index approximates the share of total income which has to be taken from those above the mean, and transferred to those below the mean in order to achieve equality. (It is an approximation since it is based on data grouped by deciles.) Algebraically, it is half the mean deviation divided by the mean. Here, in view of its simple interpretation, we refer to it as the *Robin Hood Index* (RHI). From Table 2.3 Robin Hood would have less work to do in Hungary and Czechoslovakia and quite a lot more work in the UK, where he would have to transfer 21 per cent of total income.

Table 2.4

	Share	Contribution to maximum equalization percentage
7 decile	10.6	0.6
8 decile	12.0	2.0
9 decile	14.1	4.1
10 decile	21.1	11.1

The Hungarian statistical office has used a variation on this measure of inequality: the ratio of average income above the mean to average incomes below the mean (see Éltetö and Frigyes, 1968). (The relationship between this measure and the Robin Hood Index changes as the proportion of the population above the mean changes.) The values of the *Hungarian Inequality Measure* (HIM) are shown in Table 2.3. In the UK the average income of those above the mean is 2.75 times that of those below the mean, which is quite a lot higher than in Poland and the USSR where the ratio is double. In Hungary, the value is 1.8, and Czechoslovakia has again the least inequality, with a value of 1.75.

Peter Hart has argued forcefully (for example, in Hart, 1978) for preferring *parametric* estimators of inequality to the non-parametric indices used so far in this section. As he notes,

> if an income distribution approximates a standard theoretical statistical distribution, the choice of inequality measure is considerably simplified because we can use the estimated parameters of the theoretical distribution. (Hart, 1981, p. 3)

As in his work, we have used the lognormal distribution. First, we plotted the cumulative distributions on log probability paper (that is, plotting log income against a normal probability scale), which 'although [it] can hardly be regarded as a rigorous statistical test of lognormality . . . nevertheless provides a quick method of judging whether the population may feasibly be lognormal' (Aitchison and Brown, 1957, p. 32). If the distribution were lognormal, this procedure would yield a straight-line graph. The approximate linearity in our plots suggested that the lognormal provided a reasonable fit, judged by eye, for the fifth to ninety-fifth percentiles in Hungary, the USSR and UK, but that there was a slight perceptible upward curve in Czechoslovakia, and that the fit was less good in Poland. Secondly, we obtained an estimate of the variance of logarithms from the ratio of the (interpolated) eighty-fourth and sixteenth percentiles. (The estimated standard deviation is equal to half the natural logarithm of the ratio; see Aitchison and Brown, 1957, p. 32.) The resulting estimates of the variance of logarithms are shown in the final column in Table 2.3. Again there appear to be three groups: (a) Czechoslovakia, followed by Hungary, with the lowest variance; (b) then Poland and the former USSR, although with a more noticeable gap between them; and (c) finally, the UK with the largest estimated variance.

2.4 LIMITATIONS OF THE EVIDENCE

The conclusions drawn from these statistics may change when we take account of the deficiencies of the data. In section 2.2 and in Atkinson and Micklewright (1992), we have described the sources of data on household incomes and indicated some of their limitations. All data are imperfect, and one advantage of the comparative perspective is that it allows us to see how the shortcomings of the Eastern European data compare with those of Western data. At the same time, it should be remembered that it is not just *differences* in methods of collecting data that may cause problems. Statistical deficiencies which are common to East and West may have different implications because of the social and economic differences. Household budget surveys exclude the homeless, an omission which is more significant in some countries than others. Inadequate coverage of income from the underground economy is likely to be more important in Eastern Europe. The omission from income data of capital gains is more serious in Western countries with substantial private ownership of capital and land.

One major reference point in assessing the quality of the data has been comparisons with the national accounts. In the case of the USSR, Alexeev and Gaddy (1991), drawing on work by Treml (1990), have compared the aggregate incomes of several types recorded in the Family Budget Survey (FBS) with those shown in national accounts. The differences were an over-statement of 11 per cent of state wages and salaries, and of 6.5 per cent of collective farm pay, and an under-statement of 10 per cent in state transfers. Alexeev and Gaddy argue that these figures 'conclusively demonstrated the unrepresentativeness' (1991, p. 22) of the FBS.

These discrepancies should, however, be compared with those found in Western sources. In the case of the Family Expenditure Survey (FES) data from the UK, we have investigated the divergence between income aggregates recorded in the survey for the years 1970–7 and those shown in the national accounts (Atkinson and Micklewright, 1983). The results from this exercise for 1977 show a shortfall for earnings in the FES of 6 per cent, a figure which is described in the official FES Report (Central Statistical Office, 1989, p. v) as indicating that earnings in the survey are 'slightly deficient'. For social security benefits, the deficiency was 9 per cent – a figure very similar to that quoted for state transfers in the USSR Family Budget Survey. When we come to income from self-employment and occupational pensions, we find that there is a shortfall of around one-quarter; and for investment income as much as one-half of total income appears to be missing from the FES.

The fact that such large income shortfalls should be observed in the UK FES, a survey which is widely recognised within the UK and elsewhere to be of a high standard, leads us to be cautious in reaching critical conclusions about the data for Eastern Europe. We find relatively reassuring the finding that per capita personal income recorded in the 1987 Hungarian income survey was 96 per cent of that indicated by aggregate sources (*Statistical Yearbook*, 1988, p. 427). Similarly, we were told that per capita money income in the 1988 Czechoslovak microcensus was 86 per cent of that suggested by aggregate data but that at least half the shortfall could be attributed to differences in definition, something which we found to be important in the comparison of the UK FES with the national accounts (and which has been allowed for in the comparison quoted).

At the same time, there are clearly weaknesses in the available household income data. Here we concentrate on those which may have caused inequality to be *under*stated in Eastern Europe, and those which may cause inequality to be *over*stated in the UK.

Sample Design

The first reason for understatement of inequality in the USSR is the problem of sample design. As a result of the way that the sample is drawn for the Soviet FBS, there can be no doubt that the survey is unrepresentative. The under-representation of pensioner households may be expected to cause inequality to be understated, although this under-representation may be less serious in the 1980s than in the past. A second major problem is that the panel nature of the FBS leads it to be unrepresentative of the working population, in that it is biased towards those with longer service records. This again may cause inequality to be understated.

In the three Central European countries the sample design is comparable with that in the UK, except for the exclusion in Poland of households whose principal source of income is the private non-agricultural sector. The latter exclusion may cause inequality to be understated. Differential non-response, in all three countries, may have the same effect: for example, there are signs that response is lower in large cities, where there may be more of both high- and low-income households. It should be noted that the level of response is different across countries and that in the case of Poland non-respondents were substituted with other households with similar characteristics.

Missing Income

Among respondents there is a problem of incomplete reporting or coverage of income. The incomplete coverage of agricultural production affects Eastern Europe to a greater degree than the UK. In the case of Czechoslovakia, the distribution examined here does not include the value of farm production for own-consumption. This may cause the degree of inequality to be overstated in so far as this source of income is proportionately more important at the bottom of the scale. In the case of the other Eastern European countries, an estimate of this income is included but there are issues concerning the valuation of output. The use of state prices for farm produce may cause incomes such as those of collective farmworkers in the USSR to be understated.

One of the most important problems is the omission or under-recording of income from private business activity, from illegal activities and from overseas remittances. Assessing the possible effect of un-recorded incomes on the *distribution* of income is a daunting task. An impressive attempt to do so is the study for Hungary by Éltetö and Vita (1989). They took as their starting point the microdata in the 1982 Hungarian income survey. The survey sample for this year was divided into 71 sub-groups on the basis of sex, occupation and type of residence, and the individuals in each were subjected to a separate micro-simulation treatment in respect of 'hidden' income, defined by the authors as 'unauthorized and/or tax-evading productive and service activities, tips, gratitude payments' (Éltetö and Vita, 1989, p. 4). This simulation increased the incidence and/or recorded amounts of hidden income in each sub-group, with, for example, high values of these parameters for doctors, dentists, hairdressers and beauticians living in Budapest. Within each group, simulated amounts of hidden income for each individual were drawn from a lognormal distribution. The recorded data in the 1982 survey indicated that these forms of income accounted for only 2 per cent of personal income. Éltetö and Vita experimented with three different assumptions increasing the proportion of hidden income in 'low', 'medium' or 'high' variants to 6, 8 or 11 per cent respectively. The effect of the simulations was to increase inequality of incomes; we estimate from Éltetö and Vita's results that the decile ratio rose after adjustment from 2.6 to 2.9 under the 'high' variant. Referring back to Table 2.2, even taking the 'high' variant and even supposing no upward adjustment to be necessary to the UK figures, there remains noticeably less inequality in Hungary (the UK decile ratio is 3.9). The results from this exercise cannot, of course, be seen as necessarily representative of the impact of under-recording of income in Central Europe. However, certain aspects of the Hungarian situation may be applicable, and it gives an impression of the possible quantitative impact. In the case of the USSR, there has been debate as to the distributional impact of illegal incomes. It has been suggested that illegal earnings in different jobs were inversely related to the official rates of pay. Alexeev and Gaddy make use of data for a sample of some 1000 families which emigrated from the USSR to the United States in the late 1970s and early 1980s. The results show that the Gini coefficient for total income from all sources, legal and illegal, was only one percentage point higher than that for legal incomes for those coming from Russia, Belarus, Ukraine, Moldavia and the Baltic republics, but that it was seven percentage points higher for those from the Trans-caucasus and Central Asian republics (Alexeev and Gaddy, 1991, Table 5.1). It should be noted that the results are based on a small and largely urban sample.

Non-monetary Privileges of the Elite

One of the features of the former USSR that has attracted considerable Western attention is the provision of substantial benefits in kind to a small 'elite' group of *nomenklatura*: top Party and government officials, army officers, managers, scientists and academics (see, for example, the study by Matthews, 1978). These included the provision of superior housing, provision of cars and chauffeurs, holiday homes (dachas), access to foreign currency for travel, and access to foreign-currency shops where imported goods could be purchased. At the same time, non-cash benefits were not limited to the elite, and the more evident privilege at the top should be seen as part of structured pattern of differential remuneration. Particularly in the USSR, the 'quality' of the enterprise one worked for was a most important determinant of living standards independent of the level of earnings.

What is the likely impact of such benefits in kind on the degree of income inequality in Eastern Europe? One brave attempt to estimate the effect of benefits for the *nomenklatura* was that of Morrisson (1984). He started from estimates for the size of the 'privileged' population varying from 0.2 to 1.5 per cent in the USSR and of 0.7 per cent in Poland. As has been noted by several writers, adjustment for the missing income of a group of this size would not affect the estimated decile ratio or other percentiles below the elite group. (These measures *would*, of course, be affected by more generally distributed non-wage benefits received by those lower down the distribution.)

The shares in total income and the Gini coefficient would however be affected. In order to show what he believed to be the *maximum* impact of special advantages of the 'privileged', Morrisson made an adjustment to the data on household income distribution for a number of Eastern European countries, including the four we considered here, by assuming that these advantages in every country represented at most half the recorded income of the top 5 per cent of the distribution. Summary inequality measures of the income distribution were then estimated for each country with and without the adjustment for top incomes. In between these, Morrisson argued, 'the true distribution certainly lies' (Morrisson, 1984, p. 126).

To treat the elite population as being as extensive as the top 5 per cent seems to be casting the net wide. In contrast, Bergson (1984, p. 1070) took the elite population as 0.3 per cent of the urban population, and Morrisson himself (1984, p. 126n) referred to 1.5 per cent. Here we present an alternative calculation, taking the latter figure to represent the elite population, and asking how large the payments to the top 1.5 per cent would have to be for the Gini coefficient in Eastern Europe to equal that in the UK in 1985 (29.7 per cent). It should be borne in mind that this can only be an approximate calculation since we are interpolating in an open upper interval to arrive at the share of the top 1.5 per cent. (Also, since this is only an illustrative calculation, we use the linearized Lorenz curve drawn in terms of deciles to calculate the Gini coefficient.) The calculation shows that the increase in their income necessary to raise the

Gini coefficient to the UK level would be around 125 per cent in the USSR and Poland: that is, we would have to more than double the income of the top 1.5 per cent. In the case of Hungary, the income of the top 1.5 per cent would have to be multiplied by a factor of some 4.5; for Czechoslovakia it would require a factor of 5. This calculation is clearly arbitrary, and attributes no value to what may admittedly be the lesser but none the less widespread non-wage benefits received by those at lower points of the income distribution.

In the West, these benefits in kind are referred to as 'fringe benefits', but this should not be taken as meaning that they are necessarily small in scale or extent. Indeed, in a country such as Britain, minor 'perks' or better working conditions associated with better-paid jobs are so widespread as scarcely to warrant mention. Substantial benefits are available to top managers in the private sector. Obtaining quantitative evidence about the scale and distribution of payments in kind is not easy. In Britain, the Royal Commission on the Distribution of Income and Wealth (1979) distinguished between 'welfare' benefits, generally available to all employees in a firm, including free or subsidized meals, sports facilities, and goods at discount prices, and benefits intended to attract and retain staff, particularly executives, which were concentrated at the top end of the earnings scale. The survey evidence quoted by the Commission showed that 67 per cent of executives had full use of a company car, 62 per cent had free life assurance, 44 per cent had free medical insurance, and 10 per cent had low interest loans (1979, Table 9.9). The overall conclusion of the Royal Commission was that 'there is little doubt that if account were taken of employee benefits, working conditions and other aspects of employment, the dispersion of the earnings distribution would be increased. The effect within the top one per cent of employees must be particularly marked' (Royal Commission, 1979, p. 233).

The United Kingdom Data

There are also factors which may cause the degree of inequality in the UK to be overstated. The measurement of income over a week or month may lead to a higher recorded degree of inequality than annual income. Estimates of the possible effect have been made by Nolan using the same data source as in Table 2.2, but for the earlier year of 1977. The effect on the inequality of pre-tax income is to reduce the Robin Hood Index from 24.9 per cent to 24.2 per cent (Nolan, 1987, Table 5.1, p. 71). On this basis we could account for only a modest part of the difference. Moreover, against this must be set a number of factors which may cause inequality to be understated in the UK. These include the lower response of the self-employed to the FES, the tendency for self-employment and investment income to be understated, and the omission of fringe benefits already discussed.

2.5 CONCLUSIONS

This chapter has summarised the evidence about the distribution of household income in three countries of Central Europe and the former USSR, compared with the United Kingdom. The evidence refers to the mid-1980s, and it should be noted that the trends over time in the five countries have been rather different (see Atkinson and Micklewright, 1992, ch. 5), so that the conclusions may differ for this reason from those reached in earlier studies.

Results for the mid-1980s confirm the earlier finding that income inequality in Czechoslovakia is substantially less than in the UK. The Gini coefficient is some ten percentage points less, and the decile ratio is 2.4 compared with 3.9. Put another way, if the price of economic progress in Czechoslovakia is a fall in the share of the bottom 10 per cent to that in the UK, then an increase of 40 per cent in real average income is necessary for the lowest 10 per cent simply to maintain their absolute level of income.

At the same time, our findings bring out the differences, not just between East and West, but also *within Eastern Europe*. The distribution for Hungary appears relatively close to that in Czechoslovakia: the share of the bottom 10 per cent is the same, and the Gini coefficient in Hungary is only one percentage point higher. But the Lorenz curves for these two countries lie comfortably inside those for Poland and the former USSR. The Gini coefficients for these latter two countries are some four to five percentage points higher. So that, while we find the recorded degree of inequality to be less in all four countries than in the UK, they should not be regarded as identical.

The above summarizes briefly *what the statistics show* about the distribution of household income in Eastern Europe. The italicized phrase is important, since we have emphasized the shortcomings of the statistical data in both Eastern Europe and the United Kingdom. We should also stress the problems of interpretation which surround the concept of income in Eastern Europe, notably those that arise in an economy where goods are rationed (this aspect is discussed further in Atkinson and Micklewright, 1992).

NOTE

1. The chapter draws on material on the distribution of income in Eastern Europe described in more detail in Atkinson and Micklewright (1992). We are most grateful to the many people in Eastern Europe who made data available to us and provided information about sources. In analysing and interpreting the data, we have been greatly helped by Gianna Giannelli, Joanna Gomulka, Denise Marchant and Sheila Marnie. We thank the referee for his helpful comments.

REFERENCES

Aitchison, J. and J.A.C. Brown (1957): *The Lognormal Distribution* (Cambridge: Cambridge University Press).

Alexeev, M.V. and C.G. Gaddy (1991): *Trends in Wage and Income Distribution under Gorbachev: Analysis of New Soviet Data*, Berkeley-Duke Occasional Papers on the Second Economy in the USSR, no. 25 (Durham, N.C.: Duke University).

Atkinson, A.B. and J. Micklewright (1983): 'On the reliability of income data in the Family Expenditure Survey 1970–77', *Journal of the Royal Statistical Society*, Series A, **146**, 33–61.

—— (1992): *Economic Transformation in Eastern Europe and the Distribution of Income* (Cambridge: Cambridge University Press).

Bergson, A. (1984): 'Income inequality under Soviet socialism', *Journal of Economic Literature*, **22**, 1052–99.

Boldyreva, T. (1989): 'Columns of figures or an instrument of social policy?', *Problems of Economics*, **32**, 89–102.

Bruinooge, G., Ö. Éltetö, G. Fajth and G. Grubben (1990): 'Income distributions in an international perspective – the case of Hungary and The Netherlands', *Statistical Journal of the United Nations*, **7**, 39–53.

Central Statistical Office (1989): *Family Expenditure Survey 1988* (London: Her Majesty's Stationery Office).

Chenery, H., M.S. Ahluwalia, C.L.G. Bell, J.H. Duloy and R. Jolly (1974): *Redistribution with Growth* (Oxford: Oxford University Press).

Ellman, M. (1990): 'A note on the distribution of income in the USSR under Gorbachev', *Soviet Studies*, **42**, 147–8.

Éltetö, Ö. and E. Frigyes (1968): 'New income inequality measures as efficient tools for causal analysis and planning', *Econometrica*, **36**, 383–96.

Éltetö, Ö. and L. Vita (1989): 'A micro-simulation experiment for the estimation of the possible effect of incomes from the underground economy on the income distribution: methods and results', 47th Session of the International Statistical Institute, Paris, 29 August–6 September.

Grossman, G. (1987): 'Roots of Gorbachev's problems: private income and outlay in the late 1970s', in *Gorbachev's Economic Plans* (Washington, D.C.: US Congress Joint Economic Committee).

Hart, P.E. (1978): 'Redundant inequalities', National Institute of Economic and Social Research Discussion Paper no. 18 (London: NIESR).

—— (1981): 'The statics and dynamics of income distribution: a survey', in N.A. Klevmarken and J.A. Lybeck (eds), *The Statics and Dynamics of Income* (Clevedon: Tieto) 1–20.

Hungarian Central Statistical Office (1975): *Hungarian Survey on Relative Income Differences* (Budapest: KSH).

Lydall, H.F. (1979): 'Some problems in making international comparisons of inequality', in J.R. Moroney (ed.), *Income Inequality: Trends and International Comparisons* (Lexington, Mass.: D.C. Heath).

Matthews, M. (1978): *Privilege in the Soviet Union* (London: Allen & Unwin).

McAuley, A.N.D. (1979): *Economic Welfare in the Soviet Union* (Madison: University of Wisconsin Press).

Morrisson, C. (1984): 'Income distribution in East European and Western countries', *Journal of Comparative Economics*, 8, 121–38.

Nolan, B. (1987): *Income Distribution and the Macroeconomy* (Cambridge: Cambridge University Press).

Pryor, F.L. (1973): *Property and Industrial Organization in Communist and Capitalist Nations* (Bloomington: Indiana University Press).

Royal Commission on the Distribution of Income and Wealth (1979): *Fifth Report on the Standing Reference* (London: Her Majesty's Stationery Office).

Shenfield, S. (1984): *The Mathematical-Statistical Methodology of the Contemporary Soviet Family Budget Survey*. PhD thesis, Faculty of Commerce and Social Science, University of Birmingham.

Shenfield, S. and Hanson, P. (1986): *The Functioning of the Soviet System of State Statistics (Findings from Interviews with Former Soviet Statistical Personnel)*, CREES Special Report SR–86–1, Centre for Russian and East European Studies, University of Birmingham.

Statistical Yearbook 1988, Budapest, Hungary: KSH.

Treml, V.G. (1990): 'Note on the unrepresentativeness of the Goskomstat Household Budget Survey', unpublished research memorandum for the Berkeley-Duke Project on the Second Economy in the USSR, Department of Economics, Duke University, Durham, N.C.

UN Economic Commission for Europe (1967): *Incomes in Postwar Europe: A Study of Policies, Growth and Redistribution* (Geneva: United Nations).

Wiles, P.J.D. (1978): 'Our shaky data base', in W. Krelle and A.F. Shorrocks (eds), *Personal Income Distribution* (Amsterdam: North-Holland) 167–92.

3. Wage Rate Mobility and Measurement Errors: An Application to Swedish Panel Data

N. Anders Klevmarken[1]

3.1 EARNINGS MOBILITY AND THE GALTON MODEL OF REGRESSION TOWARDS THE MEAN

Mobility of earnings over the life-cycle has gained increased research interest as more panel data have become available and because earnings mobility has become of greater concern in economic policy. In a recent survey Atkinson, Bourguignon and Morrisson (1992) mention a number of reasons for this. From the point of view of distributional equity, earnings mobility is of instrumental importance because in a society with high mobility the inequality in life-cycle earnings is in general smaller than in a society with low mobility. The debate on the future of public pension systems has also generated an interest in earnings mobility because some pay-as-you-go systems have a rule that the size of the pension depends on the earnings obtained during, for instance, the 15 or 20 best years. To predict pension expenditures for these systems, a model of earnings mobility is needed. Also, most income tax systems include some provision for smoothing wildly fluctuating incomes.

Atkinson *et al.* (1992) also suggest that high earnings mobility might be evidence of economic efficiency and also possibly of a labour market which is relatively free from regulations and discrimination. In quoting Hart (1980, p. 9) they propose that mobility might have a beneficial impact on incentives: 'it is mobility which provides the sticks for those who do not want to move down the distribution and the carrots for those who wish to move up'.

There is a variety of definitions of earnings mobility. Following Creedy, Hart and Klevmarken (1980) this chapter takes the Galtonian regression model as its starting point. For further analysis, see Chapter 1 above. Assume the following model:

$$y_{it} - m_{it} = \beta(y_{it-1} - m_{it-1}) + u_{it} \qquad (3.1)$$

where y_{it} is the log of earnings for individual i at time point t, m_{it} the average log earnings profile to be defined later, u_{it} a random error with zero expectation and β a parameter. Mobility relative to the average profile m_{it} is determined by the sign and size of β and the properties of u_{it}, in particular its variance. If β equals one, people tend to hold their relative earnings positions except for purely random shifts, the size of which depends on the variance of u_{it}, while a positive β less than one gives regression towards the mean, and a positive β greater than one, movement away from the mean. If β equals zero there is only random mobility around the mean income. A negative β implies that people alternate between relatively high and low earnings. If β equals minus one they tend to alternate between positions of equal distance from the mean, and if β is greater than minus one but less than zero the alternating process tends towards the mean, while it leads away from the mean if β is less than minus one. There are thus two values of β, zero and one, for which there is only random mobility and no systematic mobility.

When the Galtonian model has been used as a descriptive tool it has frequently been applied to earnings data. This has the disadvantage that the wage rate process is not distinguished from the hours of work process. Each has its separate explanation, and to understand earnings mobility a model of each process is needed. However, this chapter is limited to the wage-rate process, and its focus is on estimating the mobility of this process. In the following, y_{it} refers to logarithmic hourly wage rates.

The properties of u_{it} and the size of β depend on the specification of the average profile m_{it}. This study relies on a wage rate function of the Mincer type which allows the mean profile to depend on schooling, experience, age and seniority. The empirical analysis is limited to men. An analysis of women would have the additional complexity of treating the self-selection problem caused by a smaller female labour force participation.

A potential problem with this model is that ordinary and generalized least squares estimators give biased and inconsistent estimates of β if there are measurement errors in the wage-rate variable. This might not be a great problem with earnings data measured over a long period and if they come from company records, or from tax files or national insurance records as in the case of Hart (1976) and Creedy, Hart and Klevmarken (1980). But if they are weekly earnings data or hourly wage rates, then there may be noise arising from transitory components. If data originate from a survey with self-reported earnings or wage rates, measurement errors are certainly a problem. The validation study comparing company records and survey responses and reported in Duncan and Hill (1985), Bound *et al.* (1990) and Rodgers *et al.* (1991) confirms this. If measurement errors have the properties of random noise, β will in general be underestimated. This validation study, however, indicates that measurement errors have a more complicated structure, the consequences of which might become even worse.

In section 3.2 measurement errors are introduced and the model is reformulated in the form of a conventional earnings function which has no lagged values to the right of the equality sign. This brings the parameter β into the covariance matrix of the reformulated model. The advantage of this reformulation is not only that it facilitates the estimation of a model with measurement errors, it also links the Galtonian approach to mobility analysis with earnings models which elaborate on the 'fine structure of earnings', that is, on the structure of the residual covariance matrix. Section 3.3 describes the data used and section 3.4 presents results. In a preliminary analysis the average wage-rate function is first estimated by OLS, ignoring any residual covariance structure, and the residuals used to compute the empirical variance–covariance matrix. This analysis suggests minor revisions of the model, before it is estimated by the maximum likelihood method taking the full variance–covariance structure into account. The final section summarizes the findings and includes suggestions for additional research.

3.2. A MODEL OF WAGE RATE MOBILITY WITH MEASUREMENT ERRORS IN THE WAGE RATE VARIABLE

Assume the following adjustment model:

$$y_{it}^{*}-m_{it}=\beta(y_{it-1}^{*}-m_{it-1})+\varepsilon_{it} \tag{3.2}$$

where y_{it}^{*} is the true log hourly wage rate of individual i at years of experience t, m_{it} is the average log wage rate for individuals of the same type as i, and ε_{it} is a random error with expectation zero and variance σ_{ε}^{2}. The average wage rate profile will become defined below in the human capital tradition.

The individual wage rate is not directly observed, but has a measurement error,

$$y_{it}=y_{it}^{*}+u_{it} \tag{3.3}$$

where y_{it} is the observed wage rate and u_{it} the measurement error.

Measurement errors in the wage rate variable might have many causes. In this chapter data were obtained from survey questions on pay and normal hours worked. For people who are not paid by the hour but, for instance, by the month, an estimate of the hourly wage rate is obtained by dividing the monthly pay by the product of 4.3 weeks and reported normal hours per week. In general, one might expect reporting errors both in pay and in hours and the properties of these errors might depend on how each individual is paid. For instance, white collar employees with regular monthly salaries and regular hours probably report their pay and hours more accurately than employees on piece-rate and with unregular working hours. There are also individual differences in ability and care in responding to survey questions. The following assumes that the measurement error in (3.3) is decomposed into two components:

$$u_{it} = \lambda_i + z_{it} \tag{3.4}$$

where λ_i is a permanent individual error component and z_{it} an independent white noise component.

Assume also that there are unobserved individual characteristics which determine mobility, that is, the random error of the adjustment mechanism (3.2) is assumed to have the following error component structure:

$$\varepsilon_{it} = \delta_i + v_{it} \tag{3.5}$$

where δ_i is a permanent individual component and v_{it} a white noise component. All random components are assumed to have zero expectation and constant variances: σ_δ^2, σ_v^2, σ_λ^2, σ_z^2, respectively. They are also independent of all variables indexing the average wage rate profile. The white noise components of equations (3.4) and (3.5) are assumed to be independent of each other and of the permanent components, but a non-zero correlation between the latter two is in principle allowed, that is:

$$E(\delta_i v_{it}) = E(\lambda_i z_{it}) = E(v_{it} z_{it}) = 0; \qquad \forall\ i,t \tag{3.6}$$

$$E(\delta_i \lambda_i) = \sigma_{\delta\lambda}; \qquad \forall\ i \tag{3.7}$$

The initial condition of each individual process, that is, the wage rate of the first job of a career is given by

$$y_{i0}^* = m_{i0} + \varepsilon_{i0} \tag{3.8}$$

and the observed initial wage rate by

$$y_{i0} = \overset{*}{y}_{i0} + u_{i0} \tag{3.9}$$

The random errors of (3.8) and (3.9) also have the error component structure of (3.4) and (3.5). From (3.2) and (3.8) we obtain:

$$\overset{*}{y}_{i1} - m_{i1} = \beta \varepsilon_{i0} + \varepsilon_{i1} \tag{3.10}$$

and, with (3.9) inserted,

$$y_{i1} = m_{i1} + \beta \varepsilon_{i0} + \varepsilon_{i1} + u_{i1} \tag{3.11}$$

In general it holds that

$$y_{it} = m_{it} + \sum_{j=0}^{t} \beta^j \varepsilon_{it-1} + u_{it}; \qquad \forall \ i, t = 0, \dots \tag{3.12}$$

Denote by e_{it} the composite error term of equation (3.12). From the assumptions made it follows that

$$e_{it} = \sum_{j=0}^{t} \beta^j (\delta_i + v_{it-j}) + \lambda_i + z_{it} =$$

$$\begin{cases} \delta_i \dfrac{(\beta^{t+1} - 1)}{\beta - 1} + \sum_{j=0}^{t} \beta^j v_{it-j} + \lambda_i + z_{it} \ ; & \text{if } \beta \neq 1 \\[2mm] \delta_i(t+1) + \sum_{j=0}^{t} v_{it-j} + \lambda_i + z_{it}; & \text{if } \beta = 1 \end{cases} \tag{3.13}$$

Thus,

$$E(e_{it}) = 0 \tag{3.14}$$

$$E(e_{it}^2) = \begin{cases} \sigma_\delta^2 \dfrac{(\beta^{t+1} - 1)^2}{(\beta - 1)^2} + \sigma_v^2 \dfrac{\beta^{2(t+1)} - 1}{\beta^2 - 1} + \sigma_\lambda^2 + \sigma_z^2 + 2\sigma_{\delta\lambda} \dfrac{\beta^{t+1} - 1}{\beta - 1}; & \text{if } \beta \neq 1 \\[2mm] \sigma_\delta^2(t+1)^2 + \sigma_v^2(t+1) + \sigma_\lambda^2 + 2\sigma_{\delta\lambda}(t+1) \ ; & \text{if } \beta = 1 \end{cases} \tag{3.15}$$

$$E(e_{is}e_{it}) = \begin{cases} \sigma_\delta^2 + \dfrac{(\beta^{s+1} - 1)(\beta^{t+1} - 1)}{(\beta - 1)^2} + \sigma_v^2 \dfrac{\beta^{s+t+2} - \beta^{t-s}}{\beta^2 - 1} + \\[2mm] \sigma_\lambda^2 + \sigma_{\delta\lambda} \dfrac{(\beta^{s+1} - 1) + (\beta^{t+1} - 1)}{\beta - 1}; & \forall \ s < t; \quad \text{if } \beta \neq 1 \\[2mm] \sigma_\delta^2(s+1)(t+1) + \sigma_v^2(s+1) + \sigma_\lambda^2 + \sigma_{\delta\lambda}(s+1+t+1) \ ; \\[1mm] \hspace{5cm} \forall \ s < t \ ; \ \text{if } \beta = 1 \end{cases} \tag{3.16}$$

Expression (3.15) and (3.16) show that when β equals zero the model reduces to an ordinary variance component model with constant residual variance and covariance. In this case the covariance between two residual deviations from the average wage rate profile is thus independent of the time span between the two observations. When β deviates from zero the variance around the average wage rate profile will increase with increasing experience. If the absolute value of β is less than one it will increase at a decreasing rate of increase. Thus regression towards the mean tends to moderate the increase in wage-rate inequality with increasing experience, while it is magnified by regression away from the mean.

The covariance between successive wage-rate observations show the same general pattern with experience, provided the covariance between the two permanent variance components is not negative and large in absolute value.

The correlation between successive wage-rate observations as a function of experience may take various shapes, but for a wide range of parameter values it is an increasing function. If measured by the correlation coefficient, mobility is thus higher in the beginning of the career than at the end.

The assumption that everyone has the same β might seem very restrictive. However, the adjustment mechanism (3.2) can be written on the following form:

$$y^*_{it} - m_{it} = \left(\beta + \frac{\varepsilon_{it}}{y^*_{it-1} - m_{it-1}} \right) (y^*_{it-1} - m_{it-1}) = \left(\beta - \frac{\varepsilon_{it}}{\varepsilon_{it-1}} \right) (y^*_{it-1} - m_{it-1})$$

$$(3.17)$$

The model can thus be viewed as a proportional adjustment mechanism with individually varying proportionality factors. If ε is assumed to be a normal variate, the second term within large parentheses is the ratio between two correlated normal variates. The distribution of this ratio will have thick tails, which implies that in each period a few individuals will experience drastic changes in their relative earnings positions; the ratio follows a Cauchy distribution; see Arnold and Brockett (1992).

When the model is formulated as a wage rate profile in equation (3.12) all mobility parameters of interest are found in the variance–covariance matrix. In the literature on earnings profiles, several studies have elaborated on the structure of the variance–covariance matrix. For instance, in a theoretical analysis of optimal investments in human capital, von Weizäcker (1988) derived a life-cycle model of individual earnings. He assumed that each individual had its own initial stock of human capital and efficiency in aquiring new human capital. Both variables were random variables. In the present notation the residual structure of von Weizäcker's model can be written (there were no measurement errors):

$$e_{it} = \varepsilon_{i0} + a(t)\delta_i \qquad (3.18)$$

where ε_{i0} is interpreted as the individual deviation from the mean return on the initial endowment of human capital, δ_i an individual component related to efficiency in learning, and $a(t)$ a generally increasing function of years of experience.

Lillard & Willis (1978) generalized a conventional errors component model by making the individual and time varying component autoregressive. Their residual model can be written:

$$e_{it} = \delta_i + v_{it} = \delta_i + \rho v_{it-1} + \eta_{it} \qquad (3.19)$$

They estimated their model on seven contiguous years of data from the Michigan Panel Study of Income Dynamics. The selected subsample included only male household heads who had reported positive annual hours and earnings each year. The estimates depended on which of two alternative specifications of the average profile they used. When only race, years of schooling and experience, and time dummies were used the individual heterogeneity component σ_δ exceeded the white noise component σ_v but with a richer specification including a number of interaction terms the two components were approximately of the same size. The estimate of ρ was close to 0.4 and the corresponding correlation coefficient approximately 0.5.

This model was further generalized in Hause (1977, 1980), who used the following residual specification:

$$e_{it} = \phi_{i1} + \phi_{i2}t + u_{it} = \phi_{i1} + \phi_{i2}t + \rho_{t-1}u_{it-1} + \varepsilon_{it} \qquad (3.20)$$

The individual heterogeneity component is no longer constant but depends on experience. The individual level and slope variables ϕ_{i1} and ϕ_{i2} are random variables with variances θ_{11} and θ_{22} respectively and covariance θ_{12}. Human-capital theory suggests that this covariance is negative. This follows from the assumption that people with a given level of schooling who join the labour force can choose between jobs which offer a relatively low initial wage, rich investment opportunities and relatively high future wages, and jobs which pay relatively good wages from the beginning but offer fewer investment opportunities and thus a lower wage progression. This theory thus predicts, first, a movement towards the mean and then away from it. It also follows that the variance of earnings around the average profile will first decrease towards a minimum relatively early in the career, the so-called 'overtaking point', and then increase.

Hause's model also generalizes that of Lillard and Willis by allowing for non-constant ρ and heteroskedasticity in the innovation ε_{it}. His model was applied to a small sample of white-collar Swedish males born in 1943 and restricted to those who had positive annual earnings every year from 1964 to 1974. When the full model was estimated the θ parameters were not estimated with good precision but the covariance estimate had the expected negative sign. The variances of the innovations decreased with increasing experience. The variance for the first year was eight to nine times that of the sixth year. The ρ parameters were of the order 0.3–0.5. These estimates imply that the residual variance increases with increasing experience except at the very beginning of the career.

Lillard and Weiss (1979) used a model very similar to that of Hause but with somewhat more restrictive assumptions:

$$e_{it} = \delta_i + \nu_{it} + \xi_i(t-\bar{t}) = \delta_i + \xi_i(t-\bar{t}) + \rho\nu_{it-1} + \eta_{it}; \qquad (3.21)$$

ρ and the variance of the innovations η are both constants in this model. Lillard and Wise applied their model to a panel sample of scientists with PhDs who continued to report earnings at two-year intervals over the decade 1960–70. The estimates of the heterogeneity parameters were relatively well determined but the correlation between δ and ε was positive. The residual variance thus increased as a function of experience. The estimate of the heterogeneity variance at mean experience was larger than the estimate of σ_ν^2. The estimate of ρ was approximately 0.5.

An essential feature of the last two models is thus that they predict mobility towards the mean at the beginning of the career and then mobility away from the mean. In the present model this could be accomplished by either making β a function of t (before the overtaking point the absolute value of β would be less than one, and after, greater than one) or by assuming that ν_{it} is heteroskedastic.

3.3 DATA

Data come from the HUS panel surveys (Klevmarken, 1990, Klevmarken and Olovsson, 1989). The first wave of data was collected in 1984. It was a random sample of individuals and households from the Swedish-speaking non-institutionalized population of Sweden at the beginning of 1984. In households with two spouses both were interviewed. In a few households with more than two adults a third adult was also interviewed. Information about earnings was collected in personal interviews. In 1986 the same sample was reinterviewed by telephone. A new supplementary sample was also drawn and in addition members of old sample households who had had their eighteenth birthdays after the 1984 interview and new household members who had joined old households were included in the sample. All new respondents were given a personal interview. In 1988 a small third wave of data collection was administered to respondents who participated in 1986. (No attempt was made to interview those who dropped out in 1986 and no attempt was made to include new household members.) A mail questionnaire, with non-response follow-up by telephone, was used. Net sample sizes and response rates are given in Table 3.1.

Information about pay was collected from those in the labour force at the time of the interview. A series of questions determined whether the

Table 3.1   Number of respondents and response rates of the HUS panel

	HUS84 (Hh)	HUS86 Panel (Ind)	HUS86 Suppl. (Hh)	HUS88 (Ind)
Sample size				
Gross sample	2123	2540	881	2961
Not in population	139	169	48	53
Net sample	1993	2371	833	2908
Non-response				
Refusal	433	414	296	483
Other	57	63	51	128
No of interviews	1503	1904	486	2297
Response rate (%)	75.4	80.3	50.3	78.9

Note: Because there was no information about household size for non-responding households in the 1984 sampling frame, the response rate for this year applies to households. In each household on average 1.7 individuals were interviewed. In the 1503 households interviewed in 1984 there were 2540 respondents who made up the gross sample in 1986 of which 1904 were interviewed. Similarly, the 2961 respondents of the gross sample in 1988 came partly from the 1904 panel members of 1986 and partly from the 486 new households added to the survey in 1986. Hh = households, Ind = individuals.

respondent was paid by the hour, week or month or preferred to give an earnings estimate for the whole year. In 1984 the relative shares were 13.6, 1.7, 79.0 and 0.7 per cent respectively. The earnings concept used in this study is an hourly wage rate. For those who responded for a longer time-span the response was transformed into an hourly wage rate by dividing by an estimated number of hours worked per week, month or year respectively. These estimates were obtained by a series of questions on normal hours per week and number of weeks worked in the previous year. In the case of those who gave the amount of their pay by the week, an estimate of the hourly wage rate was obtained by dividing by normal weekly hours; and for those who gave monthly pay rates, the normal weekly hours were multiplied by 4.3. For the few respondents who gave an estimate of their annual earnings we divided by the product of normal weekly hours and weeks worked during the previous year (interviews were typically carried out between February and April).

Separate questions were asked about pay, hours and weeks in the main job (including overtime and overtime pay) and in a second job, if any. The hourly wage rates in the main job and in any secondary job were weighted together to produce an overall wage rate with weights proportional to normal weekly hours in each job.

The explanatory variables used in the average earnings profile are the conventional human capital variables: schooling, years of labour market experience and seniority. The age of the respondent is also included. The schooling variable is defined as the number of full-time-equivalent schooling years (SCH). The experience variable used in the average earnings profile is also a full-time-equivalent transformation of years of experience ($EXPFTE$); while the experience variable used to index time in the labour force (s, t, w) is not adjusted for part-time work (EXP). Seniority (SEN) is not adjusted either, but is a straightforward measure of the number of years employed with the present employer. Before estimating any model data were standardized.

There are obviously errors both in reported earnings and hours, and when earnings are reported for a longer period than a week we have to divide by a second-best approximation of hours worked. The variance of reporting errors is likely to depend on the interview method. Personal interviews probably stimulate people to give more reliable responses than do telephone interviews and mail questionnaires. We thus expect that measurement errors will be smaller in the first wave of data than in the second and third. It is more difficult to have any *a priori* belief about the relative size of measurement errors in telephone interviews and mail questionnaires, but one might guess that people are less careful in responding when there is no personal contact with an interviewer.

Table 3.2   OLS estimates of an average log wage rate profile

Variable/parameter	Estimate	Std
D84	2.48521	
D86	2.62854	
D88	2.75983	
SCH	0.06152	(0.00738)
SCHQ	−0.00079	(0.00027)
EXPFTE	0.00592	(0.00352)
EXPFTEQ	−0.00011	(0.00006)
AGE	0.02771	(0.00628)
AGEQ	−0.00024	(0.00006)
SEN	0.00451	(0.00066)
R^2	0.380	
N	2527	

Note: The OLS standard errors are biased and inconsistent if the residual covariance matrix is nonscalar.

The HUS surveys do not include a validation study, so it is not possible to have any direct information about the properties of these measurement errors, and we have to rely on other sources. The validation study by the Survey Research Center at the University of Michigan for the Panel Study of Income Dynamics has produced interesting results for a survey instrument which includes questions on earnings and hours (Duncan and Hill 1985; bound *et al.*, 1990; and Rodgers *et al.*, 1991). These questions were not exactly the same as those used in HUS and the validation study was limited to blue-collar workers in one big firm, but this is probably the only major validation study of earnings measures and some of their results might be transferable to our case. The Michigan study included three different measures of earnings: annual earnings; earnings for the previous pay period; and usual pay. The corresponding measures of hours worked were also recorded. There were thus also three alternative estimates of hourly wage rates. They did not find any major bias in the wage rates but the error variance was as high as 70 per cent of the total variance. The correlation between interview reports and records data from the firm was 0.6 for the wage rate calculated from annual data, but only 0.2–0.3 for wage rates obtained from data for the previous and usual pay period. They found almost no correlation between the measurement error and the true (record) scores when annual data were used to calculate wage rates, while there was a small negative correlation for the previous and usual pay period. In the latter cases, people with high wages thus tended to report with smaller errors than people with low wages. The correlations between the errors in the hourly wage rates and the age, seniority and education of the respondents were generally rather small, and there was no evidence of strong correlation across waves in errors in reports of hourly wages. Rodgers *et al.* (1991) also investigated any heteroskedasticity in the measurement errors but found only small correlations between the absolute discrepancy scores and the three variables of age, education and job tenure.

3.4 ESTIMATION AND RESULTS

In a preliminary analysis of the covariance structure, without imposing any particular structure *a priori* and ignoring the fact that many individuals have contributed more than one observation, all observations were stacked on top of each other, the average log wage rate function estimated by OLS, and the resulting residuals retrieved for analysis. The OLS estimates of the log wage rate-function are given in Table 3.2.

The model in general implies heteroskedastic residuals, and if $\beta \neq 0$ the variance will increase with experience. If there are measurement errors in the wage-rate variable, they could make it difficult to see any relation in a plot of the residuals on experience. For this reason the mean residuals for those who contributed a wage rate for all three years were plotted against experience in 1986, but there was no trace of heteroskedasticity, and when all squared residuals were plotted against experience, there was little evidence of heteroskedasticity related to experience either. This result indicates that β may be small.

Additional evidence about the covariance structure is obtained from the empirical covariance matrix. Table 3.3 gives covariance matrices computed from OLS residuals using observations from all individuals and only from those who had a positive wage rate in all three years. For this subsample matrices were also computed for four subgroups defined by years of experience. These estimates show that the residual variance increased from 1984 to 1988. Official statistics show that there was a small increase in the dispersion of earnings during this period (see, for instance, *Wages and Salaries in Sweden 1982–1989*, Table 6, Statistics Sweden) but the difference between our sample variance estimates of 0.63 for 1984 and 0.98 for 1988 is so large that another explanation is needed. One possible explanation is that the measurement error variance has increased due to a

Table 3.3   Empirical covariance matrices based on OLS residuals

Empirical CV-matrix for all cases
(N = 1297)

	1984	1986	1988
1984	0.6363	0.3562	0.3112
1986		0.7269	0.3030
1988			0.9815

Empirical CV-matrices for individuals observed all three years
0≤EXP≤10 (N = 400)

	1984	1986	1988
1984	0.4852	0.3359	0.3014
1986		0.5026	0.3350
1988			0.6013

0<EXP≤10 (N = 34)

	1984	1986	1988	$\bar{s}_{tt}$	$\bar{s}_{t,t+1}$
1984	0.4703	0.3633	0.2488	0.5394	0.3569
1986		0.7305	0.3505		
1988			0.4177		

10<EXP≤20 (N = 130)

	1984	1986	1988	$\bar{s}_{tt}$	$\bar{s}_{t,t+1}$
1984	0.3895	0.2521	0.2475	0.4812	0.2825
1986		0.4814	0.3230		
1988			0.5726		

20<EXP≤30 (N = 119)

	1984	1986	1988	$\bar{s}_{tt}$	$\bar{s}_{t,t+1}$
1984	0.5328	0.3711	0.2328	0.5033	0.3137
1986		0.4441	0.2563		
1988			0.5331		

30<EXP (N = 117)

	1984	1986	1988	$\bar{s}_{tt}$	$\bar{s}_{t,t+1}$
1984	0.5476	0.3853	0.4465	0.6077	0.4047
1986		0.5196	0.4242		
1988			0.7559		

Note: The residuals were obtained from an OLS regression (Table 3.2) on standardized variables. To retransform the empirical CV-matrices to ln (wage)-scale, multiply by $(0.308)^2$.

change in survey instrument, as pointed out above. An alternative possibility is that we see the effect of an increase in variance due to increased experience. For panel members average experience has increased by almost four years, 1984–88. This, however, is not a very likely explanation. As already noted, there is no strong cross-sectional evidence of an experience-dependent heteroskedasticity, Table 3.3 shows no monotone increase in variances and covariances with increasing experience, and in the full sample (including non-panel observations) there is no systematic increase in average experience over time, yet the residual variance increases (see the first empirical moment matrix of Table 3.3).

Another observation which suggests large measurement errors is that the covariances of successive residuals are 50–60 per cent of the variances. This indicates that there is an independent variance component, for instance, a measurement error of white-noise type. Finally, Table 3.3 shows a weak but non-uniform indication of a smaller (positive) covariance between residuals four years apart than two years apart. This could again be explained by the model if $\beta > 0$, but it could also be the result of an error structure with autocorrelated errors, like the one in (3.19).

One conclusion is that the model must allow for a shift in the measurement error variance due to survey wave. Assume that there is a unique variance of the z_{it} component for each wave. Thus,

$$\text{Var}(z_{it}) = \sigma_{zj}^2; \qquad j = 1984, 1986, 1988 \qquad (3.22)$$

The very low correlation between measurement errors of successive waves found in the Michigan validation study might be used as an excuse to assume that there is no permanent individual measurement error component, that is:

$$\sigma_\lambda^2 = \sigma_{\delta\lambda} = 0 \qquad (3.23)$$

An addition assumption introduced at this point is $\beta \geq 0$. The alternating behaviour caused by a negative β, which implies that every year people tend to move from one side of the average profile to the other, is rather implausible.

The model was estimated by maximum likelihood using all observations: the sample was not restricted to those who responded in all three years. Define a vector

$$y_i = \{y_{it_1}, y_{it_2}, \ldots, y_{it_T}\}' \qquad (3.24)$$

of log wage rate observations for each individual i. This vector will have one, two or three elements, depending on the number of waves in which i participated. Assume that

$$m_{it} = x'_{it}\alpha \tag{3.25}$$

where x_{it} is a K-vector of explanatory variables and α a parameter vector. In addition to the explanatory variables already mentioned in section 3.3, x_{it} also includes three dummy variables, one for each calendar year. Define

$$X_i = \begin{Bmatrix} x'_{it_1} \\ \vdots \\ x'_{it_T} \end{Bmatrix}_{T \times K} \quad ; \quad 1 \leqslant T \leqslant 3 \tag{3.26}$$

The number of rows of X_i equals the number of observations contributed by individual i. If y_i is assumed independently multivariate normal, then the log-likelihood function is

$$\ln L = -\frac{N}{2} \ln (2\pi) - \frac{1}{2} \sum_{i=1}^{N} \ln |\Omega_i| - \frac{1}{2} \sum_{i=1}^{N} (y_i - X_i\alpha)'\Omega_i^{-1}(y_i - X_i\alpha) \tag{3.27}$$

where N is the total number of individuals in the sample and Ω_i the covariance matrix of individual i. Ω_i is a function of the previously defined parameters β, σ_δ^2, σ_ν^2 and σ_{zj}^2. The dimension of this matrix will be 1, 2 or 3, depending on the number of responses from i. A Gauss subroutine was used to maximize the log-likelihood function (3.27) which resulted in the estimates exhibited in the first column of Table 3.4.

The three intercept estimates show that the nominal wage rates on average increased by about 15 per cent in each two-year period. The return to schooling is about 6 per cent for each additional year of schooling. The estimate for the squared schooling variable is negative, indicating a small decrease in return to schooling. The estimated return to experience shows the conventional decrease with increasing experience, but the estimates are small. At the beginning of the career the return is only about 1 per cent for each additional year of full-time work. Apparently the age variable picks up much of the effect of increased experience. The correlation between the two variables is relatively high: 0.94. However, it is still remarkable that the age variable is stronger than the experience variable in spite of the effort to compute a good

Table 3.4   *Maximum likelihood estimates of average wage rate profiles and their covariance structure*

Variable/ parameter	Homoskedastic measurement errors		Heteroskedastic measurement errors	
	estimate	asy.std	estimate	asy.std
D84	2.5358	(0.1376)	2.4834	(0.1412)
D86	2.6802	(0.1378)	2.6284	(0.1415)
D88	2.8150	(0.1380)	2.7623	(0.1417)
SCH	0.0565	(0.0095)	0.0585	(0.0095)
SCHQ	−0.0006	(0.0004)	−0.0007	(0.0004)
EXPFTE	0.0092	(0.0041)	0.0095	(0.0042)
EXPFTEQ	−0.0002	(0.00007)	−0.0002	(0.00007)
AGE	0.0251	(0.0075)	0.0266	(0.0077)
AGEQ	−0.0002	(0.00008)	−0.0002	(0.00008)
SEN	0.0035	(0.0007)	0.0035	(0.0007)
β	2.0E-08	(0.0005)	5.3E-07	(0.0002)
σ_δ^2	0.0512	(0.0029)	0.0521	(0.0029)
σ_ν^2	6.2E-09	(1.2E-05)	0.0158	(0.0013)
σ_{z84}^2	0.0142	(0.0018)	1.9E-06	(0.0003)
σ_{z86}^2	0.0247	(0.0021)	0.1877	(0.0309)
σ_{z88}^2	0.0500	(0.0036)	0.5983	(0.0914)
Mean ln L	−2.29579		−2.29244	
N	1297		1297	

Note: β was constrained to be greater than or equal to zero.

experience measure. For young males their wage rate increases *ceteris paribus* on average about 2.5 per cent per year. The increase then levels off to zero at about the age of 55 after which the age variable gives a negative contribution. Seniority gives a relatively small return: only 0.35 per cent for each additional year.

The estimate of β is virtually zero and the model almost reduces to an ordinary variance components model. There is thus no gradual movement towards or away from the mean, but mobility is purely random around each individual mean profile.

If β is zero, σ_ν^2 and σ_{zj}^2, $j = 84, 86, 88$; are not all identified. The estimate of β is so close to zero that the numerical identification of these variances might balance on a thin thread. If we can trust the estimated standard errors the results indicate, however, that the individual heterogeneity variance is much larger than the white-noise variance. We also find that the estimates of the measurement error variances show the expected pattern. Telephone interviews give larger measurement errors than personal interviews and a mail questionnaire larger errors than telephone interviews. The differences in quality are relatively large and the measurement errors are large compared to the true deviations from the average profile.

In an attempt to capture the mildly U-shaped relation between residual variance and experience observed in Table 3.3 (see the mean variances $\bar{s}_{tt}$) it was assumed that the measurement error variance is inversely proportional to years of experience. Young people at the beginning of their careers have temporary jobs and irregular hours and might find it more difficult to give reliable responses to survey questions than older people with permanent jobs and regular hours. (It is also possible that exactly these circumstances might result in a relatively high variance of the 'true' residual at the very beginning of the career, as found by Hause (1980).) Thus,

$$\mathrm{Var}(z_{it}) = \frac{\sigma^2_{zj}}{(t+1)}; \qquad j = 1984, 1986, 1988 \qquad (3.28)$$

The corresponding estimates are given in the last two columns of Table 3.4. The mean log-likelihood is marginally higher compared to the previous model. All estimates except the last four variance estimates are close to those obtained with the assumption of homoskedastic measurement errors. The variance of the white-noise component increases and the measurement error variances adjust to the new model specification. Their relative magnitudes are, however, approximately preserved.

The estimated residual variance as a function of experience is rapidly declining at the beginning of the career. This is entirely due to the assumption of measurement error variances inversely proportional to experience. The estimated 'true' residual variance has almost no relation to experience.

Disregarding the measurement errors, the model almost reduces to a traditional variance component model with one heterogeneity component and one white-noise component. This model generates a covariance matrix with covariances of the same size independently of the time span between the two covariates. The empirical covariances in Table 3.3 do not clearly reject this property but one might trace a weak tendency of a declining covariance with increasing time span. This justifies an attempt to estimate the same model as in Lillard and Willis (1978), that is, to permit the error component which depends both on individual (i) and on experience (t) to follow a first-order autoregressive process (see 3.19).

With a maximum of three observations per respondent all parameters of the covariance matrix are unfortunately not identified. One constraint is needed, and $\sigma^2_{z,84}$ was constrained to zero. This implies that we cannot distinguish between the heterogeneity variance and the measurement error variance for 1984.

The results of Table 3.4 show no strong mobility towards or away from the mean profile and thus no experience-related heteroskedasticity caused by such mobility. The particular form of heteroskedasticity in (3.15) is, however, only one of many conceivable. It is also possible that there is a heteroskedasticity more closely related to the age variable than to years of experience, although the two are highly correlated. The model was thus not only estimated for all age groups, but also for the three disjunct groups: up to 35, 36–50 and 50+ years, in order to explore any relation between mobility and age. From human-capital theory it follows that σ^2_δ should decrease to the 'overtaking point' and then increase. The first age interval is, however, so wide that it probably covers part of the increasing phase. All we can expect to find from the estimates for the three age groups used is thus an increase in σ^2_δ, if there is any change at all.

Young people at the beginning of a career usually have high job mobility. They try new jobs and move into and out of the labour force. Young labour with little seniority is also more exposed to the risk of lay-off and unemployment than more experienced people. A high mobility in wage rates is likely to follow from high job mobility.[2] When people gain experience and, in particular, firm-specific experience, their job mobility decreases and the same is probably true of the mobility of wage rates. Changes in job mobility might thus lead us to expect that σ^2_ε decreases and ρ increases with increasing age.

This model was also estimated by maximum likelihood using the log-likelihood function (3.27) with the appropriate reparametrization of Ω implicitly given by equation (3.19). The variables used to explain the average wage rate profile were the same as in the previous model. The estimates are presented in Table 3.5. The first two columns give the parameter estimates and corresponding estimated standard errors for all age groups. The following three pairs of columns are the estimates for each age group separately.

When the model is estimated for all age groups, we find that the variance of the heterogeneity component is 2.5 times that of the temporary component. Measurement errors are most important in the last wave (mail questionnaire). The estimate of ρ is significantly negative. The same result was obtained when different starting values were tried and negative estimates were also obtained for all three age

Table 3.5   *Maximum likelihood estimates of wage rate functions with an autoregressive covariance structure*

	All males		Males aged	
		$\leqslant 35$	36–50	51+
D84	2.5004 (0.13805)	2.5467 (0.4495)	3.1006 (0.6300)	−1.0990 (1.3481)
D86	2.6482 (0.13826)	2.7388 (0.4476)	3.2250 (0.6314)	−0.9634 (1.3588)
D88	2.7843 (0.13840)	2.9046 (0.4478)	3.3905 (0.6321)	−0.8786 (1.3562)
SCH	0.0584 (0.0095)	0.0266 (0.0228)	0.0537 (0.0135)	0.0525 (0.0172)
SCHQ	−0.0007 (0.0004)	−0.0002 (0.0009)	−0.0006 (0.0005)	−0.0003 (0.0007)
EXPFT	0.0079 (0.0041)	0.0096 (0.0092)	0.0114 (0.0079)	0.0286 (0.0103)
EXPFTQ	−0.0001 (0.0000)	−0.0008 (0.0004)	−0.0004 (0.0002)	−0.0004 (0.0002)
AGE	0.0263 (0.0074)	0.0427 (0.0323)	−0.0100 (0.0321)	0.1361 (0.0472)
AGEQ	−0.0002 (0.0000)	−0.0004 (0.0006)	0.0003 (0.0004)	−0.0011 (0.0004)
SEN	0.0035 (0.0007)	0.0034 (0.0028)	0.0032 (0.0010)	0.0033 (0.0012)
ρ	−0.2653 (0.1004)	−0.1514 (0.1991)	−0.7047 (0.1039)	−0.5979 (0.1171)
σ^2_δ	0.0500 (0.0029)	0.0239 (0.0039)	0.0472 (0.0036)	0.0768 (0.0080)
σ^2_υ	0.0193 (0.0013)	0.0286 (0.0030)	0.0110 (0.0021)	0.0195 (0.0028)
$\sigma^2_{z,86}$	0.0088 (0.0017)	0.0283 (0.0064)	0.0035 (0.0033)	0.0000 (0.0000)
$\sigma^2_{z,88}$	0.0240 (0.0038)	0.0000 (0.0000)	0.0354 (0.0052)	0.0339 (0.0103)
σ^2_η	0.0180 (0.0017)	0.0279 (0.0034)	0.0055 (0.0025)	0.0125 (0.0040)
n	1297	385	582	330
Mean ln L	−2.32023	−2.15634	−2.25500	−2.33049

groups. This implies that people tend to alternate between positions above and below their 'normal' earnings level. One interpretation is that people get major individual pay increases every second year and lag behind in the meantime. These results diverge from those of Lillard and Willis (1978). When they limited the number of explanatory variables to years of schooling, experience, experience squared and a few time dummies, they got a ρ estimate of about 0.4 and the heterogeneity variance was 50 per cent larger than the variance of the temporary component.

A comparision of the estimates across age groups shows that the heterogeneity variance increases with age and the variance of the temporary component is largest for the youngest age group, as expected. In absolute value the ρ estimate increases with age. The wages of the youngest thus contain more random noise than the wages of older people, while the alternating behaviour is more pronounced among older people.

The estimates of the average profiles conform more or less with previous results. We again find that the age variable dominates the experience variable. A coefficient-by-coefficient comparison shows that most differences between the age groups could be random. However, the large difference in intercept estimates between the oldest age group and the two younger groups indicates that the model specification could be improved.[3]

3.5 CONCLUSIONS

The results from the model which was estimated first showed that we have to reject the Galton type of gradual regression towards (or away from) the average wage rate profile. The relatively high estimate of β one would get if equation (3.1) was estimated by OLS is primarily the result of a large heterogeneity component which makes the OLS estimate of β biased. (Independent measurement errors tend, however, to bias the OLS estimate in the opposite direction.) From the analysis of the first model we concluded that people tend to keep their relative wage rates and that there is only random mobility around each individual's relative position.

This conclusion had to be modified slightly after the second model (equation 3.19) was estimated. These new results showed that people move around their individual mean wages in an alternating pattern, switching between wage rates above and below their means. This result deviates from those of previous studies and it will be interesting to see if it still holds when additional waves of data become available. It could possibly be interpreted as the result of biannual cycles in Swedish pay-setting.

When the second model was estimated for each of the three age groups separately, the variance of the individual heterogeneity component increased with the age of the respondent while temporary random mobility was largest at the beginning of the career. This was given a human-capital interpretation, respectively seen as a result of high initial job mobility.

However, if the variance of the heterogeneity component increases with age, it implies that people tend to move away from the average wage rate profile; this would seem to contradict the results obtained from the first model. One explanation of these conflicting results is that the Galton regression model assumes *a priori* that both the variance of the heterogeneity component and the variance of the temporary variance component increase with experience. If the latter variance is decreasing instead, as the results from the second model indicate, then the estimate of β is forced towards zero to maintain an approximately constant variance for the sum of the two variance components. The conclusion is then that the assumption of Galtonian regression towards the mean puts too strong a constraint on the model.

An alternative explanation of these differing results is that the Galton type of model implicitly puts too much weight on years of experience to explain the covariance structure. Although years of experience and age are highly correlated in this sample, age might be a better explanatory variable. The estimates of the average profile indicate that this is the case, but then we need to understand why. An explanation could perhaps be found in the pay-setting procedures in the Swedish labour market or, more trivially, in measurement errors in the experience variable.

The properties of the residual wage-rate process depend on the specification of the average wage-rate profile. It is important in particular for the relative magnitude of heterogeneity vs. temporary deviations from each individual mean. In this study a more or less conventional Mincer-type human-capital earnings model was used and we found heterogeneity relatively more important than the temporary variance component. This relationship could be altered if additional variables were used to explain the average profile.

Measurement errors are clearly very important in the type of survey data we have used. We also found that the survey instrument is important. Personal interviews give much smaller response errors than do telephone interviews or mail questionnaires. Three waves of data are insufficient to test if these errors correlate over time. Part of the correlation between wages in successive years, which is now attributed to the 'true' wage process, might be the result of more or less permanent measurement errors. To distinguish between these two sources of correlation more waves of data are needed, and ideally one would need a validation study.

In general, three waves of data are the minimum necessary to generate interesting results about the residual process. More waves will allow sharper tests and a more general error specification.

In 1984 80 per cent of the females and 90 per cent of the males in the age bracket 18–64 years were in the labour force, according to the HUS survey. Although the labour force participation rate of men is high, sample selectivity caused by wage-rate-dependent decisions to participate in the labour force might be a problem. A similar selectivity problem might arise because of selective non-response. Preliminary results from Brose and Klevmarken (1991) showed that attrition in the HUS panel depended on the wage rate, but not to the extent that estimates of an earnings function were severely affected.

Another neglected problem which deserves additional attention in future research is the possibility of correlation between the individual heterogeneity component and the explanatory variables of the average earnings profile. If the assumption of independence does not hold, all estimates are in general biased and inconsistent (cf. Hausman and Taylor, 1981).

NOTES

1. Constructive comments from Anthony B. Atkinson and an anonymous referee are gratefully acknowledged.
2. In a study of job mobility and subsequent wages in Sweden, Björklund and Holmlund (1989) found that those who quit their job gained on average about 8 per cent in pay per hour during the two-year period studied, somewhat more for young and somewhat less for old employees, while the change in pay for those who were laid off did not significantly differ from the average change.
3. A chi-square test rejects the hypothesis that all age groups follow the same model. The test statistic is 195.36 with 32 degrees of freedom.

REFERENCES

Arnold, B.C. and P.L. Brocket (1992): 'On distributions whose component ratios are Cauchy', *American Statistician*, **46**, (1), 25–6.

Atkinson, A.A., F. Bourguignon and C. Morrison (1992): 'Empirical studies of earnings mobility', in *Empirical Studies of Earnings Mobility* (Chur.; Harwood Academic Publishers).

Björklund, A. and B. Holmlund (1989): 'Job mobility and subsequent wages in Sweden', in J. van Dijk *et al.* (eds), *Migration and Labor Market Adjustment* (Dordrecht: Kluwer Academic Publishers).

Bound, J., C. Brown, G.J. Duncan and W.L. Rodgers (1990): 'Measurement errors in cross-sectional and longitudinal labor market surveys: validation study evidence', in J. Hartog, G. Ridder and J. Theeuwes (eds), *Panel Data and Labor Market Studies* (Amsterdam: North-Holland) 1–19.

Brose, P. and N.A. Klevmarken (1991): 'Modelling non-response in a panel survey', paper presented at the 48th session of the International Statistical Institute, Cairo, September.

Creedy, J., P.E. Hart and N.A. Klevmarken (1980): 'Income mobility in Great Britain and Sweden', in N.A. Klevmarken and J.A. Lybeck (eds), *The Statics and Dynamics of Income* (Clevedon: Tieto) 195–211.

Duncan, G.J. and D.H. Hill (1985): 'An investigation of the extent and consequences of measurement errors in labor economic survey data', *Journal of Labor Economics*, **3**, 508–22.

Galton, F. (1889): *Natural Inheritance* (London: Macmillan).

Hart, P.E. (1976): 'The comparative statics and dynamics of income distributions', *Journal of the Royal Statistical Society*, Series A, **139**, (1), 108–25.

——: 'The statics and dynamics of income distributions: a survey', in N.A. Klevmarken and J.A. Lybeck (eds), *The Statics and Dynamics of Income* (Clevedon: Tieto) 1–20.

Hause, J.C. (1977): 'The covariance structure of earnings and the on-the-job training hypothesis', *Annals of Economic and Social Measurement*, **6**, 73–108.

—— (1980): 'The fine structure of earnings and the on-the-job training hypothesis', *Econometrica*, **48**, (4), 1013–29.

Hausman, J.A. and W.E. Taylor (1981): 'Panel data and unobservable individual effects', *Econometrica*, **49**, (6), 1377–98.

Klevmarken, N.A. (1990): *Household Market and Nonmarket Activities (HUS). Design, Field Work and Nonresponse*, Memorandum no. 144, Department of Economics, Gothenburg University.

—— and P. Olovsson (1989): *Hushållens ekonomiska levnadsförhållanden (HUS). Teknisk beskrivning och kodbok*, Department of Economics, Gothenburg University.

Lilliard, L.A. and Weiss, Y. (1979): 'Components of variation in panel earnings data: American scientists, 1960–70', *Econometrica*, **47**, (2), 437–54.

Lilliard, L.A. and Willis, R.J. (1978): 'Dynamic aspects of earnings mobility', *Econometrica*, **46**, (5), 985–1012.

Rodgers, W.L., G.J. Duncan and C. Brown (1991): 'Errors in survey reports of earnings, hours worked and hourly wages', Working Paper, Survey Research Center, University of Michigan.

Weizäcker, R.K. von (1988): 'Age structure and income distribution policy', *Journal of Population Economics*, **1**(1), 33–56.

4. Higher Education: Grants, Taxation and Lifetime Inequality

John Creedy and Patrick Francois

4.1 INTRODUCTION

This chapter examines the redistributive effects of subsidies for higher education. Section 4.2 begins by isolating several crucial issues in any study of redistribution, and examines previous studies. Most studies of the redistributive effects of higher education grants use a static or annual approach. However, a lifetime approach is necessary since both the costs and benefits of grants are borne over the entire working life. It is also suggested that treating the government's funding decision as exogenous abstracts from the nature of social decision-making. For example, Majumdar (1983) argues that since individuals receive varying degrees of benefit from state-funded education, it is essential that the means of social decision-making be explicitly considered. Section 4.3 constructs a framework employing a lifetime approach and endogenizing the level of a tax-financed grant. Higher education grants are a special form of selective benefit received by those of higher income-earning ability and are therefore regressive when considered in isolation. It is of interest to consider how the preferred level of the grant is affected by this regressivity, and how the choice of grant is affected by the introduction of other transfers such as a minimum income guarantee.

Section 4.4 adds selective benefits to the basic model. The framework is used in section 4.5 to determine the effects on lifetime inequality of changes in the level of the grant. It is demonstrated that ignoring the influences on the level of the grant of progressive selective benefits can be misleading, as the net redistributive effects of changes in the grant depend on their causes. Such effects cannot be predicted *a priori*, since they depend on the relative sizes of some crucial magnitudes. For this reason simulation methods are used to provide orders of magnitude. Section 4.6 presents brief conclusions.

4.2   SOME CONCEPTUAL ISSUES

In examining redistribution, a decision must first be made about the time period of analysis. Secondly, the income unit must be specified and this will often be linked to the decision on the time period. Thirdly, it is necessary to consider any externalities generated. Fourthly, changes in eligibility for benefits and the way in which this is altered by changes in the level of spending need to be taken into account. Finally, an appropriate counter-factual must be specified. Previous studies can be distinguished according to their treatment of these aspects, which are considered in turn below.

The Time Period of Analysis

Most authors recognize that the benefits of education vary over the lifetime, but nevertheless take a partial approach. For example, some have attempted to allow for life-cycle effects by arguing that income units should only be compared at similar points in the life-cycle. Crean (1975) argues for a comparison of benefits and contributions only within cohorts of equivalently aged children. McGuire (1976) limits his analysis to a cohort of families where the family head is between 39 and 60 years of age, but ignores taxes. James and Benjamin (1988a) consider the aggregate income distribution but adjust the incomes of families which may have children of university age. In listing the proportion of units receiving subsidies, within an income group, these authors exclude individuals who are ineligible for benefits in view of their age and find that those in the lower percentiles of the population are more highly represented among the beneficiaries of subsidies.

Hansen and Weisbrod (1969a) and Pechman (1970) compare benefits received in terms of annual data irrespective of age. Pechman (1970) emphasizes the lifetime nature of redistribution but uses this approach in order to demonstrate that, even with the same data as used by Hansen and Weisbrod (1969a), different results will be obtained when comparisons are made between different groups. Those units who are, due to their age, ineligible to receive benefits are counted as not receiving a benefit in the same way as are individuals who are of an eligible age but who do not, for whatever reason, receive benefits. Thus some variability in benefits received is mistakenly attributed to differences in wealth instead of differences in age.

Most authors do not allow for the enhanced earnings of the educated. Crean (1975) and McGuire (1976) restrict their analyses to annual data, listing both the direct benefits received within the specified age groups and the taxes paid over that period. James and Benjamin (1988a) are more ambitious, assuming that, within a cohort, individual relative incomes remain constant. They track age groups through time and calculate both the direct educational receipts and lifetime tax payments of families within each group. They extrapolate from a cross-sectional income distribution to a lifetime income distribution by assuming that relative incomes within a cohort do not vary. Conlisk (1977, p. 154) also argues that the way in which earnings are altered by the subsidy needs to be taken into account.

Hansen and Weisbrod (1969b, p. 56) attempt to calculate the extra tax payment of the educated over time by estimating the lifetime tax payments of the arithmetic mean educated individual. But this is not the approach most favoured by them. It represents an attempt to incorporate a lifetime approach, but leads to internal inconsistency as they allow the increased earnings of the educated to affect their lifetime tax payment but take no account of the extra earnings of the educated which contribute to the lifetime benefit.

Contributions to costs of subsidies through tax payments occur over the working life of educated and non-educated persons. Benefits generally accrue over time as a result of increased future earning potential. An annual approach ignores increased earnings and the partial deferred payment of fees, via taxation, after education. Hence, a lifetime approach to both costs and benefits is needed.

The Income Unit

In the choice of income unit, the major distinction is between the family and the individual. Hansen and Weisbrod (1969a, 1969b) and Pechman (1970) consider a cross-section of families, while Conlisk (1977) uses a cross-section of individuals where earning potential and the likelihood of investing in higher education are related to parental characteristics. Shackett and Slottje (1987) consider data on individual incomes, using a time-series of cross-sections.

There is, however, an advantage in limiting the analysis of life-cycle effects to a single cohort of individuals. This is not to deny that a component of the lifetime redistribution is between cohorts, but merely makes explicit the distinction between intra- and inter-cohort effects. In general, a within-cohort lifetime analysis cannot be undertaken for a comparison between families, as a family is composed of individuals from different cohorts. However, Crean (1975), McGuire (1976) and James and Benjamin (1988a, b) all apply a within-cohort family analysis by ranking families according to the age of the family head. McGuire (1976) considers parental income for parents aged between 39 and 60 without allowing that some students may be financially or legally independent of their parents. This approach may be justified in an annual framework, but in a lifetime context the problems raised by families being composed of individuals of different ages cannot be overcome by focusing on the head of the family. Through time, the composition of the family unit changes along with the distribution of income within the family. One way around this is to concentrate on a within-cohort, lifetime analysis focusing on individuals.

External Effects

Few authors have attempted to allow for external effects. Conlisk (1977) accounts for extra taxes paid by the educated through their enhanced earning potential but includes no provision for any external effects. Shackett and Slottje (1987) analyse a time series of incomes, with higher education used as one of the explanatory variables. Even though education is found to have a significant effect on inequality, it is not clear whether the effects are a consequence of external economies or direct benefits in the form of grants.

Given the uncertainty surrounding the size and nature of externalities generated by higher education it would seem best to compare results obtained using differing assumptions about externalities. If measured inequality is found to be sensitive to the assumed size and nature of these externalities then this should be made explicit.

Endogenous Educational Choice

Most authors assume that educational choice is not responsive to changes in subsidies. Subsidies represent a transfer towards some members of the population who may anyway have chosen to become educated. However, it is likely that there are some individuals who, without subsidies, find the costs too high in relation to the benefits and, even where capital markets are perfect, will not invest in education. Conlisk (1977) attempts to account for these individuals by including a parameter which can vary with the income background of students, and emphasizes the ambiguity of changes in tuition subsidy on inequality. However, it seems from his discussion that much of the ambiguity stems from the response of previously uneducated individuals. This response can be more fully analysed when educational decisions are considered in a lifetime context. If an individual's decision is framed in terms of choosing that course of action which maximizes the net present value of lifetime income, then the effects of an increase in grants have direct implications for the educational decision.

The Counter-factual Situation

Finally, it is important to establish a well-defined counter-factual situation. It has already been noted that most authors consider only the direct changes in tuition costs and their immediate extra tax burden. Only Conlisk (1977) considers the interaction of individuals' education decisions with the government's provision of tuition grants, subject to a budget constraint. A further interdependency is the effect which individual actions have on the level of funding chosen by the government. James and Benjamin (1988b) consider government subsidies as the endogenous outcome of political processes. In their analysis, the Japanese system of funding for higher education is explained in terms of the behaviour of vote-maximizing political agents. A similar approach can be applied to analyse the level of government grants for education where the inequality effects of such grants are the focus of investigation.

4.3 A FRAMEWORK OF ANALYSIS

This section presents a framework dealing with the many interdependencies raised in the previous section, concentrating on the life earnings of a single cohort. The analysis of a single cohort can be regarded as a necessary first stage in a more complete analysis. Each individual's net lifetime income is assumed to depend upon inherited characteristics and the degree to which they are developed through education. The form of the relationship between parents' and individuals' characteristics is complex, but if the analysis is restricted to a single cohort, it is not necessary to specify the transformation. The approach assumes that enrolment in higher education raises an individual's income earning potential and is the only means by which this can be done. The working life can be divided into two periods of unequal length where each individual faces the choice of either working or enrolling in higher education during the first period. The determinants of this choice will be analysed in the next sub-section. The second period can be thought of as the rest of the individual's working life. The income received in this period also depends upon ability as well as education, and will therefore vary across members of the cohort.

Educational Choice

Each individual has an endowment of y_i $(i=1, \ldots, N)$, which determines both income in the first period and the ability to benefit from education. Higher education raises the earnings of the educated by an amount proportional to their initial endowment. In addition, the overall rate of growth of incomes, g, depends on the proportion of individuals educated. The cost of education per student is denoted c, a proportion of which, pc, is financed through income taxation. Education involves the opportunity cost of foregoing a proportion, h, of first-period earnings.

If the interest rate is denoted r, then the present value of net lifetime earnings of the ith person, if educated, V_i^E is given by:

$$V_i^E = (1-h)(1-t)y_i - c(1-p) + y_i(1+s_i+g)(1-t)/(1+r) \qquad (4.1)$$

Here s_i is the direct effect of education on the growth of the individual's earnings, while g measures the public good element of education. It is assumed that $s_i = uy_i$ and that g is an increasing function of the proportion of the cohort educated, p, so that $g = g(p)$. The income tax system involves a proportional tax at the rate t. If capital markets are perfect, the cost of education can be met during either the first or the second period.

The present value of net lifetime earnings of the ith person, if uneducated, is given by:

$$V_i^N = (1-t)y_i + y_i(1+g)(1-t)/(1+r) \qquad (4.2)$$

The endowment level at which $V_i^E = V_i^N$ may be called the 'educational choice margin', y^*. Equating (4.1) and (4.2) and rearranging yields the margin as the positive root of the quadratic:

$$y^{*2}\frac{u(1-t)}{1+r} - y^*(1-t)h - c(1-p) = 0 \qquad (4.3)$$

It is assumed that as p rises the average cost of education falls, because of the existence of high fixed costs, according to the following function:

$$c = d_1(p+\theta)^{-d_2} \qquad (4.4)$$

Increasing d_2 and reducing θ causes costs to vary more rapidly with p, while d_1 changes only the absolute size of costs.

Deficit Neutrality

It is necessary to obtain the tax rate required to finance higher education. This depends on the proportion, p, of individuals who receive higher education, which in turn is equal to the proportion having $y_i > y^*$. If $F(y)$ denotes the distribution function of y, then $p = 1 - F(y^*)$. Suppose in addition that the revenue per person required to finance non-education expenditure is equal to the fixed amount R. Hence the deficit neutrality condition requires that taxation must raise an amount per person, R_t, such that:

$$R_t = \rho c\{1 - F(y^*)\} + R \tag{4.5}$$

Since a separate cohort is being considered, R_t is the present value of tax payments. In order to obtain an expression for tax revenue, it is necessary to derive the tax base in each period. The total income per person in the first period is:

$$\int_0^{y^*} y \, dF(y) + \int_{y^*}^\infty (1-h) y \, dF(y) \tag{4.6}$$

while total income per person in the second period is:

$$\int_0^{y^*} (1+g) y \, dF(y) + \int_{y^*}^\infty (1+uy+g) y \, dF(y) \tag{4.7}$$

The expressions in (4.6) and (4.7) can be simplified using the concept of the ith moment distribution of y, denoted $F_i(y)$ and defined by:

$$F_i(y) = \int_0^y v^i dF(v) / \int_0^\infty v^i dF(v) \tag{4.8}$$

For a detailed analysis of the use of moment distributions, particularly in the context of inequality measurement, see Hart (1975). If $\bar{y}$ and η_y denote respectively the arithmetic mean and coefficient of variation of y, it can be shown that (4.6) and (4.7) can be written respectively as:

$$\bar{y}\{h + (1-h)F_1(y^*)\} \tag{4.9}$$

$$\text{and } \bar{y}\left[(1+g) + u\bar{y}(\eta_y^2 + 1)\{1 - F_2(y^*)\}\right] \tag{4.10}$$

Rewrite (4.10) as $\bar{y}\Psi$, where Ψ is the term in square brackets. The deficit neutrality condition then gives the tax rate as:

$$t = \frac{R+\rho c\{1-F(y^*)\}}{\bar{y}\{h+(1-h)F_1(y^*)+\Psi/(1+r)\}} \tag{4.11}$$

In considering (4.11) it is important to recognize that g is a function of p, which in turn depends on y^* and the form of F. A convenient form of $g(p)$ which depends on only one parameter, and has the property that the rate of increase in g decreases as p increases, is:

$$g=\delta p/(1+p) \tag{4.12}$$

Unfortunately, empirical studies have not attempted to link the proportion with higher education to the growth rate. However, the large literature on the external benefits of education may be used to ascertain reasonable values of δ.

An appropriate form for $F(y)$ which also has convenient first and second moment distributions is the lognormal, $\Lambda(y|\mu,\sigma^2)$, where μ and σ^2 are respectively the mean and variance of the logarithms of y. The moment distributions are given (see Aitchison and Brown, 1957) by:

$$\Lambda_j(y|\mu,\sigma^2)=\Lambda(y|\mu+j\sigma^2,\sigma^2) \tag{4.13}$$

For any set of parameter values, equations (4.3) and (4.11) can be solved simultaneously for t and y^* using an iterative approach. This can be repeated for alternative values of ρ and the net lifetime income of any individual evaluated.

Majority Choice of Grant

Suppose that the government sets the level of ρ, which affects the grant, preferred by the majority of the cohort. The value of ρ which, combined with the appropriate tax rate, maximizes the net lifetime income of any individual (given y) can be obtained numerically using the procedure outlined in the previous subsection. The determination of the majority choice is considerably simplified in the present framework by the property that all individuals below the education choice threshold agree about their preferred value of ρ. This can be seen by appropriate differentiation of equation (4.2), where the term y disappears from the first-order condition for a maximum with respect to ρ. In view of the fact that a substantial majority of any cohort chooses not to invest in higher education, there will clearly be a majority voting equilibrium. The variation in V^N with ρ need only be examined for a single relatively low value of y, so long as $y < y^*$ (and $p < 0.5$).

4.4   SELECTIVE BENEFITS

This section shows how selective benefits, in the form of social transfers to low-income individuals and a higher education grant having a 'taper', can be introduced into the basic model of section 4.3. The approach in each case is necessarily highly stylized, but helps to illustrate the effects of these further types of interdependency.

A Guaranteed Minimum Income

Suppose the transfer system raises the incomes of those with a pre-tax income below a specified level, m, to the level $(1-t)m$. Hence all those below m receive the same after-tax-and-transfer income as an individual with a pre-tax income of m. If m remains constant in real terms, the effect of the general growth of earnings (which results from a higher proportion of the cohort investing in higher education) is to reduce the number of individuals below m. The consequent reduction in the total amount of transfer payments compensates to some extent for the higher cost of financing higher education as ρ is increased. The median voter's choice of ρ therefore increases.

For those with $y \leqslant m$, the amount of the transfer is equal to $(1-t)(m-y)$. Hence in the first period the total amount required to finance transfer payments is equal to the size of the cohort multiplied by:

$$(1-t) \int_0^m (m-y)dF(y) \qquad (4.14)$$

This expression can be simplified to:

$$(1-t) \{mF(m) - \bar{y}F_1(m) \} \qquad (4.15)$$

The first term in (4.15), after multiplying by the size of the cohort, is the amount that would need to be given to those below m in order to bring them up to $(1-t)m$, if they had no income. The second term reflects the total amount of income, after paying tax at the rate t, obtained by those with $y<m$. The difference between the two terms measures the total net transfers required.

In the second period all incomes are increased by a proportion g. As those below the threshold, m, obviously do not invest in higher education, the amount needed to finance transfers in the second period is:

$$(1-t) \{mF(m) - \bar{y}(1+g)F_1(m) \} \qquad (4.16)$$

The total amount of income tax raised is of course precisely the same as shown in section 4.3. Rewrite (4.15) as $(1-t)A$ and (4.16) as $(1-t)B$, and let the present value of the total tax revenue per person be written as tC. Then the budget constraint facing the cohort is:

$$(1-t) \left(A + \frac{B}{1+r}\right) + R_t = tC$$

thus

$$t = \frac{A+B/(1+r)+R_t}{A+B/(1+r)+C} \qquad (4.17)$$

The deficit neutrality condition is therefore easily modified, while the determination of the educational choice margin is unchanged. The population must be divided into four groups, rather than two (for those above and below the educational choice margin). Net lifetime income, V, is given by equation (4.1) for $y>y^*$ and by equation (4.2) for $m<y<y^*$. The other two groups are specified as follows:

for $(1+g)y>m>y$;

$$V=(1-t)m+(1-t)(1+g)y/(1+r) \qquad (4.18)$$

for $m>(1+g)y$;

$$V=(1-t)m \{1 + 1/(1+r) \} \qquad (4.19)$$

Equation (4.18) corresponds to the case where an individual receives the transfer in only the first period, while (4.19) applies to an individual receiving a transfer in both periods.

A Means-tested Grant

Each person above the educational choice margin has been assumed to receive a grant of pc towards the cost of education. This means that some individuals receive a larger grant than is necessary to induce them to invest in education. Suppose, however, that a taper is introduced such that only those at the margin receive the full grant, which is reduced progressively for $y > y^*$. Assume that the grant, $G(y)$, is determined according to:

$$G(y) = \rho c - \gamma(y - y^*) \qquad \text{for } y^* \leqslant y \leqslant y^* + \rho c/\gamma = y_u \qquad (4.20)$$
$$= 0 \qquad \text{for } y > y_u$$

The educational choice margin, y^*, may be determined in the usual way using equation (4.3). As long as y_u is sufficiently large, those above y^* still have an incentive to become educated despite the reduction in their grant. The cost per member of the cohort of financing any given value of ρ is no longer $\rho c\{1 - F(y^*)\}$, but is:

$$\int_{y^*}^{y_u} \{\rho c - \gamma(y - y^*)\} \, dF(y) \qquad (4.21)$$

This expression may be rearranged to give:

$$\rho c \{F(y_u) - F(y^*)\} - \gamma \bar{y} \left[\{F_1(y_u) - F_1(y^*)\} - (y^*/\bar{y}) \{F(y_u) - F(y^*)\} \right] \qquad (4.22)$$

The deficit neutrality condition in (4.17) can be modified simply by altering the expression for R_t. The examination of lifetime inequality now requires additional consideration of the separate group having $y > y_u$, whose members receive no grant. The lifetime income of those with $y^* < y < y_u$ is reduced by an amount equal to $\gamma(y - y^*)$.

4.5   SOME COMPARISONS

As outlined in section 4.2, the approach taken in the previous literature has been to attempt to estimate the effect of a given level of funding on the dispersion of incomes in comparison with a situation of no funding. It is hard to imagine such a properly constructed study showing anything other than a regressive effect. The framework outlined in section 4.3 takes a fundamentally different approach. Here, the level of funding provided by the government is endogenous such that changes in the level of funding of higher education are seen to be caused by changes in some of the exogenous conditions specified in the model. Increases in funding, considered alone, are still regressive. But because funding levels respond to other variables, it is inadequate to consider the size of the grant independently of the context in which it is provided. It is not appropriate to specify the effect of a change in the grant on the distribution of incomes without considering the cause of that change. This section shows that, in some situations, increases in grants for higher education can be associated with falls in the inequality of net lifetime income.

Government Transfers and the Grant

The grant can usefully be expressed as a proportion, ρ, of the cost of education per person, c. Table 4.1 presents results which show the change in ρ caused by changes in both the minimum income guarantee and the degree to which the grant is means-tested. Denote by γ the rate of taper in the means-testing of the grant, and suppose that the minimum income guarantee is operated such that all those with incomes below y_m have their income increased to the post-tax value of y_m. The variance of logarithms of the basic distribution of ability is denoted by σ^2. Table 4.1 gives two columns for each set of parameter values. The first applies to the counter-factual situation in which there is no grant, while the second column refers to the value of ρ preferred by the majority of the cohort.

Table 4.1   *Inequality and the level of grant: zero grant and majority choice of grant*

	Example 1 $\sigma^2=0.223$ $\gamma=0$ $ym=0$		Example 2 $\sigma^2=0.223$ $\gamma=0$ $ym=6$		Example 3 $\sigma^2=0.223$ $\gamma=0.4$ $ym=0$		Example 4 $\sigma^2=0.243$ $\gamma=0.3$ $ym=0$	
ρ	0	0.35	0	0.40	0	0.90	0	0.75
t	0.294	0.299	0.303	0.308	0.294	0.300	0.286	0.291
p	0.105	0.148	0.104	0.154	0.105	0.268	0.118	0.237
c	4.18	3.95	4.19	3.92	4.28	3.95	4.11	3.60
$I(1.6)$	0.203	0.210	0.171	0.180	0.203	0.208	0.203	0.210

Note: The cost of education per student is given by $c=2.6\,(p+0.1)^{-0.3}$. The above results were obtained for the following parameter values: $r=0.6$, $R=6$, $h=0.2$, $u=0.1$, $\delta=0.7$.

A rise in the minimum income guarantee induces a rise in the grant. This is explained by considering two changes. First, providing a guaranteed minimum income raises the tax rate, t, required to support government expenditure and, as shown in section 4.3, reduces the proportion educated, p. As additional growth generated by the proportion educated is assumed to be marginally diminishing, a fall in the proportion educated ensures that the external benefit from inducing the marginal person to invest in education rises. The combined effect of these two factors is seen to raise the median voter's preferred level of the grant; this is seen by comparing the preferred value of ρ for examples 1 and 2 in Table 4.1.

Means-testing of benefits will also raise the majority's desired level of the grant. With means-testing, the tax rate required to support a given grant falls and therefore the proportion educated for that level of grant rises. Thus the marginal benefit, to the majority, of inducing another person to invest in education falls. However, the marginal cost to the majority will also fall because, with the means-testing of benefits, inducing the marginal person to invest in education costs relatively less. The relative magnitude of these effects, which depends upon both the concavity of the external growth function and the degree of means-testing, determines whether the grant rises with increased means-testing. It is shown in Table 4.1 by comparing the preferred level of the grant in examples 1 and 3, that the net effect of means-testing is to raise the level of funding the majority is prepared to support.

Lifetime Inequality and the Grant

It is necessary to consider the two effects on inequality which stem from a change in conditions. The first is the direct effect on inequality of a change in either the minimum income guarantee or the extent to which the grant is means-tested, while the second is the effect on inequality of the induced change in the level of funding accompanying the initial change. The net result will determine the overall effect of a change on the dispersion of incomes.

The results cannot be obtained analytically but require simulation methods. The measure of inequality reported is Atkinson's measure, based on an inequality aversion parameter of 1.6 (see Atkinson, 1970). A wide range of inequality measures was found to give similar results. The analysis is complicated by the need to divide the population into four subgroups as follows: individuals who are both uneducated and below the minimum income guarantee in both periods; those who are uneducated and below the minimum income guarantee in the first period but above it in the second; those who are uneducated and above the minimum income guarantee in both periods; and those who are both educated and above the minimum income guarantee. A simulated population of 15 000 individuals was produced.

A rise in the minimum income guarantee leads directly to a fall in dispersion for a given grant as all members of the population below the guaranteed minimum income have their incomes raised. However, as shown in the previous section, this leads to an increase in the grant which counteracts the direct effect. Comparison of these two effects, as presented by the measures of inequality in Table 4.1, shows that Atkinson's measure of inequality falls from 0.210 to 0.180 whilst the majority choice of grant rises from 0.35 to 0.40. This can be explained by referring to Figure 4.1. Schedule A shows the relationship between

Atkinson's measure and the level of the grant for the case of no means-testing and no minimum income guarantee. Schedule B, which lies below schedule A, shows the same relationship when there is a minimum income guarantee. With the grant initially at 0.35, Atkinson's measure is shown by schedule A. However a rise in ρ to 0.4, which occurs as a result of the introduction of a minimum income guarantee, yields an inequality measure shown by the lower schedule B. Thus the downward shift in the

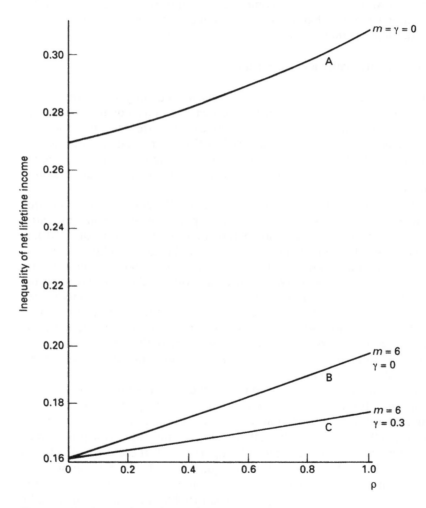

Figure 4.1   Inequality of net lifetime income

schedule means that a rise in the minimum income guarantee leads to a fall in inequality, despite the endogenous rise in the level of the grant.

Means-testing of benefits can also be viewed in terms of its direct and indirect effects on the dispersion of incomes. The direct effect reduces the dispersion, as high income individuals receive a progressively smaller grant. However, the indirect effect of an induced rise in funding causes a rise in dispersion. The inequality measures in examples 1 and 3 in Table 4.1 show the relative magnitude of these effects. It is seen that, despite the large induced rise in the grant, inequality in the distribution of net lifetime income falls. This can again be explained by referring to Figure 4.1. Schedule C shows the relationship between inequality and the grant where the grant is means-tested. Means-testing serves to flatten the schedule considerably, so that a rise in funding leads to a smaller increase in the dispersion of incomes. This ensures that even the considerably large increase in ρ to 0.90 yields less dispersion than a value of 0.3, when the grant is not means-tested. Thus a higher grant is again associated with a lower dispersion of the distribution of net lifetime income.

In reality it is possible that more than one factor may change at a time. The difficulties presented by this can again be shown by referring to Table 4.1. Example 4 presents results when both the initial dispersion of income earning ability and the degree to which the grant is means-tested are simultaneously varied. In this situation, while both factors lead to an increase in the grant, they affect the dispersion of incomes in conflicting ways and in total lead to an unaltered dispersion of incomes. A partial analysis may have concluded in this situation that state funding of higher education is neutral in its effect on the dispersion of incomes.

4.6 CONCLUSIONS

The analysis of this chapter has suggested some explanations for the confusion that surrounds studies of the effects of higher education subsidies. In the framework used here higher education grants are, *ceteris paribus*, regressive. However, depending on the nature of changes which cause the grant to change, the net effect on the distribution of net lifetime income of an increase in funding may be progressive. This has been demonstrated for two cases of variation in a government-controlled variable: the introduction of a minimum income guarantee and the means-testing of higher education grants.

These examples serve to highlight the difficulty in explaining the lifetime incidence of expenditure on higher education grants. It is not surprising that the more partial approach of many authors leads to a disparity in results. This study suggests that incidence studies of higher education should not ignore the factors that determine the level of expenditure on higher education as the incidence of such expenditure will, in part, depend on its determinants.

REFERENCES

Aitchison, J.A. and J.A.C. Brown (1957): *The Lognormal Distribution with Special Reference to its Uses in Economics* (Cambridge: Cambridge University Press).

Atkinson, A.B. (1970): 'On the measurement of inequality', *Journal of Economic Theory*, 2, 244–63.

Conlisk, J. (1977): 'A further look at the Hansen–Weisbrod–Pechman debate', *Journal of Human Resources*, 12, 147–163.

Crean, J.F. (1975): 'The income redistributive effect of public spending on higher education', *Journal of Human Resources*, 10, 116–22.

Creedy, J. and P. Francois (1990): 'Education: taxes, fees and majority voting', *Journal of Public Economics*, 24, 181–200.

Greene, K.V. (1973): 'Collective decision making models and the measurement of benefits in fiscal incidence studies', *National Tax Journal*, 26, 177–85.

Hansen, W.L. and B.A. Weisbrod (1969a): 'The distribution of costs and direct benefits of public higher education: the case of California', *Journal of Human Resources*, 4, 176–91.

—— (1969b): *Benefits, Costs and the Finance of Public Higher Education*, (Chicago: Markham Publishing Co.).

Hart, P.E. (1975): 'Moment distributions in economics: an exposition', *Journal of the Royal Statistical Society*, Series A, 138, 423–34.

Haveman, R.H. and B.C. Wolfe (1984): 'Schooling and economic well being: the role of non-market effects', *Journal of Human Resources*, 19, 377–407.

James, E. and Benjamin G. (1988a): 'Educational distribution and income redistribution through education in Japan', *Journal of Human Resources*, 23, 469–89.

—— (1988b): *Public Policy and Private Education in Japan* (London: Macmillan).

Johnson, G.E. (1984): 'Subsidies for higher education', *Journal of Labour Economics*, 2, 303–18.

Majumdar, T. (1983): *Investment in Education and Social Choice* (Cambridge: Cambridge University Press).

McGuire, J.W. (1976): 'The distribution of subsidy to students in California public higher education', *Journal of Human Resources*, 11, 343–53.

Pechman, J.A. (1970): 'The distributional effects of public higher education in California', *Journal of Human Resources*, 5, 230–6.

Shackett, J.R. and D.J. Slottje (1987): 'Labour supply decisions, human capital attributes, and inequality in the size distribution of earnings in the U.S., 1952–81', *Journal of Human Resources*, 22, 82–100.

5. Will Younger Cohorts Obtain a Worse Deal from the UK State Pension Scheme?

Richard Disney and Edward Whitehouse

5.1 INTRODUCTION

How well do successive generations fare in public pay-as-you-go pension schemes? In the United Kingdom, as in many other countries, there have been frequent variations to the rules governing benefit entitlements, to eligibility criteria and to contribution schedules, and in consequence different generations can expect to obtain widely differing rates of return from their contributions to the public pension scheme. In general, however, the retrenchment of pension provision in the 1980s, in the light of concern as to the ageing of the population in industralized countries (Heller, Hemming and Kohnert, 1986) implies that current younger and future generations may expect to earn a lower return on their membership of the public pension scheme than earlier generations.

This chapter focuses on the measurement of expected rates of return to the United Kingdom public pension scheme for successive generations of male earners born between 1935 and 1960. Variation in rates of return between generations implies a degree of intergenerational redistribution in the context of a pay-as-you-go pension scheme. The issue of measuring redistribution is discussed more fully in the next section.

Central to calculations of rates of return on public pension scheme membership is a precise calculation of the accrual of individual pension entitlements over time. This involves a careful specification of the parameters governing the schedules of contributions and benefits, and, where contributions and benefits are related non-linearly to income, consideration of the dynamic process by which individual lifetime earnings profiles are generated. The latter should be undertaken on a disaggregated and plausible basis rather than by using either an average, 'representative' individual, or growth factors attached to, say, the current wage bill. As Peter Hart (1976a, p. 561) has pointed out: 'any forecast of the costs of pension based merely on the average path, or even worse, merely on the average income in a cross-section, is likely severely to underestimate the future pension burden'.

Although the United Kingdom pension scheme revalues individual lifetime earnings in such a way that the impact of misplaced aggregation on the *average* future pension burden is unclear, the *distribution* of pension entitlements, and rates of return both within and between cohorts, will be distorted by inappropriate modelling of earnings dynamics.

In a series of papers, Peter Hart has shed light on the dynamics of earnings distributions (Hart, 1976a, 1976b; Creedy and Hart, 1979). Using data on the earnings of a number of cohorts of individuals for several years, Hart showed how the inequality of earnings changed over the life-cycle, how measured inequality was affected by entries and exits, and the impact of earnings mobility on the inequality of earnings. This fascinating analysis used 'pure' cohort earnings data drawn from official national insurance records. Unfortunately, few cohort data sets have become available in the UK since that time, and those that have emerged have problems of panel attrition.

Nevertheless, Peter Hart's strictures as to calculations of aggregate pension burdens based on data on the growth of average earnings, or a cross-section of earnings averaged across age-groups, remain pertinent. An appropriate methodology requires a disaggregated approach and consideration of cohort and time as well as age effects on lifetime earnings. Section 5.3 shows how pooled cross-section data can generate a distribution of heterogeneous lifetime earnings profiles which, although lacking a stochastic structure to the earnings generation process, can underpin plausible values of the distributions of pension entitlements for successive generations.

Section 5.4 considers the parameters of the contribution schedule and the benefit system within the UK pension scheme and describes how differential mortality among individuals, and mortality improvements, are modelled. The empirical results are then considered: summary measures of the expected rates of return on the basis of their contributions to the pension scheme for four generations born between 1935 and 1960, assumed to retire between 2000 and 2025. In these tabulations, it is assumed that all workers are contracted-in to the state scheme (a discussion of the returns to contracting-out for individuals is contained in Disney and Whitehouse, 1992a, 1992b), and also only returns on the pension scheme accrued since 1978, when the state earnings-related pension scheme (SERPS) was introduced, are considered.

The results suggest both that rates of return to earlier cohorts are higher and that there are significant inter-decile variations in rates of return within generations. The reason for the higher returns to earlier cohorts is primarily the accelerated accrual of benefits in SERPS for earlier members of the scheme. Indexation of the basic pension post-retirement to earnings rather than prices, as well as indexation of the national insurance contribution floor and ceiling to earnings, raises the rate of return to all generations within the sample.

The results reveal that rates of return by decile *within* generations are monotonically decreasing from lowest to highest decile, irrespective of the method of post-retirement indexation of pension benefits (and pre-retirement indexation of the national insurance floor and ceiling on contributions) when uniform mortality by occupational group is assumed. However, when differential mortality by occupational class is incorporated, the relationship becomes highly non-linear across deciles, with the lowest and highest deciles as the main beneficiaries.

5.2 MEASURING REDISTRIBUTION IN PENSION SCHEMES

When measuring the extent of intergenerational redistribution we are, almost by definition, examining a pension scheme which is not in steady state. In stylized form, a pay-as-you-go public pension scheme implies that generation B is supporting generation A in retirement, and is itself subsequently supported in its retirement by generation C. Redistribution between generations will take place unless generation birth rates, life expectancy and participation rates are constant and there are no changes to the benefit and contribution regime.

Many of these changes, such as demographic trends, are incremental over time. However, changes to the benefit and contribution regime can have substantial effects over a short period, as, for example, when the UK government decides to increase the basic pension or alter the terms of the earnings-related component or the contribution schedule. Even changes to the method of indexation of benefit rates or contribution schedules can have impacts which accumulate rapidly, as described in section 5.4.

It is often desirable to examine the redistributive impact of the pension scheme in steady state, as a means of examining intragenerational redistribution under the condition of lifetime revenue neutrality. In a PAYG pension scheme in steady state with demographic composition and structural factors held constant, the average rate of return should equal the sum of the growth of population and real wages (Aaron, 1985), which is akin to studying the scheme as if it were a funded scheme. To put it another way, an appropriate measure of revenue neutrality in such a framework is obtained, the average contribution rate is set such that the aggregate value of contributions to retirement is equal to the aggregate value of benefits at retirement, discounted at the sum of these rates of growth. In such circumstances, the equilibrium tax rate for the scheme can be found and simulations undertaken with alternative assumptions as to benefit and contribution schedules. An example of such an approach for a single cohort in the British pension scheme is Creedy, Disney and Whitehouse (1992); see also Creedy (1982).

However, this method of calculating revenue neutrality is not available when out of steady state, and individual cohorts or generations may earn average returns which differ from their 'steady state' return. So a more rough and ready approach to revenue neutrality is adopted here. It is assumed that the Government Actuary's (1990) projections of contribution rates into the future under the two main variants (price or earnings indexation of the basic pension and national insurance contribution floor and ceiling) are approximately accurate, although they are built on stylized growth factors.

These projections, suitably adjusted to take account of projected expenditure on other national insurance benefits, are assumed to be those rates paid over time by each generation, with benefits projected on the basis of the existing (post-1986) benefit formula plus accrued entitlements under the 1978–86 formula. Thus the requirement of steady state average lifetime revenue neutrality is replaced by the assumption of period-by-period revenue neutrality (that is, the statutory provision that the National Insurance Fund must approximately balance its income and outgoings in each financial year).

A further question concerns the interpretation of measured redistribution. Some studies, typically utilizing data on observed pension recipients, examine redistribution *ex post*, taking account of observed differences in household characteristics (such as composition of the observed pensioner families, disabilities and so on), while imputing directly or indirectly past earnings histories and contribution records. Often, however, such comparisons have simply taken the form of static measured within-period transfers from current workers to pensioners. The latter case does not capture the dynamic aspect of intergenerational redistribution.

Alternatively, as in the approach adopted here, *ex ante* intergenerational redistribution is considered: that is, prior to knowledge of such factors as family composition after attaining pensionable age (which will determine eligibility for dependants' or survivors' benefits) and state of health (likewise for receipt of disability benefits). In addition, examining the expected rates of return solely to men means that cohort returns as a whole are biased downwards: given the differential mortality (and, currently, pensionable age) of men and women, and the built-in redistributive features of the benefit regime, the state pension scheme in Britain involves significant intragenerational transfers to women as a group (Hemming and Kay, 1982).

5.3 LIFETIME EARNINGS PROFILES

The data for this simulation analysis of rates of return are lifetime earnings profiles constructed in Disney and Whitehouse (1991). Nine years of FES data from 1978 to 1986 were pooled and a series of regressions of individual earnings for occupation and industry sub-groupings were obtained, including age, education, region and time dummies among the regressors. A sample of over 30 000 individuals was utilized. We focus here on the earnings profiles from 1978 onwards of four 'generations' born in 1935, 1945, 1955 and 1960, which comprise over 3000 individuals.

Individual lifetime earnings profiles were projected to state pension-able age and simulated recursively where necessary back to 1978, from the individual's earnings observation in the FES data set using the occupation and industry-specific age quadratic, time dummies, and assumed 2 per cent productivity growth post-sample period. In the case of the cohort born in 1960, reported date of labour market entry was obtained from the education variable, and only the FES from 1982 onwards was utilized, in order to gain a sufficient sample of late entrants who had engaged in tertiary education. Even so, mean earnings of this cohort are somewhat lower than expected (see section 5.5).

Stochastic intra-occupation and industry fluctuations in earnings are ruled out, as are individual moves between industries and occupations and spells of interruption to employment; the occupational and industrial affiliation observed in the FES sample record are assumed to persist over the lifetime. In the context of *ex post* redistribution, the assumption of no interruptions to employment will bias downwards the degree of variation in pension entitlements that will actually occur, given that spells of work interruption tend to correlate with low average lifetime incomes. The direction of the bias stemming from the other assumptions is unclear. In any event, there is a high degree of variation in lifetime incomes among the sample even under the restrictive assumptions used here.

5.4   THE PENSION SCHEME IN BRITAIN: A BRIEF DESCRIPTION

The UK pension scheme is a pay-as-you-go system funded by the scheme of national insurance contributions, notionally levied on employees and employers. Contracted-in employees pay the full rate of NI contributions and, subject to obtaining an adequate contribution record, are entitled to receive both the basic flat-rate pension and the earnings-related 'tier', SERPS. Individuals who are contracted-out of the NI scheme pay a reduced rate of contribution and are only entitled to the flat-rate component of the pension, but we assume here that all individuals are contracted-in.

National Insurance Contributions

Employee
Employees' national insurance contributions are currently payable above a lower earnings limit (LEL), set approximately equal to the basic flat-rate pension for a single person, and up to an upper earnings limit (UEL) fixed by statute as a multiple of between 6.5 and 7.5 times the flat-rate pension. Typically, in recent years it has been near the 7.5 multiple. To avoid the 'threshold effect' of the marginal contribution rate at the LEL, earnings below the LEL once the LEL is attained are taxed at a lower rate (see Dilnot and Webb, 1989).

   Using the following notation: time indexed by tax year 0 (1978) . . . t . . . R where R = year of reaching pensionable age and refers to *end year* values. Thus y_R refers to earnings in the tax year preceding retirement; y is individual earnings in nominal terms; c_e is employee's contribution rate and LEL and UEL are lower and upper earnings limit respectively. Then the contribution schedule can be described as:

$$c_{et} = 0 \text{ for all } t \text{ where } y_t < \text{LEL}_t \tag{5.1}$$

$$c_{et} = c_{e1}y_t \text{ for all } t \text{ where } y_t = \text{LEL}_t \tag{5.2}$$

$$c_{et} = c_{e1}y_t + c_{e2}(y_t - \text{LEL}_t) \text{ for all } t \text{ where } \text{LEL}_t < y_t < \text{UEL}_t \tag{5.3}$$

$$c_{et} = c_{e1} + c_{e2}(\text{UEL}_t - \text{LEL}_t) \text{ for all } t \text{ where } y_t \geqslant \text{UEL}_t \tag{5.4}$$

$$C_e = \sum_{t=0}^{R} c_{et} \tag{5.5}$$

Employer
The employers' national insurance contribution schedule is graduated, with four bands, and no UEL. Each incremental rate becomes payable on the *whole* of earnings. Defining the employers' contribution rate as c_z, then the schedule is summarized as:

$$c_{zt} = 0 \text{ for all } t \text{ where } y_t < \text{LEL}_t \tag{5.6}$$

$$c_{zt} = c_{z1}y_t \text{ for all } t \text{ where } \text{LEL}_t \leq y_t < b_1 \tag{5.7}$$

$$c_{zt} = c_{z2}y_t \text{ for all } t \text{ where } b_1 \leq y_t < b_2 \tag{5.8}$$

$$c_{zt} = c_{z3}y_t \text{ for all } t \text{ where } b_2 \leq y_t < b_3 \tag{5.9}$$

$$c_{zt} = c_{z4}y_t \text{ for all } t \text{ where } b_3 \leq y_t \tag{5.10}$$

$$C_z = \sum_{t=0}^{R} c_{zt} \tag{5.11}$$

Pension Benefits

Flat-rate pension
Entitlement to flat-rate benefit B (paid at two rates: single person and for a married couple) is contingent on having accumulated a sufficient value of contributions. For those with an almost-full NI contribution record (nine-tenths of the working life), full benefit is payable. It is reduced for those with interrupted contributions histories, subject to a minimum number of years of credited contributions of roughly 20 per cent of the working life. However 'home responsibilities protection' waives this rule for those who can show that he or she was precluded from regular employment by looking after children or the disabled, and for such individuals a 50 per cent contributory record is adequate for a full pension.

SERPS
Those contracted-in to the pension scheme are also entitled to state earnings-related pension, which was introduced in the Social Security Act 1975 and radically modified in the Social Security Act 1986 (Hemming and Kay, 1982; Creedy and Disney, 1988). Although SERPS provides significant protection for widows and widowers, it is the schedule concerning the individual's own entitlements which is central here.

Define:

> S = total SERPS entitlement at pensionable age (£ per week). Incre-
> ments in SERPS accrued per time period are denoted s and time
> indexed.
> w = average economy-wide earnings in nominal terms.
> x = pension accrual rate (specific to each R) see Table 5.1:
> We assume that earners retire on reaching state pensionable age
> (currently 65 for men and 60 for women).

The four possible outcomes for any period t are described in equations
(5.12) to (5.15), with total SERPS entitlement given by (5.16):

$$s_t = 0 \text{ for all } t \text{ where } y_t < \text{LEL}_t \tag{5.12}$$

$$s_t = 0 \text{ for all } t \text{ where } (w_R/w_t).y_t < \text{LEL}_R \tag{5.13}$$

$$s_t = \{ (w_R/w_t).y_t - \text{LEL}_R\}.x_R \text{ for all } t \text{ where } \text{LEL}_R \leqslant (w_R/w_t)y_t < \text{UEL}_t \tag{5.14}$$

$$s_t = \{ (w_R/w_t). \text{UEL}_t - LEL_R\}.x_R \text{ for all } t \text{ where } w_t \geqslant \text{UEL}_t \tag{5.15}$$

$$\text{and: } S_z = \sum_{t=0}^{R} s_t \tag{5.16}$$

The salient features of this schedule of benefits are:

(a)   only earnings below the UEL 'count' towards SERPS entitlement;
(b)   both earnings and the earnings limits are indexed, but are currently
       asymmetrically indexed: the LEL (approximately equal to the basic
       flat-rate pension) and the UEL are indexed to prices, while eligible
       earnings are revalued to an average earnings index. This has some
       interesting redistributive effects, explored in Creedy, Disney and
       Whitehouse (1992);
(c)   at pensionable age, revalued earnings are averaged and the LEL in
       the year prior to reaching pensionable age (which is the basic
       pension: see above) is deducted from the total to obtain eligible
       SERPS earnings. A cohort-specific accrual rate is then applied to
       this amount in order to derive the SERPS entitlement. As with the
       basic pension, the SERPS entitlement post-retirement is currently
       indexed to price inflation.

The present focus is on the accumulation of pension entitlements since

1978, both of the basic flat-rate pension and of the additional component (SERPS). As with many new PAYG pension schemes, SERPS involved the accrual of pension increments at an accelerated rate for early participants. Originally, individuals retiring in 1998 could draw a full SERPS entitlement of 25 per cent of their average revalued eligible earnings over these 20 years. As more years of pensionable earnings accrued, individuals could, under the 1975 legislation, select their '20 best years' of revalued earnings for calculating the pension entitlement.

However, the Social Security Act 1986 ended the '20 best years' rule (although rights obtained from 1978–86 were preserved) and reduced the fraction of average earnings replaced to 20 per cent by stages (Creedy and Disney, 1988). Selected accrual rates applicable to various cohorts by year of reaching pensionable age are shown in Table 5.1 and it is apparent that earlier cohorts will obtain the better return on their SERPS contributions. Indeed, for the cohorts selected here, the accrual rate for the oldest cohort is three times that for the youngest cohort.

Table 5.1 SERPS accrual rate by year of retirement

Year of retirement	Age in 1990	Accrual rate
1995–96	60	25/20 = 1.25%
2000–01	55	25/21 = 1.19%
2005–06	50	22.5/26 = 0.87%
2010–11	45	20/31 = 0.65%
2015–16	40	20/36 = 0.56%
2020–21	35	20/41 = 0.49%
2025–26	30	20/46 = 0.43%
2027–28 onwards	28 and under	20/49 = 0.41%

Source: Government Actuary (1990).

A slight offsetting factor is mortality improvement: on the basis of projections by the Government Actuary, we forecast that the youngest cohort will live on average just over a year longer than the oldest cohort, and the two cohorts born 1955 and 1960 are therefore given a one year mortality improvement (as the simulation deals with discrete years rather than fractions of a year).

Some calculations also take account of differential mortality between occupations and industries. The expected length of life for individuals in each sector can be obtained using the industry and occupation-specific standardized mortality ratios (SMRs) described in OPCS (1990). These SMRs are applied to individuals in our cohort according to their industry and occupational affiliation observed in the relevant FES.[1]

5.5   COMPARISONS OF RATES OF RETURN

Previous Studies

Studies of intergenerational rates of return are rare, and those that are undertaken generally utilize stylized age-earnings profiles. In the only major study for the UK, Atkinson (1970) examined the Labour Party's proposals for national superannuation which were ultimately aborted by the 1970 General Election (although they contained some of the features ultimately included in the 1975 legislation). Atkinson assumed that national earnings would grow at 6 per cent per annum in nominal terms, and then compared expected scheme returns at earnings levels of varying proportions of national average earnings over the lifetime. Given the progressive benefit structure, the assumption that employers' national insurance contributions were borne by consumers, and the absence of differential mortality in his study, it was not surprising to find that, in steady state, rates of return were highest among the lower paid.

Atkinson considered expected average rates of return for a series of cohorts born in 1907, 1917, 1927, 1937 and 1951. Benefit accrual was considered from age 21, and so the cohort retiring in 1972 would receive no benefits from national superannuation. Thereafter, an accelerated proportion of benefits would be paid under the new scheme until 1992, whereafter a full entitlement would be obtained. Given the favourable terms of partial accrual, he found that the highest nominal returns were obtained by the oldest generation (who had paid very low national insurance contributions in their early working lives) and the next two generations who received partial superannuation benefits on favourable terms. The last generation, born in 1951, was projected to receive a rate of return some 3 per cent below the second generation (but still positive at 9 per cent). Atkinson's results therefore confirm that returns in steady state are typically lower than those obtained when new pension schemes are introduced.

A study of the United States pension scheme confirms this result. Hurd and Shoven (1985) merged the Retirement History Survey with Social Security administrative records in order to calculate contribution 'histories' for a sample of individuals aged 58 to 64 in 1969. These individuals were reinterviewed twice, in 1975 and 1979, in order to obtain a picture of transfers received post-retirement. In terms of the discussion in section 5.2, this study was composed of a mixture of *ex ante* and *ex post* assumptions, unlike the present study and that of Atkinson, which utilize an *ex ante* approach.

Hurd and Shoven show that rates of return fell significantly from eldest cohort to youngest cohort, from 9.4 per cent to 7.0 per cent on 1969 benefit provisions, even for a sample with a seven-year range in ages. Again, this is attributed to the more favourable accrual rates of earlier cohorts in the social security programme. Married couples appeared to earn a higher return than single people, and whites relative to blacks (given differential mortality), although some of these interpretations were questioned by Aaron (1985).

Results

The following results distinguish between cases of uniform mortality and differential mortality by occupations, and between price and earnings indexation. Using the simulated individual earnings profiles, the benefit and contribution schedules defined in section 5.4, the projected average contribution rates of the Government Actuary, and forecast differences in life expectancy over time and across occupations, real internal rates of return (IRRs) were calculated for all men in the four age cohorts. These returns were calculated for the cases of uniform and differential mortality and under two indexation assumptions.

In the first case (the status quo), all values other than lifetime earnings are indexed in line with prices and uniform mortality is assumed. In the second case, differential mortality across occupations is incorporated. In the third case, the basic pension in payment, the national insurance LEL and the UEL and lifetime earnings were all revalued in line with average earnings with uniform mortality, and in case four, differential mortality is again applied. The important summary results are grouped in Table 5.2.

The interpretation of the baseline case of price indexation and uniform mortality is straightforward. Mean returns decline from the oldest cohort, born 1935, through to the youngest, born 1960. The slight improvement in average mortality (modelled as a jump of one year from the cohort born in 1945 to that born in 1955) does not outweigh the advantage of accelerated SERPS accrual for older cohorts and the projected impact of the worsening dependency ratio on contribution rates after 2000. Indeed, for men in the two younger cohorts, mean expected real rates of return in the scheme are negative.[2]

Mean average lifetime earnings are higher for younger cohorts: a consequence of real productivity growth. The exception is the fall in average earnings between the cohorts born 1955 and 1960, which we infer stems from the lack of some potential high earners from the FES data set for this cohort, some of whom may still have been in tertiary education in 1982 – the first year of our sample for the 1960 cohort.

Table 5.2 reports the standard deviation of returns, and the real rate of

Table 5.2   Rates of return: the basic results

Cohort, and assumptions	Mean	Rate of return (%) s.d.[a]	d2[b]	Median	d8	Average lifetime earnings[d] Mean	s.d.
Price index: uniform mortality							
c35	2.4	1.1	3.3	2.5	2.1	234	122
c45	0.4	1.0	1.2	0.6	−0.1	277	129
c55	−0.2	0.8	0.3	−0.1	−0.5	313	126
c60	−0.3	0.8	0.4	−0.2	−0.7	286	107
Price index: differential mortality							
c35	1.0	3.1	0.5	0.0	2.2	as	
c45	0.2	2.6	−0.1	0.1	0.5		
c55	−0.9	2.6	−1.0	−1.2	−0.5	above	
c60	−0.7	1.9	−0.5	−0.9	−0.8		
Earnings index: uniform mortality							
c35	4.0	1.2	5.1	4.2	3.4	as	
c45	1.7	1.1	2.9	1.9	1.1		
c55	0.9	1.0	1.8	1.0	0.2	above	
c60	0.8	0.9	1.7	0.9	0.2		
Earnings index: differential mortality							
c35	3.6	3.0	3.7	3.3	3.5	as	
c45	1.6	2.5	1.7	1.5	1.7		
c55	0.2	2.7	0.3	−0.1	0.4	above	
c60	0.4	2.0	0.7	0.1	0.0		

Notes:
[a] c[xx] refers to cohort born in 19[xx].
[b] s.d. is standard deviation.
[c] d[x] refers to xth decile (d1 is lowest).
[d] Average lifetime earnings are £ per week at 1990 levels.

return for the median and the second and eighth deciles of average lifetime earnings, for each case. It is apparent from inspection of the returns according to earnings decile that, on the assumption of uniform mortality, the progressivity of the benefit formula (the flat rate component to the pension) implies that lower lifetime earners receive a better return on their contributions. The same phenomenon is revealed in the case of earnings indexation of the basic pension in payment and the floor and ceiling of national insurance contributions, although in this case all real rates of return are positive. Figure 5.1 plots the rates of return by

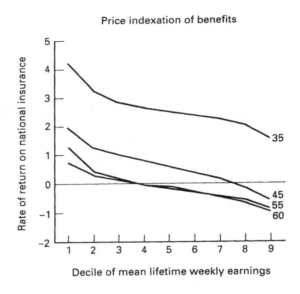

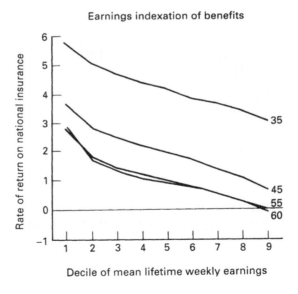

Figure 5.1   Rate of return on national insurance contributions for selected cohorts, assuming uniform mortality

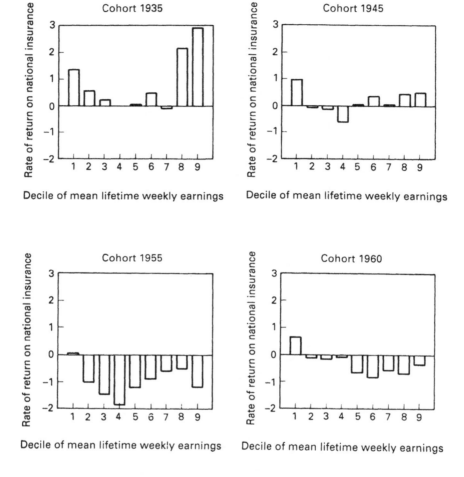

*Figure 5.2   Rate of return on national insurance contributions for selected
cohorts, occupation and industry-specific mortality*

the deciles of average earnings for the cases of price and earnings indexation under uniform mortality for all four cohorts. The two salient features, higher returns for younger cohorts and for lower lifetime earners, are clear.

The introduction of differential mortality by occupation alters the story substantially. Real rates of return are on average somewhat lower than the uniform case, although there is much greater variation.[3] The fall in real rates of return for younger cohorts is also apparent, although the cohort born in 1960 appears to earn a slightly higher return than the 1955 cohort in the price indexation case, and a slightly higher positive return in the earnings indexation case. Moreover, the variation in real return across deciles is of some interest, with the eighth decile earning a greater return than the second decile, reversing the uniform mortality case. In fact, the relationship between earnings decile and return is non-linear, as can be illustrated in greater detail.

Figure 5.2 plots real rates of return by decile of average earnings for each of the four cohorts in the case of price indexation and it is apparent for the two older cohorts that the first decile, and the higher deciles, earn the highest returns. (The case of earnings indexation tells a similar story.) For the two younger cohorts, there are different orderings, although, other than the first decile, the lower deciles fare worst.

Finally, Figure 5.3 provides plots of *individual* real rates of return in the differential mortality case against average lifetime earnings, with price indexation for the cohort born in 1960. The separate impacts of the benefit formula and occupational-specific differences in mortality are clear: the former in the weak negative gradient of the occupation-specific 'lines' according to earnings which are apparent in the data, and the latter in the differences in returns between occupations.

5.6   CONCLUSIONS

The results presented here confirm the results of earlier studies: older cohorts will do better from the public pension scheme than younger cohorts. However, there is a good deal of variation in returns to individuals, arising from the heterogeneity of their earnings profiles, the non-proportional contribution and benefit schedules, and differential mortality across occupations. These general results are fairly familiar, but no study in the United Kingdom to our knowledge since Atkinson (1970) has calculated these returns, nor at such a disaggregated level.

What policy conclusions stem from these results? One issue is whether the calculated average returns offer a satisfactory return to members of

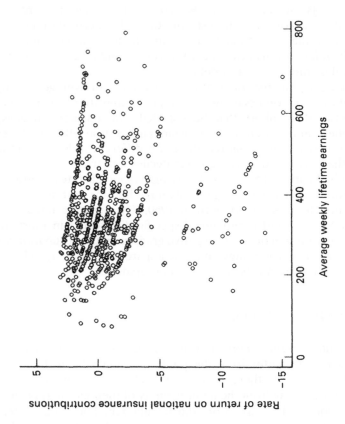

Figure 5.3 Rates of return: no contracting-out, differential mortality

individual generations, defining satisfactory by reference to outside alternatives. On the face of it, therefore, the results suggest that younger cohorts of men are going to earn negative real returns to their public pension scheme membership. This might be a source of some concern. Individuals earning lower returns have the ability to contract-out of the earnings-related component (SERPS) and into an occupationally provided defined benefit scheme or a money-purchase pension scheme such as a personal pension. Elsewhere we have suggested by a similar disaggregated analysis that this is exactly what has happened (Disney and Whitehouse, 1992a, 1992b). Problems of adverse selection in the public pension scheme may emerge which will make its continued funding politically unviable.

However, it should be noted that the negative real rates of return occur in part because we have focused on male contributions and pension entitlements. Had we adopted the steady state revenue-neutral methodology, most returns for all cohorts would have been strictly positive (although still declining over time by generation). The within-period revenue-neutral contribution rate is higher because most men will retire as part of a family unit in which they will be entitled to the married couple's pension, and where the woman will typically outlive the man. Incorporating these aspects, it can be calculated, would raise internal rates of return by several percentage points. Again, however, the return, while positive, could easily be exceeded by returns on other schemes, such as money-purchase pensions.

Since *ex post* the higher returns to earlier generations cannot be changed, the issue arises as to whether the lower returns to later generations should be raised. In part, their lower returns stem from the change to the benefit formula in the Social Security Act 1986 and a reversion to previous practice would improve their returns. However, there is a range of policy options, of which this is one, which would also involve variations in the degree of *intragenerational* redistribution (Creedy, Disney and Whitehouse, 1992). It is not self-evident to us that, say, a restoration of pre-1986 SERPS accrual rates, as opposed to indexing the basic pension to earnings (although these are not revenue-neutral alternatives), is the superior option in raising the return to later cohorts. It is to be hoped, however, that discussion of these alternatives will be facilitated by the type of disaggregated analysis undertaken here.

NOTES

1. The assumption of no individual mobility between industries and occupations is

important here and, indeed, we arbitrarily reduced the SMR adjustment for the mining industry to next-highest industry SMR in order to ensure that all workers could expect some pensionable period.

2. Given that the pension scheme is highly redistributive to women, this does not, of course, imply that real returns to the whole cohort are negative. See section 5.6 below, and Hemming and Kay (1982).

3. The wide disparity in mean and median returns by generation is something of a puzzle. The SMRs have been slightly altered in the analysis (see note 1) but this would imply a slightly higher return in the differential case. The main reason would seem to be our assumption that all earners survive to retirement. Given that a significant number do not, and that these tend to be concentrated in occupations with below-average earnings, our FES sample of earners 'oversamples' low earners, who are assumed to earn lower returns after reaching retirement.

REFERENCES

Aaron, H.J. (1985): Comment, in D.A. Wise (ed.), *Pensions, Labor and Individual Choice* (Chicago: Chicago University Press) 215–21.

Atkinson, A.B. (1970): 'National superannuation: redistribution and value for money', *Oxford Bulletin of Economics and Statistics*, 32 (August), 171–85.

Creedy, J. (1982): *State Pensions in Britain*, National Institute of Economic and Social Research Occasional Paper (Cambridge: Cambridge University Press).

—— and R. Disney (1988): 'The new pension scheme in Britain', *Fiscal Studies*, 9 (May), 57–71.

——, R. Disney and E. Whitehouse (1992): 'The earnings-related state pension, indexation and lifetime redistribution in the UK', Institute for Fiscal Studies Working Paper no. W92/1.

—— and P.E. Hart (1979): 'Age and the distribution of earnings', *Economic Journal*, 89 (June), 280–93.

Dilnot, A.W. and S. Webb (1989): 'Reforming National Insurance contributions: a progress report', *Fiscal Studies*, 10 (May), 38–47.

Disney, R. and E. Whitehouse (1991): 'Occupational and industrial earnings over time: the use of pooled cross-section data', Institute for Fiscal Studies, Working Paper no. 91/7.

—— (1992a): 'Contracting out and lifetime redistribution in the state pension scheme in Britain', University of Kent Studies in Economics no. 92/4.

—— (1992b): *The Personal Pensions Stampede*, Report Series (London: Institute for Fiscal Studies).

Government Actuary (1990): *National Insurance Fund: Long-term Financial Estimates*, Second Quinquennial Review (London: Her Majesty's Stationery Office).

Hart, P.E. (1976a): 'The dynamics of earnings, 1963–1973', *Economic Journal*, 86 (September), 551–65.

—— (1976b): 'The comparative statics and dynamics of income distributions', *Journal of the Royal Statistical Society*, Series A, 139, 108–25.

Heller, P.S., R. Hemming and P.W. Kohnert (1986): *Aging and Social Expenditure in the Major Industrial Countries, 1980–2025*, Occasional Paper no. 47 (Washington D.C.: International Monetary Fund).

Hemming, R. and J.A. Kay (1982): 'The costs of the state earnings-related pension scheme', *Economic Journal*, 92 (June), 300–19.

Hurd, M.D. and J.B. Shoven (1985): 'The distributional impact of social security', in D.A. Wise (ed), *Pensions, Labor and Individual Choice* (Chicago: Chicago University Press) 193–215.

OPCS (1990): *Longitudinal Study: Mortality and Social Organisation 1971–81* (ed. P. Goldblatt) (London: Her Majesty's Stationery Office, for Office of Population Census and Surveys).

PART II

Industrial Concentration

6. Are Industrial Economists Still Interested in Concentration?

Michael Waterson

6.1 INTRODUCTION

Peter Hart's interests in industrial economics are very much linked with his interests in concentration. This is evident in his papers with Prais (1956) and Morgan (1977) and book with Clarke (1980) as well as in his sole-authored papers. They encompass the effects of concentration and, in particular, its determinants. Concentration plays a central part in his vision of the subject, I believe. But does it still for others? This chapter argues that concentration, in the sense of the use of concentration measures and analysis of their determinants, currently plays a relatively small part in the field of industrial economics, particularly in the North American, industrial-organization version. The reasons which underlie this lessening emphasis are then explored. Some indications of a revival of interest in concentration as a subject are then examined. After a brief consideration of links to the stochastic approach, the final section provides some concluding remarks, setting out what I see as desirable developments.

6.2 THE CURRENT TEXTBOOK IMPORTANCE OF CONCENTRATION

With reference to the current North American field of industrial organization and its relative neglect of concentration, consider two main pieces of evidence. They are the *Handbook of Industrial Organisation* (Schmalensee and Willig, 1989) and Tirole's (1989) *Theory of Industrial Organisation*. The former is bound to become a standard reference work in the field, whilst the latter is a standard graduate text. They will influence the direction of the subject through those who use them as texts and works of reference.

The *Handbook* is more extensive in its coverage than is Tirole; this is not surprising, given its very considerable length (1600 pages). But only five of the 26 chapters contain any reference to concentration. It is in the more theoretical sections that contributions are particularly sparse. Jacquemin and Slade (ch. 7) illustrate some derivations of relationships between the Lerner index of monopoly power and concentration indices and there is a short section in Chapter 15 by Carlton, entitled 'Market Structure Means More than Just the Degree of Concentration', which implicitly discusses limitations of concentration measures. But that is all, regarding theory.

Schmalensee's survey of empirical work (Chapter 16 of the *Handbook*) has a short (1¼ page) section on measures of concentration. It also has a section on empirical studies of concentration and profitability including some 'stylized facts', a brief discussion of endogeneity of (the Herfindahl index of) concentration in covering intra-industry differences, and a few sentences on the influence of concentration on cyclical behaviour of price –cost margins, a topic also touched upon by Carlton.

Schmalensee's chapter also contains the most sustained passage relating directly to determinants of concentration within the whole *Handbook*. This is section 6.1, which incorporates a number of stylized facts relating to concentration levels between countries and between industries, and plausible influences on these patterns.

There is additional material in Cohen and Levin's chapter on 'Innovation and Market Structure', relating essentially to empirical tests of the Schumpeterian hypothesized relationship between monopolistic markets and innovative performance. A number of tests which examine the link beween market concentration and R&D are reported upon. Finally, Caves's chapter on international differences in industrial organization contains a brief discussion of cross-country concentration differences, focusing on empirical findings.

Thus the most obvious omission from the *Handbook* in its treatment of concentration is any systematic consideration of the determinants of industrial structure. This is not to forget Panzar's Chapter 1, with its section on industry configurations based upon scale economies, but this in any case is not linked directly to concentration measures. Yet it is symptomatic that some empirical work in volume II discusses concepts that have not been covered in volume I; concentration indices are hardly covered theoretically, for example. Thus empirical analyses of differences in firm size between industries, and differences in concentration across countries, are not backed up by theory. There is only one reference to Gibrat's law in volume I, and it reads: 'Also, the finding that firms grow roughly in accordance with Gibrat's Law (growth rates are independent of size; see Mansfield 1962, and Evans, 1986) must be attended to' (p. 78).

This is not clarified in the only other reference, in Schmalensee's chapter (p. 994). Moreover, neither Panzar's chapter, nor Eaton and Lipsey's (on 'Product Differentiation') discuss natural monopoly and oligopoly caused by the nature of demand; that is, where consumers' willingness to pay may continually be enhanced by increases in fixed-cost expenditure without increasing variable costs. This, as will be seen in section 6.3, is a key feature of Sutton's (1991) recent treatment.

Tirole's (1989) text devotes if anything proportionately less time to concentration as a topic than does the *Handbook*. The main treatment is a two-page section on concentration indices and industry profitability. This first discusses the concentration ratio, Herfindahl index and entropy index, together with some general considerations, then gives examples of the link between concentration and profitability. The only other references are rather scattered. For the most part, they occur in two-firm models in which there is an incumbent and a potential entrant, where the question is whether entry will in fact take place, and in similar models concerning patent races, concerned with pre-emption issues. One such discussion, in a war of attrition model, has, it may be worth noting, a stochastic element.

As with the *Handbook*, then, Tirole's treatment is distinguished by paying relatively little attention to industry concentration. Tirole's book is a text in industrial economic theory, and it is not an introductory treatment. But it eschews any theoretical discussion of the determinants of concentration, apart from indirect references to economies of scale as an influence.

The pattern in these recent books contrasts quite sharply with older traditions. Stepping back a generation in texts, Hay and Morris's (1979) first edition has an extensive, chapter-length discussion of cost and supply conditions. This leads into a chapter that contains sections discussing the effect of concentration on a market, measures of concentration, and classification problems. In a later chapter there is an extensive discussion of stochastic models of growth, effects on concentration and so on. These are in addition to empirical material on the effects of concentration on profitability. The second edition (1991) has essentially the same sections. Similarly, Waterson (1984) has a chapter on the determinants of market structure, as well as material on its effects.

This difference in treatment is not peculiar to British texts. Scherer's (1970) first edition has two chapters on the detail of industry structure. The first (ch. 3) was an extensive coverage of concentration measures and concentration in the US. The second chapter (ch. 4) has an in-depth analysis of the determinants of market structure, focusing on scale economies at various levels and merger waves, but also covering stochastic determinants. In Scherer's second edition (1980), the discussion of the determinants of market structure is, if anything, more extensive than in the previous edition, due in particular to reporting on his co-authored study (Scherer *et al.*, 1975) on the economics of multiplant operation. The extensive coverage continues along similar lines in the third edition (Scherer and Ross, 1990), the main change being to separate out the discussion of mergers from Chapter 4 to form a new Chapter 5. Scherer clearly still believes, as do Hay and Morris, that concentration is an important issue.

Slightly earlier, Stigler (1968) was unequivocal in a chapter entitled 'What Is Industrial Organisation?' His definition, of a typical course in the subject, is worth quoting:

> These courses deal with the size structure of firms (one or many, 'concentrated' or not), the causes (above all the economies of scale) of this size structure, the effects of concentration on competition, the effects of competition upon prices, investment, innovation, and so on. (p. 1)

Note in particular the *order* in which these items are listed.

Concentration and its determinants were of primal importance in the subject of industrial economics 20 to 25 years ago. And this was not just because the subject was more empirically orientated and non-theoretical. Stigler himself made substantial theoretical as well as empirical contributions. His book contains a whole part, six chapters out of 22, on the determinants of concentration. These chapters are primarily empirical, but there are theoretical contributions on the measurement of concentration and other concentration-related matters in other parts of the book.

Concentration, and in particular the Herfindahl index, also plays a large role in the US 'merger guidelines', discussed by Michael Utton in Chapter 8 below. The anti-trust tradition relies heavily on concepts of concentration levels and changes in concentration. Thus the policy branch of the subject, as well as some parts of the empirical branch, makes use of concepts which remain largely undiscussed and poorly defined in recent authoritative text and reference contributions.

6.3 REASONS FOR THE DECLINE OF INTEREST IN CONCENTRATION

The obvious question is why industrial economics/industrial organization theory has moved away from consideration of concentration and its determinants. I argue that this is not due directly to a decline of interest in empirical work. Rather, it is due to a combination of factors, mainly the methodological position of the 'New IO', the interrelated influence of game theory and the development of contestability theory. This has in turn had an influence on the type of empirical work which is commonly pursued in recent studies.

A useful discussion of what is meant by the 'New IO' is provided in Davies and Lyons (1989, p. 7):

> Characteristic features are that the mode of analysis is mathematical and often couched in game-theoretic terms, and the treatment of economic welfare is usually explicit. Furthermore, and probably most importantly the . . . methodology . . . specifies the conduct of firms in terms of an *equilibrium concept*.

It has very frequently been pointed out that Bain's (1962) Structure–Conduct–Performance paradigm held a central role for concentration as a major element of structure. He acknowledged that structure was not immutable, but believed it to be slow-changing. Structure was supposed to influence conduct strongly, so that performance was largely determined by structural elements. Therefore it was important to study structure in order to capture the influences on performance and, as a secondary task, to go one stage back to identify the underlying basic influences on structure.

The big change, from the viewpoint of current theory, is in the shift of emphasis in analysis from structure to conduct. Industries with essentially similar structures are now seen as exhibiting a wide variety of behaviours arising from different equilibrium concepts, and so performing very differently. In turn, the task of measuring structure has reduced in importance.

The triumph in the importance of behaviour over conduct arguably reaches its zenith in contestability theory (Baumol *et al.*, 1982). In perfectly contestable (single-product) markets,

> For production by a single firm to be sustainable that firm must (i) produce an output quantity for which it is a natural monopoly (i.e. at which cost is subadditive), and (ii) it must set the lowest price which is equal to the average cost of producing the output demanded by the market. (p. 28)

A similar condition holds in multiproduct markets, save that restrictions on the relationship between prices follow Ramsey-optimality rules.

In other words, in perfectly contestable markets, even if they be natural monopolies and populated by a single firm, that firm is forced to set prices which only barely secure break-even. This further extends the

Bertrand equilibrium result on pricing, that even with only two firms in the industry, prices can be as low as average costs, to one-firm cases.

Perfect contestability does demand some conditions on structure to be satisfied. Dixit (1982) for example suggests the following four conditions are appropriate:

a.   That all producers have access to the same technology
b.   That this technology may have scale economies which in turn may arise through fixed costs but not sunk costs.
c.   Incumbent firms can change prices only with a non-zero time lag.
d.   Customers respond to price differences with a shorter time lag.

Baumol *et al.* (1982) would argue that these conditions are unnecessarily restrictive, though they would agree that the first two are necessary.

However, the important point remains, whether one considers Dixit's four conditions as definitive or not. None of the condition sets has any *necessary* implications for concentration. Thus perfect contestability, though it involves conditions on basic structural elements, involves no conditions on concentration.

With this point accepted, the link from concentration as structure to performance is broken. Any degree of concentration, between monopoly and competition, is consistent with prices at average cost levels. Scale economies and similar factors may, probably will, influence concentration as structure but not performance. Clear predictions from concentration to price–cost margins or profitability cannot be entertained, although barriers to entry *are* still likely to influence profitability.

Indeed, Baumol *et al.* did, perhaps paradoxically, have a great deal to say about the theory of industry structure as exhibited in concentration (or at least numbers of firms). But at the same time they downgraded the importance of measuring structure with any predictive purpose in mind. What they had to say about structure was also linked closely with technological factors – the shapes of cost curves and so on. It did not relate to *differences* in firm sizes within an industry.

Game theory has had a rather more subtle influence on the importance of concentration in industrial economics. In the subject area, overwhelmingly the applications have come from the Nash equilibrium concept and its refinements, subgame perfection and so on. Classic applications in industrial economics include those arising from the Prisoners' Dilemma game. Thus the method has been used to *illustrate* how, for example, firms can be better off colluding yet be unable to reach that outcome. A lot of time has also been spent on demonstrating counter-intuitive results rather than on examining general tendencies.

It is not clear to what extent game theory has useful predictive, as against explanatory, power from the point of view of things industrial economists can measure. Certainly, it can be useful in understanding the behaviour of economic agents. But many people have noted how outcomes depend on rather fine details of the game structure. Behaviour and the factors influencing behaviour – the strategy sets available to players – come to the fore. Again, as with contestability theory, basic structural elements but not concentration come into play here in determining the outcome. But these fine details of strategy sets are not easily observed and measured. Moreover, in multiperiod games there is the famous (or perhaps infamous) Folk Theorem. Any individually rational feasible outcome of a game can be achieved as an equilibrium outcome of that game in infinite repetition. Thus the use of equilibrium concepts need not be constraining on conduct. Again, therefore, the link between structure and performance (here the outcome of the game) is weakened.

Game theory's influence extends beyond this, though; this is why it was described as more subtle. Much recent modelling in industrial economics has been in what is sometimes called the 'MIT tradition' of using stripped-down models to illustrate points simply. Game theory is an ideal tool for doing this. But simple games as used by modellers are almost invariably two-person games. They illustrate points well, but the real world seldom corresponds to a duopoly. Quite commonly, to make things even more stark and straightforward, symmetric duopolies are chosen for examples. Perfect information is often assumed. There are even fewer such real-world cases where these are even approximately true.

Even without that, game theory lends itself relatively poorly to comparisons between two-, three-, four- and more person games. Equilibria tend to multiply as the number of players increases. Thus game theorists naturally tend to shun many-person games in industrial economics. The fact that game theory is commonly used simply to illustrate possibilities makes the limitations perfectly legitimate, but it does not help much to illuminate the real-world empirical influence of concentration.

One factor which both contestability theory and most game theoretic approaches have in common and which makes the relating of concentration to theoretical analysis problematic, is as follows. Neither naturally concern themselves with the *distribution* of firm sizes. But it is fundamental that concentration is a function not only of firm numbers but also firm sizes. Contestability theory, with its emphasis on technology as determining structure, has no real scope for distributions of firm sizes within an industry. Game theoretic approaches, with their emphasis on demonstration, have no need for firms to be unequally sized. Indeed, this would introduce an element of arbitrariness into the analysis.

To put it slightly differently, both approaches are deterministic, and commonly models assume certainty rather than being in any way stochastic. Yet empirically the stochastic tradition appears to have at least something to say about the distribution of firm sizes, as Hart and Prais (1956) and references cited in Schmalensee's *Handbook* (1989) chapter (at p. 994) would attest. This is yet another reason (apart from the shift of focus from structure to conduct) why there is a relative de-emphasis of concentration.

Running alongside the trend in the theory is a switch in emphasis of empirical work in the subject. What is currently considerably in vogue is the single-industry, often time-series study. Examples include Porter (1983) and Slade (1987) and Bresnahan surveys them in the *Handbook* (Schmalensee and Willig, 1989, pp. 1011–57). These are, without doubt, interesting studies, and the careful linking of microdata with theory and sophisticated econometrics is in many senses a considerable advance. It renders testable relatively fine hypotheses, for example about types of behaviour patterns. Thus the pursuit of monopoly power in individual industries continues. Considerable detailed knowledge about mono-polistic practices and other factors will in due course be built up.

However, one major difference is obvious between these studies and those in the older tradition dating from Bain (1951) involving cross-sectional analysis. Single-industry time-series studies by definition need no measure of concentration as an explanatory variable, as long as concentration is (or alternatively its underlying determinants are) slow-moving. Cross-sectional studies naturally employ explanatory variables such as concentration which differ from industry to industry.

To be sure, not all studies in the modern empirical tradition are without a cross-sectional element; some outliers will receive more extensive treatment in the next section. But there is again, empirically as well as theoretically, a shift of emphasis.

6.4   SIGNS OF A REVIVAL?

Is concentration being dropped from the advanced industrial economist's set of 'big questions'? This would seem to be the case, based upon Tirole (1989) and the *Handbook* (Schmalensee and Willig, 1989). Yet there is at least one significant pointer to a revival in interest.

Analysis of concentration never disappeared, despite the paucity of reports in some recent treatments. (This is quite apart from the obvious milestone of Baumol *et al.*, 1982). There is, for example, the work of Clarke and Davies (1982) on the determinants of concentration in terms of the coefficient of variation of costs; also Davies and Lyons (1982), which links the technological and the stochastic schools of thought. But, particularly in the US, analysing its determinants became a minority pursuit.

Moreover, the recent flowering of interest in microeconometric work in industrial economics largely ill-suits investigation of concentration. However, a significant exception within this new tradition (if that is not a contradiction in terms) is Bresnahan and Reiss (1990), which makes use of the geography of the US to investigate the determinants of concentration among car dealers, in terms of monopoly and duopoly, in a series of isolated towns in that country. The major question investigated is the relationship between the minimum size of town needed to support one dealer and the minimum size needed to support two. This relationship is influenced by scale economies, strategic considerations and also by the extent of product differentiation. Thus the cross-section is generated *within* the industry.

But a far more significant development is represented by Sutton (1991). This book takes a quite different tack. It acknowledges that game-theoretic analysis is very sensitive to the precise specification, and therefore tends to have been employed in single-industry studies and to have questioned the rectitude of cross-industry analysis. But it does not accept that single industry studies are the only response. Instead, his response is to draw out as results from game-theoretic analysis some robust predictions which hold across a variety of model specifications. This can lead to a development of the theory of determinants of concentration, providing a new foundation for cross-industry studies.

The theory is developed separately for the cases of exogenous sunk-cost industries and endogenous sunk-cost industries. The former essentially can be dealt with using the traditional technological explanation of concentration. This runs in terms of the relationship between minimum efficient scale and market size (or, as Sutton puts it, the ratio of sunk set-up costs to market size). Briefly, if minimum efficient scale of operation is, say, one-tenth of market size, we can expect in equilibrium no more than ten firms in the industry, and a minimum four-firm concentration ratio of 40 per cent.

With the latter industries, sunk-cost expenditures – in Sutton's examples, advertising expenditures – enhance willingness-to-pay for a given product without increasing variable cost. The mechanism at work may be demonstrated along the following lines, using Figure 6.1. Initially, average and marginal costs are represented by AC^1 and MC respectively. In a small market (demand D_s^1) there will be scope for only a

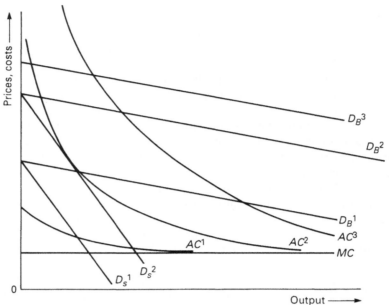

Figure 6.1   Effects of sunk costs on industry equilibrium

few firms (as drawn, probably only one) whereas in a big market (demand D_B^1) there is scope for many firms. This is very similar to the technology school's approach. However, now introduce the possibility that by an addition to the fixed and sunk costs of advertising, yielding costs AC^2, willingness to pay can be enhanced. In the small market (D_s^2) nothing will happen; no one will take up the possibility. But in the larger market some firms will want to move to the higher-cost, higher returns to scale and greater sales position on D_B^2. At this level, though, there will not be room for as many firms in equilibrium. In some circumstances, these large firms will co-exist with small firms, as long as the equivalent of D_B^1 is not shifted down too much. A further move might then be made to D_B^3 and AC^3, involving higher fixed and sunk costs generating greater scale economies, and correspondingly fewer firms in such a position. Thus, with endogenous sunk costs, those firms which have made the expenditures are able to capture a non-negligible share of the market, however large that market becomes. This theoretical development, based upon Sutton's work with Shaked (for example, Shaked and Sutton, 1987) clearly involves a substantially modified mechanism compared with the technological school.

The two sets of models naturally lead to predictions in terms of minimum concentration levels rather than actual concentration – the latter can be affected by more particular strategic factors. These predictions are: that as market size increases, minimal concentration decreases smoothly in the exogenous sunk-cost industries, but in the advertising-intensive endogenous sunk-cost industries minimum concentration approaches a positive asymptote from above, as illustrated in Figure 6.2. In turn, this suggests testing on a cross-country basis, since sunk costs may be considered similar across countries whereas market size varies greatly (for products where the economies can be considered relatively closed). This is what Sutton does, with a fair degree of success, for his sample of food industries. He then goes on to look in detail at each industry in his sample to examine the dynamic factors at work.

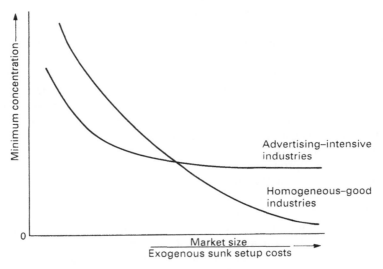

Figure 6.2   Minimum concentration levels

One feature of this work is that the theory is orientated very strongly towards testability and prediction rather than special cases and curiosa. The move back to cross-sectional work is also very noteworthy. At the same time, from our present viewpoint, since Sutton seeks to analyse only minimum concentration levels, he is developing a very partial explanation of concentration. On the issue of why it is that some firms are so much above the minimum size, his theory is naturally (and deliberately) silent. Yet it is still a considerable advance and is very likely to have a major influence on future work.

6.5   LINKS TO THE STOCHASTIC APPROACH

There is one factor noticeably absent from Sutton's (1991) recent study, also from the Bresnahan and Reiss (1990) paper, as well as the *Handbook* (Schmalensee and Willig, 1989) and Tirole (1989) treatments of concentration. This is the feature most closely linked with Peter Hart's own interests, namely, the determinants of the inequality element in concentration.

Although Sutton reports on clear and important predictions beyond those of the technological determination of concentration, his work is, in one sense at least, in the same tradition. The technology view, properly expressed, normally predicts only minimal levels of concentration. So it is with Sutton. But concentration is concerned with inequality as much as with numbers. There *is* inequality in Sutton's theoretical treatment, though of a somewhat arbitrary nature (it is not said why some firms take a lead).

Both the technological view and Sutton's extensions leave aside any prediction of the distribution of firm sizes. This is the central element in the stochastic analyses based upon Gibrat's law or similar processes. And this is the area which links Peter Hart's interests in concentration and in inequality. But stochastic analysis, as already said, sits uneasily on the shoulders of the deterministic type of framework commonly employed in game-theoretic approaches.

The 'problem' with the stochastic approach, from today's common viewpoint, is that it is only a (set of) proximate explanation(s) of the development of firm size distributions. It does not enquire into the fundamental elements but embraces them, for simplicity, as 'luck'. This is at once both a strength and a weakness. From the point of view of rigorous theory, it is a weakness not to be able to explain the ways or nature of luck. On the other hand, all modelling is a simplification. If stochastic approaches lead to distributions which are empirically commonly observed, there is arguably no need to enquire *why* 'luck' interfered. One needs simply to accept that it exists. Thus the approaches are not necessarily in conflict, and a greater acceptance of the stochastic elements when studying concentration and within industrial economics more generally appears warranted.

6.6   CONCLUDING REMARKS

In my view, the concentration of industry is one of the 'big questions' with which industrial economists should concern themselves, simply because it is a major feature of industrial economies. It is desirable to understand the positive economics of concentration. Thus the relative neglect of concentration in modern theoretical developments in the subject is undesirable, as also is the excessive search for counter-intuitive results. Advances such as Sutton's (1991) are to be welcomed. There the game-theoretic equilibrium approach has, perhaps surprisingly, led to concrete predictions which appear supported by empirical observation. This is a considerable advance on the rather sloppy *ad hoc* theorizing which characterized models of the determinants of concentration in the more empirically oriented 1960s and early 1970s.

Yet much remains to be done. As suggested in the previous section, developments on the stochastic approach are likely to provide in part the key to extending the explanation beyond minimal concentration towards actual concentration, but the grafting will be difficult. In turn, this will allow a broader look at the policy issues involved with concentration. None of the recent contributions outlined above has any real positive implications for industrial policy. Yet a substantial amount of effort has in the past been devoted to developing a link between structural observations and the screening of potential candidates for competition policy. The US merger guidelines reflect that concern. It is in this area that the approach of seeking broadly robust predictions, rather than development of interesting counter-intuitive examples, has yet to be tried. Such an extension of the provenance of modern analytical techniques seems to me to be very desirable.

REFERENCES

Bain, J.S. (1951): 'Relation of profit rate to industry concentration in American manufacturing, 1936–1940', *Quarterly Journal of Economics*, **65**, 293–324.
—— (1962): *Industrial Organisation* (New York: John Wiley).
Baumol, W.J., J.C. Panzar and R.D. Willig (1982): *Contestable Markets and the Theory of Industry Structure* (San Diego, CA: Harcourt Brace Jovanovich).
Bresnahan, T.F. and P.C. Reiss (1990): 'Entry in monopoly markets', *Review of Economic Studies*, **57**, 531–53.
Clarke, R. and S.W. Davies (1982): 'Market structure and price cost margins', *Economica*, **49**, 277–87.
Davies, S.W. and B.R. Lyons (1982): 'Seller concentration: the technological explanation and demand uncertainty', *Economic Journal*, **92**, 903–19.
—— (with H. Dixon and P. Geroski) (1989): *Economics of Industrial Organisation* (London: Longman).
Dixit, A.K. (1982): 'Recent developments in oligopoly theory', *American Economic Review* (papers and proceedings), **72**, 12–17.
Hart, P.E. and R. Clarke (1980): *Concentration in British Industry, 1935–1975* (Cambridge: Cambridge University Press).

Hart, P.E. and E. Morgan (1977): 'Market structure and economic performance in the United Kingdom', *Journal of Industrial Economics*, **25**, 177–93.

Hart, P.E. and S.J. Prais (1956): 'The analysis of business concentration: a statistical approach', *Journal of the Royal Statistical Society*, Series A, **134**, 73–85.

Hay, D.A. and D.J. Morris (1979): *Industrial Economics: Theory and Evidence* (Oxford: Oxford University Press).

—— (1991): *Industrial Economics and Organisation: Theory and Evidence* (Oxford: Oxford University Press).

Porter, R.H. (1983): 'A study of cartel stability: the joint executive committee, 1880–1886', *Bell Journal of Economics*, **14**, 301–14.

Scherer, F.M. (1970): *Industrial Market Structure and Economic Performance* (Chicago: Rand McNally).

—— (1980): *Industrial Market Structure and Economic Performance*, 2nd edn (Chicago: Rand McNally).

—— and Ross, D. (1990): *Industrial Market Structure and Economic Performance*, 3rd ed (Boston, MA: Houghton Mifflin).

——, A. Beckstein, E. Kaufer and R.D. Murphy (1975): *The Economics of Multiplant Organisation: An International Comparisons Study* (Cambridge, MA: Harvard University Press).

Schmalensee, R. and R. Willig (1989): *Handbook of Industrial Organisation*, 2 vols (Amsterdam: North-Holland).

Shaked, A. and J. Sutton (1987): 'Product differentiation and industrial structure', *Journal of Industrial Economics*, **36**, 131–46.

Slade, M. (1987): 'Interfirm rivalry in a repeated game: an empirical test of tacit collusion', *Journal of Industrial Economics*, **35**, 499–516.

Stigler, G.J. (1968): *The Organisation of Industry* (Homewood, IL: R.D. Irwin).

Sutton, J. (1991): *Sunk Costs and Market Structure: Price Competition, Advertising, and the Evolution of Concentration* (Cambridge, MA: MIT Press).

Tirole, J. (1989): *The Theory of Industrial Organisation* (Cambridge, MA: MIT Press).

Waterson, M. (1984): *Economic Theory of the Industry* (Cambridge: Cambridge University Press).

7. Trends in Concentration in UK Manufacturing, 1980–9

Roger Clarke[1]

7.1 INTRODUCTION

This chapter examines recent evidence on trends in industrial concentration in UK manufacturing industry in 1980–9. In particular, it looks at movements in average concentration (measured in terms of sales, net output and employment) for comparable samples of three-digit manufacturing industries in the period.

Average concentration in UK manufacturing industry increased markedly in the postwar period and, in particular, in the period 1958–68. Looking at the evidence available up until the end of the 1960s it seemed likely that concentration might continue its rising trend with further substantial increases in the 1970s and on. However, the evidence available for the 1970s (see section 7.2 below) suggests that concentration was relatively stable or, indeed, declining in the period. Despite high levels of merger activity in the early 1970s, traditional Census of Production data shows concentration was stable, or rising slightly, in 1970–9. Moreover, evidence on the growing importance of foreign trade (for example, Utton, 1982) leads to the conclusion that trade-adjusted average concentration was actually falling in the 1970s.

Against this background, it is interesting to consider the further trend in concentration in the 1980s. This chapter shows that this trend was negative in the 1980s and, indeed, that concentration fell markedly in the period. Moreover, in contrast to the 1970s, this trend was observed in both domestic (that is non-trade adjusted) and trade-adjusted concentration. Examination of the data also allows us to draw some conclusions concerning sectors and industries which experienced the largest falls in concentration in the period and examine the effects of using weighted and unweighted measures of average concentration change.

The available evidence on the trends in average concentration prior to 1980 are presented in section 7.2. Section 7.3 then looks at the trend in average domestic concentration in 1980–9. Section 7.4 shows the effects of adjustments for imports and exports on measured concentration. Finally, section 7.5 draws some conclusions.[2]

7.2   TRENDS IN CONCENTRATION PRIOR TO 1980

Since evidence on trends in average concentration prior to 1980 is fairly well known (see, for example, Clarke, 1985, ch. 2), this section simply outlines the main points. Data are available at the three-digit and the four-digit levels of aggregation, and trends in average concentration for comparable samples of industries are summarized in Table 7.1.[3]

Table 7.1   Trends in concentration: 1935–79

Year	(1) %	(2) %	(3) %	(4) %	(5) %
1935	26.3				
1951	29.3				
1958	32.4	36.9	55.4		
1963	37.4	41.6	58.6		
1968	41.0	45.6	63.4		58.8
1970				44.8	
1975				45.5	56.4
1977					54.8
1979				45.6	

Note: Column headings are as follows:
(1)   Average three-firm employment concentration for three-digit UK industries ($n=42$).
(2)   Average five-firm employment concentration for three-digit UK industries ($n=79$).
(3)   Average five-firm sales concentration for four-digit UK industries ($n=144$).
(4)   Average five-firm employment concentration for three-digit UK industries ($n=93$).
(5)   Average trade-adjusted five-firm sales concentration for four-digit UK industries ($n=121$).

Sources: Columns (1)–(3) Hart and Clarke (1980); column (4) Clarke (1985); column (5) Utton (1982).

Broadly speaking, three phases in the trend in concentration in the period as a whole can be identified. First, in the earliest period, 1935–58, there was a general upward trend in average concentration although, in retrospect, at a fairly modest pace. This is shown in column (1) of Table 7.1, which shows that average three-firm employment concentration at the three-digit level of aggregation rose by about 0.2 percentage points per annum in 1935–51, rising to about twice this rate (0.4 percentage points per annum) in 1951–8. The earliest period covers the Second

World War and it is not possible to say in any finer detail how the trend in concentration varied in this period. What can be said is that, overall, there was a rise in concentration in the period, which apparently increased at an accelerated rate after 1951.

Secondly, average concentration rose substantially in 1958–68. Column (2) of Table 7.1 shows that average five-firm employment concentration at the three-digit industry level rose by about 0.9 percentage points per annum in the period as a whole, with a slightly higher rise in 1958–63 than in 1963–8. Data on products at the four-digit level of aggregation (column (3)), show that average five-firm sales concentration increased by 0.8 percentage points per annum in 1958–68 although in this case there was a slightly larger rise in 1963–8 than in 1958–63.

As argued elsewhere (Hart and Clarke, 1980), it seems likely that some part of the large increase in concentration observed in the 1960s is attributable to government policy of the time; in particular, the Labour government's attempt to restructure parts of manufacturing industry in order to increase UK competitiveness abroad. In addition, merger activity reached historically high levels in the 1960s and this is also likely to have had an effect in raising average concentration.

Finally, columns (4) and (5) of Table 7.1 show the trend in concentration in the 1970s. Column (4) shows that average five-firm employment concentration for three-digit industries increased by less than 0.1 percentage points per annum in 1970–9, indicating relatively stable average concentration in the period. Column (5), which allows for foreign trade, however, suggests that average concentration fell in the 1970s. This column shows that average trade-adjusted sales concentration at the four-digit level fell on average by about 0.4 percentage points per annum in 1968–77.

Whilst there are problems in adjusting concentration data for foreign trade (as discussed further below), the best available evidence is that such adjustments reduced average concentration in the 1970s. Corrections of concentration data for earlier periods (see Utton, 1982; Cannon, 1978), however, show a more limited effect of such adjustments as far as the trend in concentration is concerned. The available evidence suggests that adjusting for foreign trade had a quite small effect on the upward trend observed before 1970.[4]

Given the continued growth in trade in the 1980s (in particular, in manufacturing imports), it would seem reasonable to expect that adjustments for foreign trade would tend to reduce average concentration in 1980–9. What is more unexpected is that average domestic concentration would also fall substantially in the 1980s.

7.3 CHANGES IN DOMESTIC CONCENTRATION, 1980–9

Consider trends in domestic concentration in 1980–9, using data from the Annual Censuses of Production. These show trends in five-firm sales, net output and employment concentration at the three-digit or *group* level of aggregation; the *group* corresponding to the most recent definition of the three-digit industry in the Standard Industrial Classification (revised) 1980 (CSO, 1979).[5]

Consider, first, the trend in simple average concentration in 1980–9. Table 7.2 and Figure 7.1 show the trend in unweighted average employment, sales and net output concentration for 100 comparable industry groups in 1980–9.[6] In contrast to the 1970s, average concentration fell markedly in 1980–9. In terms of employment, concentration fell on average by about 0.5 percentage points per annum in 1980–9, including a fall of about 0.9 percentage points per annum in 1980–4. In terms of sales and net output, concentration fell by about 0.4 percentage points per annum (in both cases) in 1980–9 with most of this fall occurring in the 1980–4 period.[7]

Table 7.2   Trends in concentration: 1980–9

	Employment	Sales	Net output
1980	44.0	44.9	45.7
1981	43.6	44.7	45.2
1982	42.9	44.1	44.4
1983	42.2	43.3	43.8
1984	40.4	41.9	42.6
1985	40.4	41.9	42.5
1986	40.1	42.2	42.6
1987	40.1	42.3	43.0
1988	39.5	42.1	43.3
1989	39.1	41.4	42.2
Change in 1980–9	−4.9	−3.5	−3.5
Change in 1970–9	0.8	0.9	1.5

Source: BSO, *Report on the Census of Production: Summary Tables*, PA1002, Summary Table 13, issues 1980–9; Clarke (1985).

These figures strongly contrast with the experience of the 1970s. Table 7.2 shows the trend in unweighted average employment, sales and net output concentration in 1970–9 for comparison with 1980–9. This clearly

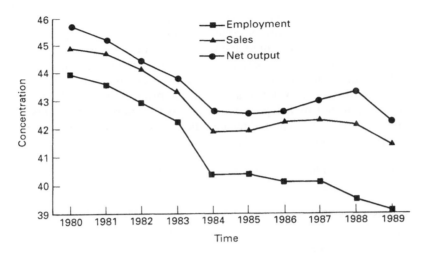

Figure 7.1   Trends in concentration, 1980–9

shows a very marked contrast of results between the 1970s and the 1980s.

Several other points should be noted in Table 7.2 and Figure 7.1. First, average employment concentration decreased by more than sales and net output concentration in the period. This could be due to larger firms increasing their labour productivity relative to smaller firms in the period. However, it could also be due to possible price effects (such as larger firms holding – or raising – their profit margins more than smaller firms in the period).[8]

Secondly, as noted above, the bulk of the fall in average concentration in the 1980s, particularly in terms of sales and net output, took place in 1980–4. This was a period of recession in UK manufacturing industry and the results lead to the somewhat surprising conclusion that, on average, leading firms cut output and employment proportionately more in this period than did their smaller rivals. One possible explanation is that some leading firms switched production overseas in the early 1980s in response to rising costs of production in the UK. Alternatively, larger firms may have engaged in a proportionately larger shakeout of employment and production in the period. Unfortunately, the data available do not allow us to distinguish between these possibilities. Some evidence exists in Table 7.2 to suggest that average concentration also turned down in the late 1980s (especially in terms of sales and net output), although it is too early to say whether this represents a further pro-cyclical change as far as concentration is concerned.

Table 7.3 presents results for weighted averages of employment concentration (with total employment weights) in 1980–9. In contrast to the fall in unweighted average concentration of 4.9 percentage points in Table 7.2, the fall in weighted average concentration was at or near 6.3 percentage points (0.7 percentage points per annum) using constant employment weights in 1980–9, shown in the last column of Table 7.3. In terms of current year weights, shown in the principal diagonal, average concentration fell by 8.1 percentage points (0.9 percentage points per annum). Thus using weighted means, the fall in average concentration is even more marked in the 1980s.[9]

Table 7.3　Weighted average employment concentration changes, 1980–9

	Averages										Change
Weights	1980	1981	1982	1983	1984	1985	1986	1987	1988	1989	1980–9
1980	**39.1**	38.5	37.9	37.4	34.8	35.1	34.8	34.3	33.1	32.7	−6.4
1981	39.2	**38.5**	38.0	37.4	34.8	35.1	34.9	34.3	33.1	32.8	−6.4
1982	39.0	38.4	**37.9**	37.3	34.6	35.0	34.8	34.2	33.0	32.6	−6.4
1983	38.7	38.1	37.6	**37.1**	34.4	34.8	34.6	34.0	32.8	32.5	−6.2
1984	38.5	37.8	37.3	36.8	**34.1**	34.5	34.3	33.7	32.5	32.1	−6.4
1985	38.2	37.5	37.0	36.5	33.7	**34.2**	34.0	33.4	32.3	31.9	−6.3
1986	38.0	37.3	36.8	36.3	33.5	34.0	**33.8**	33.2	32.1	31.7	−6.3
1987	37.9	37.2	36.7	36.2	33.4	33.9	33.7	**33.2**	32.1	31.7	−6.2
1988	37.6	36.9	36.3	35.8	33.1	33.5	33.3	32.8	**31.7**	31.3	−6.3
1989	37.3	36.6	36.1	35.6	32.8	33.2	33.0	32.5	31.4	**31.0**	−6.3
											−8.1

Note:　This table uses total employment weights for each year 1980–9. Current weights are shown in the principal diagonal.

Source:　See Table 7.2.

It is possible to draw a number of conclusions from comparison of Tables 7.2 and 7.3. First, in general, there is a simple relationship between weighted and unweighted average concentration and the correlation between concentration and the industry weights.[10] Specifically, since equal-weighted mean concentration (in Table 7.2) is generally greater than employment-weighted mean concentration in Table 7.3, employment concentration must be negatively correlated with industry employment; that is, concentrated industries were smaller on average than unconcentrated industries in the 1980s. Moreover, as discussed below, there is a tendency for concentrated industries to have grown less than average in the 1980s, as can be seen by the negative correlation becoming stronger as the decade goes on. These results are similar to those found for earlier periods at the three-digit level (Hart and Clarke, 1980, ch. 2), although in the earlier study the negative correlation tended to weaken rather than strengthen in the later periods covered.

It is also possible to decompose the change in the current weighted mean concentration into the change in concentration and the change in the industry weights.[11] Using 1980 employment weights in Table 7.3, for example, the change in the current weighted concentration average (−8.1) can be decomposed into the change in average concentration using 1980 weights (−6.4) and the change in industry weights (−1.7). Results are similar whichever year's weights are used, and this shows that about one-quarter of the fall in the current weighted mean is due to the change in industry weights, that is, the tendency for more-concentrated industries to grow by less than less-concentrated industries.

Table 7.4 provides a different view of the 1980s results, showing the change in (unweighted) average employment concentration by 1980 concentration decile. Falls in concentration were recorded on average for each opening decile (ignoring 0–9) with the exception of decile 20–29. In terms of magnitude of concentration change, deciles 50–59, 70–79 and 80–89 stand out. In decile 50–59, the unweighted average fall in concentration across 14 industries was about 1.2 percentage points per annum. Even more interesting, results for the nine industries in deciles 70–79 and 80–89 combined show a fall in average concentration of about

Table 7.4   Changes in employment concentration by 1980 concentration decile

Size class	Frequency	Average change in concentration 1980–9
0–9	−	−
10–19	16	−1.6
20–29	15	0
30–39	16	−3.2
40–49	14	−5.6
50–59	14	−10.4
60–69	12	−6.1
70–79	4	−15.2
80–89	5	−8.2
90–100	4	−3.2
Total	100	−4.9

Note: Figures for the change in concentration include corrections for 1984 Census revisions.

Source: See Table 7.2.

1.3 percentage points per annum (11.3 percentage points over the period as a whole). In other words, and in contrast to earlier periods, there were substantial falls in average concentration amongst industries in the very high concentration groups. Amongst the falls in concentration, insulated wire and cable (group 341) had a 20-point fall in employment concentration, shipbuilding (group 361) had a 26-point fall, cycles and motor cycles (group 363) had a 17-point fall, and clocks and watches (group 374) had a 28-point fall. These cases indicate the significance of falls in concentration in engineering and vehicles industries (see below); in the cases cited from initially very high concentration levels.

Further evidence on concentration change over broad industry groups is shown in Table 7.5. This table gives trends in unweighted average employment concentration classified by two-digit industry class. Significant falls in average concentration occurred in mineral oil processing and metal manufacture; electrical and electronic engineering industries; motor vehicles and other transport equipment; and instrument engineering. In the mineral oil etc. class, concentration falls were most notable in mineral oil processing (−1.7 percentage points per annum on average) and extraction of sand, clay and so on (−3.0 percentage points per annum on average). The bulk of the other major falls occurred in the motor and engineering sectors. Concentration in vehicles fell on average by about 1.3 percentage points per annum, reflecting falls in a number of groups, including motor vehicles, motor vehicle parts, cycles and motor cycles. In electrical engineering, average concentration fell by about 1.5 percentage points per annum, with notable falls in industrial electrical equipment and other electronic equipment. Finally, in instrument engineering, average concentration fell by about 1.3 percentage points per annum, with substantial falls seen in optical instruments and clocks and watches.

Two industry classes (the manufacture of non-metallic mineral products, and leather, footwear and clothing) experienced increases in average concentration in the period. In both cases the average increase was small and clearly insufficient to outweigh the general trend of falling concentration in the period. In the 100 industries considered in this section, 67 experienced falls in concentration and 33 experienced rises or no change.

The dominance of engineering industries in falling concentration can be seen again in Table 7.6. This shows those three-digit industry groups in which employment concentration changed by more than 10 percentage points in 1980–9. With the exception of extraction of sand, clay, and so on, which had a 27-point fall, all other groups with a very large concentration fall are in vehicle and engineering industries: industrial electrical equipment (−28 per cent), clocks and watches (−28 per cent),

Table 7.5 Trends in employment concentration by industry class, 1980–9

	Class	No. of industries	1980	1981	1982	1983	1984	1985	1986	1987	1988	1989	Change 1980–9[a]
Mineral oil proc., metal manuf., etc.	14, 22, 23	6	55.2	54.5	55.3	50.5	49.0	46.8	46.7	47.8	47.3	46.7	−10.5
Manufacture of non-metallic min. prods	24	8	53.5	53.0	52.9	54.8	52.1	55.1	54.9	55.8	55.0	55.4	1.0
Chemicals and man-made fibres	25, 26	7	50.4	49.1	48.9	48.7	46.4	46.6	45.1	44.9	45.6	45.3	−5.1
Manufacture of metal goods N.E.S.	31	5	21.6	20.2	23.0	22.6	22.2	20.4	17.6	17.6	16.6	15.2	−6.4
Mech. Eng. and office machinery	32, 33	11	35.6	35.0	33.5	33.5	31.5	30.6	30.8	29.4	29.4	29.2	−5.8
Electrical and electronic engineering	34	7	56.7	55.9	53.4	50.3	46.7	46.3	46.1	45.1	42.6	41.4	−13.7
Motor vehicles and other transport equip.	35, 36	7	64.7	64.7	64.1	62.7	60.4	60.1	58.1	55.3	52.7	53.1	−11.6
Instrument engineering	37	4	40.8	40.5	41.0	34.5	35.0	34.3	33.3	32.5	31.5	29.5	−11.5
Food, drink and tobacco	41, 42	15	57.6	57.1	56.1	55.9	53.6	53.5	53.8	55.3	55.2	55.7	−2.0
Textiles	43	9	42.2	43.1	41.1	42.1	40.9	42.3	42.3	42.3	41.8	40.9	−1.4
Leather, footwear and clothing	44, 45	5	22.8	23.6	24.0	24.6	22.6	24.2	25.4	26.0	28.0	28.0	5.2
Timber, wood, paper and printing	46, 47	10	23.6	23.2	23.3	23.2	23.2	23.2	22.3	23.6	22.6	21.4	−2.4
Other manufacturing industries	48, 49	6	29.8	28.8	27.2	26.3	23.8	22.5	24.2	23.3	22.8	22.8	−6.2
Total		100	44.0	43.6	42.9	42.2	40.4	40.4	40.1	40.1	39.5	39.1	−4.9

Note: [a]Figures for the change in concentration in 1980–9 include corrections for 1984 Census revisions.

Source: See Table 7.2.

other electronic equipment (−26 per cent), shipbuilding and repairing (−26 per cent), office machinery (−21 per cent) and insulated wires and cables (−20 per cent). On the other hand, only leather and fellmongery (+19 per cent) and working of stone and so on (+17 per cent) stand out with sharply increased concentration in the period. This table, therefore, confirms the large falls in concentration seen in the period, particularly in the vehicles and engineering groups.

Table 7.6   Industries with major changes in employment concentration: 1980–9

	Group	Change in concentration, 1980–9[a]
Mineral oil processing	140	−15
Extraction of sand, clay, etc.	231	−27
Working of stone, etc.	245	17
Household etc. chemicals	259	−14
Textile machinery	323	−16
Manufacture of office machinery	330	−21
Insulated wires and cables	341	−20
Industrial electrical equipment	343	−28
Telecom equipment	344	−11
Other electronic equipment	345	−26
Motor vehicles	351	−12
Motor vehicle parts	353	−12
Shipbuilding and repairing	361	−26
Cycles and motor cycles	363	−17
Optical instruments and photographic equip.	373	−15
Clocks, watches, etc.	374	−28
Bread, biscuits and flour confectionery	419	−13
Brewing and malting	427	−13
Leather and fellmongery	441	19
Pulp, paper and board	471	−16
Conversion of paper, etc.	472	−10
Rubber products	481(482)	−12
Toys and sports goods	494	−15

Note: [a]Figures include corrections for the 1984 revision of Census.
Source: See Table 7.2.

7.4 ADJUSTMENTS FOR FOREIGN TRADE

In interpreting the above results, it is important to remember that the data relate only to domestic production and do not take account of foreign trade. In the case of motor vehicles (industry group 351), for example, domestic five-firm sales concentration was 84 per cent in 1989 whilst trade adjusted concentration was just 41 per cent in the same year. Whilst the trade adjusted concentration ratio itself may contain measurement errors, it is clearly important to take account of foreign trade in measuring concentration. In the motor vehicles case, allowing for trade does not significantly affect the measured change in concentration in 1980–9. But it is clear that foreign trade could have large effects on concentration trends and we consider this in this section.

Adjustments for foreign trade can only be made on certain simplifying assumptions using available data; see Utton (1982) and Kumar (1985). First, it is necessary to assume that industries are dominated by the top five domestic firms; that is, foreign firms are not amongst the top five suppliers in the UK market. Secondly, it is necessary to assume that the top five firms do not import goods for sale in the UK. And finally, it is necessary to assume that these firms export in proportion to their sales so that no special adjustments for exports need be made.[12]

Clearly, one can think of examples where each of these assumptions would be wrong. In the case of cutlery or motor vehicles, the largest UK firms produce some of their output abroad for sale in the UK. Hence, it is not appropriate to treat all imports as competitive in such cases. Again, it is well known (see, for example, Utton, 1982) that larger firms tend to export proportionately more output than their smaller rivals, whilst in some industries (such as motor cycles) importers are dominant suppliers to the UK market. Unfortunately, in the absence of detailed knowledge of individual industries it is not possible to adjust for these factors in a systematic way. It is important, therefore, to bear this limitation in mind when interpreting the results reported below.

On the basis of the above assumptions, it can be shown that concentration adjusted for foreign trade becomes:[13]

$$\hat{C}_5 = \frac{C_5(S-X)}{S-X+M} \qquad (7.1)$$

where $\hat{C}_5$ = trade adjusted five-firm sales concentration
C_5 = unadjusted five-firm sales concentration
S = total sales (domestic production)
X = exports
M = imports

Table 7.7　Trends in trade-adjusted sales concentration, 1980–9

	Unadjusted average concentration	Adjusted average concentration
1980	43.7	30.4
1981	43.4	29.0
1982	42.8	28.2
1983	42.2	29.1
1984	40.7	25.2
1985	40.6	24.7
1986	40.9	24.8
1987	41.0	25.0
1988	40.9	25.2
1989	40.2	24.3
Change in 1980–9	−3.5	−6.1

Source: BSO, *Report of the Census of Production, 1980–89*; BSO, *Business Monitor*, MQ12.

Equation (7.1) has been used to adjust concentration ratios for all available industries in 1980–9. The detailed results of this exercise are given in the appendix and are summarized in Tables 7.7 to 7.9.[14]

Table 7.7 shows the trend in unadjusted and trade-adjusted average five-firm sales concentration in 1980–9. It is immediately apparent that allowing for foreign trade reduces average concentration substantially. In 1980, for example, average concentration without adjustment for foreign trade was 43.7 per cent whilst allowing for foreign trade it was only 30.4 per cent. Some part of this difference will be due to measurement errors in adjusting for foreign trade, in particular, the assumption that all imports are competitive. Nevertheless, it seems likely that the bulk of the difference does reflect the importance of foreign trade in UK markets. Allowing for such trade indicates that competition is *prima facie* stronger in UK markets than domestic concentration ratios would suggest.

Table 7.7 shows that over the period 1980–9 average trade-adjusted sales concentration fell by 6.1 percentage points compared with a fall of 3.5 percentage points for domestic sales concentration. The largest part of this fall occurred in 1980–4 with an estimated fall of over 5 percentage points in the trade-adjusted figures. Overall, the pattern of concentration change is similar to that for domestic sales concentration with concentration falling in 1980–4 and being fairly stable thereafter. The net effect of adjusting for foreign trade is to decrease average concentration by a

Table 7.8 Trends in trade-adjusted sales concentration by industry class, 1980–9

	Class	No. of industries	1980	1981	1982	1983	1984	1985	1986	1987	1988	1989	Change 1980–9
Mineral proc., metal manuf., etc.	14, 22, 23	3	36.0	40.0	35.7	34.3	29.7	24.3	20.7	36.7	35.3	35.7	−0.3
Manufacture of non-metallic min. prods	24	6	43.2	43.7	43.3	48.0	41.2	44.0	42.3	42.5	41.3	41.3	−1.9
Chemicals and man-made fibres	25, 26	7	33.4	30.3	28.0	27.3	25.0	24.7	24.4	25.1	26.4	26.4	−7.0
Manufacture of metal goods n.e.s.	31	5	23.2	21.8	20.2	21.4	18.6	17.6	20.0	16.6	18.2	16.2	−7.0
Mech. eng. and office machinery	32, 33	11	20.1	19.5	18.1	18.7	17.3	16.5	16.3	15.3	17.1	15.9	−4.2
Electrical and electronic engineering	34	6	41.8	38.2	35.8	32.7	29.5	25.7	26.3	26.3	25.0	23.7	−18.1
Motor vehicles and other transport equip.	35, 36	5	38.0	37.0	35.2	55.4	29.8	34.8	28.6	32.0	29.4	26.2	−11.8
Instrument engineering	37	3	9.0	6.7	8.7	8.0	6.0	4.7	4.7	2.7	3.3	2.7	−6.3
Food, drink and tobacco	41, 42	14	49.5	46.9	46.9	46.0	42.5	41.3	42.1	41.0	43.5	42.0	−7.5
Textiles	43	9	27.7	27.1	26.1	23.9	22.3	22.8	23.6	23.7	23.6	22.0	−5.7
Leather, footwear and clothing	44, 45	5	16.0	16.4	16.0	16.4	14.6	15.2	15.8	16.0	17.4	16.8	0.8
Timber, wood, paper and printing	46, 47	9	16.3	15.4	16.7	16.1	15.9	15.1	17.2	18.3	15.1	15.2	−1.1
Other manufacturing industries	48, 49	5	19.2	16.6	15.6	16.0	13.6	12.0	13.0	10.0	9.4	10.0	−9.2
Total		88	30.4	29.0	28.2	29.1	25.2	24.7	24.8	25.0	25.2	24.3	−6.1

Source: See Table 7.7.

*Table 7.9   Industries with major changes in trade adjusted sales
concentration, 1980–9*

	Group	Change in concentration, 1980–9
Working of stone, etc.	245	18
Abrasive products	246	−13
Glass and glassware	247	−17
Basic industrial chemicals	251	−18
Household etc. chemicals	259	−16
Man-made fibres	260(26)	−10
Metal doors etc.	314	−15
Power transmission equipment	326	−10
Ordnance etc.	329	−10
Insulated wires and cables	341	−30
Basic electrical equipment	342	−18
Industrial electrical equipment	343	−26
Other electrical equipment	345	−18
Electric lamps etc.	347	−12
Motor vehicle parts	353	−15
Shipbuilding and repairing	361	−22
Clocks, watches, etc.	374	−14
Organic oils and fats	411	−17
Bread, biscuits, etc.	419	−15
Brewing and malting	427	−12
Cotton and silk	432	−10
Continuous yarn	433	−14
Spinning etc. of flax	434	−12
Sawmilling, etc.	461	−10
Misc. wood articles	465	13
Conversion of paper, etc.	472	−11
Rubber products	481(482)	−17
Toys and sports goods	494	−11

Source: See Table 7.7.

further 2.6 percentage points in the period as a whole. Adjustment for foreign trade, therefore, accounts for somewhat less than half the fall in concentration observed in the period.

Table 7.8 shows changes in average trade-adjusted sales concentration by two-digit industry class. The most notable feature of Table 7.8 is the large reduction in average sales concentration in electrical and electronic engineering. The six industries in this group saw an average fall in concentration of about 1.6 percentage points per annum in domestic five-firm sales concentration and of about 2.0 percentage points per annum in trade-adjusted average concentration. The extra trade effect occurred in particular in insulated wires and cables, basic electrical equipment and miscellaneous electrical equipment (see Table 7.9). The other industry classes in Table 7.8 show a broadly similar picture to that seen in Table 7.5. Only one industry class (leather, footwear and clothing) shows an average increase in concentration in 1980–9 and this of only about 0.1 percentage points per annum in the period as a whole.

Finally, Table 7.9 shows those industries in which trade-adjusted sales concentration changed by more than 10 percentage points in 1980–9. Allowing for foreign trade leads to a slightly different picture to that found in Table 7.6, although this is partly due to the difference in the measure of firm size used and the fact that some industries in Table 7.6 are excluded in the current sample. Of the industries included in Table 7.9, three stand out with a concentration fall of over 20 percentage points: insulated wires and cables (-30 per cent), industrial electrical equipment (-26 per cent) and shipbuilding and repairing (-22 points). Again, engineering and vehicle industries are well represented in the table, although in this case there is a wider coverage of other sectors than in Table 7.6.

7.5 CONCLUSIONS

The evidence presented in this chapter suggests that concentration declined on average in UK manufacturing in the 1980s, following a period of sharply increasing concentration in the 1960s and stable or falling concentration in the 1970s. The best evidence available suggests that domestic sales concentration fell by 3.5 percentage points on average in the 1980s, and that, with adjustment for foreign trade, average sales concentration fell by 6.1 percentage points in the period. Moreover, a number of dramatic falls in concentration were observed, in particular in electrical and electronics engineering, and in engineering and vehicles industries.

Despite a number of reservations concerning the data, the general trend seems clear. Part of the fall in concentration was due to the continuing growth in foreign trade and its effects were similar to those found in the 1970s. In addition to this, however, substantial falls in domestic concentration were also observed. These could reflect the effects of government 'supply-side' policies in the 1980s or they may be associated with technological changes (for example, in electronic engineering) tending to favour smaller firms.[15] On the other hand, some part of the trend may reflect large firms moving production abroad in the early 1980s or, alternatively, large firms slimming down their production and workforce more than smaller firms in the period.

Unfortunately, it is not possible to distinguish between these possibilities from the descriptive data considered in this paper. Nevertheless, the decline in average concentration in the 1980s is of considerable interest and is an area in which further research is required. Of even more interest is the effect that these changes may have had on competition and performance in UK markets. If the falls in concentration observed do reflect underlying structural changes then we would expect to find significant effects on competition and performance in the 1980s. Further research is required to consider whether this is the case.

APPENDIX: ADJUSTMENTS FOR FOREIGN TRADE

As explained in the text, it is necessary to make a number of assumptions in adjusting domestic concentration ratios for foreign trade. Specifically, it is assumed that the top five domestic firms are the top five suppliers to the domestic market, that all imports are competitive and that the top five firms export in proportion to their sales (i.e. $X_5/X = S_5/S$).

If this is the case, then trade-adjusted five firm concentration is

$$\hat{C}_5 = \frac{S_5 - X_5}{S - X + M} = \frac{C_5(S - X)}{S - X + M} \qquad (7.A1)$$

where S_5 = domestic production of the top five domestic producers
X_5 = exports of the top five domestic producers
S = production of all domestic producers
X = total exports of domestic producers
M = total imports

In the analysis, adjustments for foreign trade were made using the ratios $R_3 = (X/S).100$ and $R_4 = (X/(S + M)).100$ in BSO, *Business Monitor*, MQ12. Specifically, trade-adjusted concentration was measured as

$$\hat{C}_5 = \frac{C_5 R_4(100 - R_3)}{R_3(100 - R_4)} \qquad (7.A2)$$

A slight complication in the analysis is introduced by the fact that published data in *Business Monitor* MQ12 includes imports for re-export and re-exports (see Wells and Imber, 1977). If we assume that the top five firms re-export (if at all) in proportion to their sales (and we also ignore any value added to re-exports in the UK), then it is easily shown that the measured trade-adjusted concentration ratio is

$$\hat{C}_5' = \frac{C_5(S-X^*)}{S-X^*+M^*} = \frac{C_5(S-X-W)}{S-X+M} \tag{7.A3}$$

where W = re-exports
  $X^* = X + W$ = exports plus re-exports
  $M^* = M + W$ = imports plus imports for re-export.

Equation (7.A3) shows that in industries where re-exports are a factor there is a tendency to understate trade-adjusted sales concentration using (7.A1) by the amount $-C_5.W/(S - X + M)$ and this may also affect the measured change in concentration. Unfortunately, in the absence of separate data for re-exports it is not possible to adjust for this factor. A by-product of this effect is that measured $R_3 = (X^*/S).100$ can exceed 100 per cent for industries where re-exports are of substantial importance, thereby producing negative trade-adjusted concentration ratios. A few instances of this can be seen in Table 7.A1.

Table 7.A1 Domestic and trade-adjusted five-firm sales concentration ratios, 1980–9

	Group	1980 C₅	1980 C₅(adj)	1981 C₅	1981 C₅(adj)	1982 C₅	1982 C₅(adj)	1983 C₅	1983 C₅(adj)	1984 C₅	1984 C₅(adj)	1985 C₅	1985 C₅(adj)	1986 C₅	1986 C₅(adj)	1987 C₅	1987 C₅(adj)	1988 C₅	1988 C₅(adj)	1989 C₅	1989 C₅(adj)	Correction factors[a]
Coke ovens	120	94	—	—	—	—	—	—	—	—	—	—	—	—	—	—	—	—	—	—	—	—
Mineral oil processing	140	71	—	75	—	69	—	60	—	58	—	58	—	60	—	61	—	64	—	63	—	—
Extract metals, ores	210	81	-1	85	-2	76	-2	84	-1	99	2	99	0	—	—	—	—	—	—	—	—	—
Iron and steel	221	75	67	82	70	83	71	83	64	85	59	85	61	87	57	95	76	—	—	95	—	-1
Steel tubes	222	75	56	81	63	80	71	76	48	75	41	76	34	65	34	76	56	72	48	73	49	0
Drawing etc. steel	223	36	29	35	31	34	28	37	30	36	27	35	23	37	31	30	27	34	31	34	31	-1
Non-ferrous metals	224	40	23	44	26	40	23	44	25	40	21	30	16	35	17	37	27	45	27	47	27	0
Extract, stone, clay, etc.	231	49	—	47	47	56	—	39	—	47	—	41	—	41	—	42	—	36	—	38	—	-8
Extract. misc. minerals	239(233)	68	—	70	—	70	—	69	—	65	—	64	—	67	—	70	—	68	—	66	—	-4
Structural clay products	241	52	52	55	55	53	53	57	57	53	53	63	63	64	—	60	—	60	—	61	—	-1
Cement, lime, plaster	242	84	84	84	84	86	86	91	91	86	86	87	87	87	87	88	—	86	—	84	—	0
Building prods	243	31	31	32	32	32	32	34	34	36	36	33	33	38	38	37	37	35	35	37	37	-2
Asbestos goods	244	88	80	88	84	89	85	88	115	81	73	90	86	88	76	94	81	91	79	94	78	0
Working of stone etc.	245	28	22	32	32	33	30	39	35	40	40	45	45	44	40	42	39	42	38	44	40	-1
Abrasive products	246	63	48	62	47	59	44	55	39	53	40	54	36	57	41	52	37	52	35	52	35	-4
Glass and glassware	247	60	50	57	44	57	44	55	40	53	36	51	34	50	35	55	38	55	36	54	33	1
Refractory etc. goods	248	33	28	29	23	31	25	32	25	29	22	37	30	32	24	31	23	34	25	33	25	0
Basic indust. chems	251	59	38	59	37	60	60	59	59	55	28	51	26	49	22	50	22	50	22	48	20	0
Paints, varnishes etc.	255	34	32	38	35	35	30	38	35	37	32	34	32	37	34	36	31	38	33	40	35	0
Specialized chems	256	31	23	30	20	29	19	28	18	25	16	22	14	23	15	27	18	26	18	29	19	0
Pharmaceuticals	257	38	32	35	28	36	29	35	27	36	27	36	27	38	28	39	30	42	32	40	30	0
Soap and toilet preps	258	50	47	46	41	47	36	45	40	41	34	47	39	46	39	45	38	52	44	54	45	0
Household etc. chems	259	64	23	55	14	53	9	52	11	53	9	52	9	48	5	52	7	53	6	52	7	0
Man-made fibres	260(26)	94	39	91	37	90	29	93	27	91	29	91	26	90	28	90	30	92	30	93	29	-1
Foundries	311	22	22	22	22	22	22	24	22	22	22	20	18	22	18	22	22	20	18	19	19	0
Forging etc.	312	25	25	26	26	21	21	22	22	20	16	20	20	18	18	17	13	19	19	18	18	0
Bolts, nuts etc.	313	17	13	15	12	15	11	15	11	13	9	13	9	14	10	13	9	13	9	13	9	1
Metal doors etc.	314	41	41	33	33	33	33	37	37	33	33	38	30	39	39	38	28	35	35	26	26	0
Hand tools etc.	316	19	15	19	16	18	14	16	13	16	13	14	11	14	11	14	11	13	10	12	12	0
Industrial plant etc.	320	19	16	18	18	21	21	19	19	19	18	24	21	23	21	19	16	17	15	15	15	1
Agr. machinery	321	68	37	70	37	67	32	70	35	69	32	62	26	64	22	72	26	76	40	76	37	-1
Machine tools	322	15	10	15	10	13	8	13	8	13	8	13	8	10	6	10	6	11	6	11	6	0
Textile machinery	323	48	14	49	12	29	8	26	10	30	10	34	10	32	8	27	5	34	9	35	6	0
Machinery for food etc.	324	16	8	16	7	24	12	22	12	27	12	26	11	22	9	20	9	20	9	20	9	0
Mining machinery	325	19	14	18	13	15	10	16	11	14	9	12	7	14	7	12	8	12	8	11	7	0

Code	Industry	1	2	3	4	5	6	7	8	9	10	11	12	13	14	15	16	17	18	19	20	21
326	Power transm. equip.	36	28	35	25	32	24	30	21	26	17	27	19	24	17	23	17	25	18	27	18	5
327	Paper etc. machinery	19	7	23	8	21	7	22	6	26	6	28	7	28	7	28	7	29	7	32	6	-1
328	Misc. machinery	16	12	15	11	15	11	14	10	12	8	12	8	11	8	11	7	12	7	13	8	0
329	Ordnance etc.	84	70	86	70	92	72	91	77	86	73	80	65	85	72	86	62	76	64	67	60	0
330(33)	Office mach. etc.	71	5	67	3	69	-4	80	-4	65	-3	65	0	65	0	62	5	57	5	53	3	3
341	Ins. wires and cables	82	77	83	72	81	72	69	61	57	54	57	47	56	47	54	45	55	45	59	47	1
342	Basic elec. equip.	49	37	49	34	48	32	47	30	42	26	43	26	43	23	44	24	39	19	39	19	0
343	Indust. elec. equip.	53	43	51	30	42	30	39	28	37	26	36	26	40	27	40	28	32	22	25	17	1
344	Telecom. equip.	50	37	50	35	50	34	39	32	48	26	48	30	42	24	42	24	41	24	38	—	1
345	Misc. elec. equip.	51	18	54	15	51	11	47	11	45	12	41	9	36	5	28	5	25	3	20	0	1
346	Domestic elec. apps.	55	37	54	34	52	34	54	34	53	30	51	32	50	28	53	30	56	33	56	32	6
347	Elec. lamps etc.	52	39	47	35	49	36	47	35	40	26	38	30	38	27	38	28	39	28	36	27	0
351	Motor vehicles etc.	91	50	90	47	90	45	90	40	91	47	91	40	92	41	84	41	83	41	84	41	0
352	Motor bodies etc.	18	16	15	15	12	11	17	15	18	15	17	16	18	15	20	15	18	16	17	15	-1
353	Motor vehicle parts	38	25	40	25	35	20	35	18	32	13	31	15	32	13	27	12	24	10	24	10	0
361	Shipbuilding	72	51	74	54	76	59	70	168	76	67	73	50	76	30	64	33	54	42	38	29	0
362	Railway vehicles	86	78	90	79	86	76	84	81	73	72	80	72	82	72	69	—	76	63	78	64	0
363	Cycles and motor cycles	76	17	69	14	71	16	73	18	77	16	75	16	64	13	69	46	73	—	74	—	0
364	Aerospace equip.	78	48	77	44	80	41	79	36	79	28	65	28	77	32	78	42	76	38	78	36	1
365	Misc. vehicles	79	72	77	69	78	69	72	61	69	61	72	57	65	60	66	12	64	—	63	—	-2
371	Measuring etc. insts	17	15	17	13	15	12	15	14	17	14	13	14	18	10	16	13	16	—	16	—	0
372	Medical etc. appls	28	13	28	—	29	13	13	11	30	11	32	11	36	5	32	6	34	—	33	7	0
373	Optical etc. insts	62	1	62	4	65	-5	51	2	52	2	44	-2	51	0	48	-1	47	6	47	2	1
374	Clocks, watches etc.	64	13	68	18	70	18	47	11	47	9	52	9	49	9	49	1	47	4	35	-1	0
411	Organic oils and fats	72	59	68	46	71	42	71	42	52	39	55	44	80	41	68	32	66	40	69	42	-2
412	Processing of bacon etc.	26	17	17	15	23	11	24	22	22	17	32	15	15	17	23	15	21	14	20	20	0
413	Prep. of milk etc.	52	45	52	45	52	45	54	22	53	40	55	46	54	40	60	46	58	51	59	53	-3
414	Proc. fruit and veg.	36	26	35	33	38	33	34	46	37	21	32	21	34	21	37	24	37	24	45	26	-4
415	Fish processing	64	34	63	38	69	32	69	22	67	28	67	30	69	28	60	25	64	26	67	27	7
416	Grain milling	65	65	63	63	63	64	64	62	62	71	62	45	68	71	63	56	64	69	66	66	0
419	Bread, biscuits etc.	67	67	67	67	65	65	46	65	65	55	65	46	46	55	60	52	69	51	52	52	-1
420	Sugar	—	—	100	—	100	59	100	79	100	65	100	—	—	—	—	56	—	55	—	59	-2
421	Ice-cream, choc. etc.	63	57	63	63	64	58	64	57	63	51	65	54	62	51	60	52	63	57	65	54	1
422	Animal foods	46	—	45	—	46	45	45	—	46	33	36	36	44	33	37	50	46	34	51	49	0
423(418)	Starch etc.	28	47	26	42	31	—	25	39	23	—	28	37	25	—	28	31	31	35	28	21	2
424	Spirit dist.	63	26	61	22	58	39	57	32	58	39	56	25	53	39	56	28	65	21	59	21	0
426	Wine, cider and perry	87	86	86	57	94	31	95	41	92	23	95	58	92	23	91	28	67	21	94	32	0
427	Brewing and malting	57	57	57	57	57	50	50	49	57	40	50	45	58	40	50	50	51	49	45	45	0
428	Soft drinks	52	52	57	37	50	49	49	49	50	33	45	45	45	33	45	36	45	50	54	54	0
429	Tobacco	100	95	100	89	99	93	99	94	98	86	99	86	99	93	99	92	98	88	99	89	0

Industry	Group	1980 C₅	1980 C₅(adj)	1981 C₅	1981 C₅(adj)	1982 C₅	1982 C₅(adj)	1983 C₅	1983 C₅(adj)	1984 C₅	1984 C₅(adj)	1985 C₅	1985 C₅(adj)	1986 C₅	1986 C₅(adj)	1987 C₅	1987 C₅(adj)	1988 C₅	1988 C₅(adj)	1989 C₅	1989 C₅(adj)	Correction factors[a]
Woollen and worsted	431	29	23	32	24	28	21	27	19	27	19	26	18	30	20	32	22	31	21	31	22	−1
Cotton and silk	432	46	19	51	18	49	18	47	16	47	15	44	14	43	13	46	12	44	12	37	9	1
Continuous yarn	433	65	41	63	36	66	38	65	31	54	23	51	16	63	23	56	26	66	31	60	27	−2
Spinning etc. flax	434	38	23	45	28	42	23	43	19	46	20	49	22	50	21	50	18	50	15	48	11	−2
Jute etc.	435	62	48	61	48	63	46	54	41	67	49	72	51	69	50	74	53	70	52	67	52	0
Hosiery etc.	436	33	23	33	22	32	22	33	23	31	20	29	20	31	20	30	18	28	16	28	16	1
Textile finishing	437	31	31	30	30	31	31	30	30	32	26	32	20	30	30	32	32	34	34	31	31	1
Carpets etc.	438	31	23	30	30	25	18	26	19	20	14	28	19	30	21	26	18	24	16	25	17	0
Misc. textiles	439	25	18	25	17	24	18	24	17	23	15	21	13	22	14	23	14	23	15	21	13	1
Leather and fellmongers	441	30	21	36	25	38	18	38	25	30	19	35	20	40	25	40	24	50	31	50	29	−2
Leather goods	442	12	5	10	4	13	6	13	6	15	6	14	5	14	5	5	4	12	4	13	4	1
Footwear	451	36	24	36	21	37	21	37	19	35	19	37	20	35	18	39	21	37	20	39	20	1
Clothing, hats and gloves	453	12	9	13	9	13	8	14	10	13	8	16	11	15	10	15	10	15	9	16	10	1
Household textiles	455	27	21	28	23	25	19	26	22	27	21	27	20	28	21	28	21	28	23	26	21	−1
Fur goods	456	28	—	24	—	27	—	27	—	37	—	21	—	16	—	15	—	24	—	—	—	—
Sawmilling etc.	461	20	10	19	9	21	10	22	11	22	11	24	12	20	20	31	31	35	35	26	0	−3
Wood processing	462	44	—	51	20	49	21	48	20	53	20	59	18	56	20	57	23	54	21	51	20	−2
Builders, carpentry	463	19	19	20	16	23	23	26	26	26	26	23	23	28	28	28	28	30	30	19	19	−1
Wooden containers	464	12	12	12	12	10	10	9	9	10	10	9	9	12	12	15	15	16	16	16	16	−1
Misc. wood articles	465	17	14	17	13	22	17	22	15	21	15	22	17	24	18	16	16	22	17	35	27	1
Cork brushes etc.	466	26	18	27	18	29	19	30	19	34	19	34	18	37	20	35	20	35	19	36	19	2
Wood furniture etc.	467	12	10	10	8	9	8	8	7	8	8	7	6	9	7	9	7	13	10	13	13	0
Pulp, paper etc.	471	46	19	40	17	39	16	40	16	38	15	36	13	37	15	37	13	35	12	31	11	0
Conv. of paper etc.	472	27	27	27	27	26	26	24	24	23	20	26	22	21	18	21	21	20	17	19	16	0
Printing and publishing	475	20	18	21	19	21	21	21	18	21	19	18	16	19	17	16	14	17	15	18	16	1
Rubber products	481(482)	60	49	56	42	50	37	49	34	46	32	46	31	47	32	46	31	46	29	47	32	0
Process plastics	483	12	10	12	10	12	9	12	9	12	10	11	8	12	9	10	7	10	8	10	8	0
Jewellery etc.	491	29	—	24	—	22	—	19	—	19	—	22	—	20	—	23	—	20	—	18	—	0
Musical insts	492	43	6	45	4	39	5	45	7	38	8	40	7	46	8	44	−2	47	−4	49	−2	−2
Photographic labs	493	—	—	—	—	—	—	—	—	44	—	50	—	47	—	50	—	45	—	48	—	—
Toys and sports goods	494	32	16	29	13	27	13	29	13	22	8	16	5	20	6	20	5	20	6	18	5	0
Misc. manufactures	495	20	15	19	14	17	14	20	17	11	10	11	9	12	10	11	9	10	8	9	7	7

Source: BSO, *Report on the Census of Production – Summary Tables*, Table 13, issues 1980–9; BSO, *Business Monitor*, MQ12, issues 1983–9.

Notes:
a This column shows correction factors for Census data revisions in 1983–4. These numbers should be added to figures for domestic concentration change in 1980–9.
— Indicates not available.

140

NOTES

1. I would like to thank Derek Baskerville, Steve Davies, Paul Geroski, Peter Hart and Mike Utton for comments on an earlier version of this paper. The usual disclaimer applies.
2. In an independently written paper, Andrew Henley reaches similar conclusions to those given below for the period 1980–7. For further details, see Henley (1991).
3. Data at the four-digit level conform more closely to an economic market than do three-digit-level data. Available evidence, however, suggests that trends in concentration at these different levels tend to be similar, at least in periods where both sets of data are available; see Hart and Clarke (1980). The level of concentration at the three-digit level has less meaning given the degree of aggregation involved.
4. See Clarke (1985, p. 38, n. 11).
5. The Business Statistics Office adopted the new Standard Industrial Classification in 1980, bringing the UK more closely into line with the EC NACE classification. This SIC distinguishes the (two-digit) *class*, the (three-digit) *group* and the (four-digit) *activity* level of aggregation.
6. Seven industries were omitted in this section due to incomplete data: coke ovens (group 120); extraction and preparation of metalliferous ores (group 210); iron and steel (group 221); railway and tramway vehicles (group 362); sugar (group 420); fur goods (group 456); and photographic processing laboratories (group 493).
7. Some data revision took place in the 1984 Census associated with a benchmark Census for that year. These changes led to the inclusion of some small firms not previously included in the Census and also to some reorganization of business units between groups. Adjustments for these changes are published by the BSO (for example, in *Business Monitor*, PA260, 1987) and these have been used in a number of tables in this section. Their net effect in Table 7.2, however, is practically zero and, in general, their effect on average concentration is quite small.
8. A similar effect was observed in Hart and Clarke (1980, p. 25) for the early 1970s: in this case against a backdrop of slightly rising concentration.
9. These figures for weighted-average concentration slightly overstate the fall in concentration in 1980–9 due to the data revisions noted in note 7. Calculations show that, for the current weighted mean, concentration fell by 7.7 percentage points when this factor is taken into account.
10. As shown in Hart and Clarke (1980, appendix 2A), the relationship between weighted and unweighted concentration (respectively C_w and C) at any particular time is given by $C_w - C = \rho_{cw}\sigma_c\eta_w$ where ρ_{cw} is the correlation coefficient between concentration and the weights, σ_c is the standard deviation of concentration and η_w is the coefficient of variation in the weights. Hence, $C_w - C$ has the sign of ρ_{cw}.
11. For any two periods, 0 and 1, the change in the current weighted means is $C_{w1} - C_{w0} = \Sigma w_1 C_1 - \Sigma w_0 C_0 = \Sigma w_0(C_1 - C_0) + \Sigma C_1(w_1 - w_0)$ where w_t $(t = 0,1)$ are the weights, C_t $(t = 0, 1)$ are the levels of concentration.
12. As noted in the appendix, the adjustments made also ignore the effects of importing for re-export and re-exports by domestic firms. The appendix shows that this tends to bias the trade-adjusted concentration measure downward in industries where re-exporting takes place.
13. See appendix.
14. Twelve industries were omitted in this section due to incomplete data: mineral oil processing (group 140); extraction of stone, etc. (231); extraction of minerals (239); structural clay products (241); cement, lime and plaster (242); telecommunication equipment, etc. (344); cycles and motor cycles (363); other vehicles (365); measuring instruments (371); miscellaneous foods (423); wood processing (462); and jewellery and coins (491).
15. Some evidence supporting this latter hypothesis can be seen in Henley (1991).

REFERENCES

Business Statistics Office (1980–8): 'Report on the Census of Production: Summary Tables', *Business Monitor*, PA1002 (London: Her Majesty's Stationery Office).

—— (1983–9a): 'Import penetration and export sales ratios for manufacturing industries', *Business Monitor*, MO12 (London: Her Majesty's Stationary Office).

—— (1983–9b): 'Overseas trade analysed in terms of industries', *Business Monitor*, MO10 (London: Her Majesty's Stationery Office).

—— (1987): 'Report on the Census of Production: Production of Man-made Fibres', *Business Monitor*, PA260 (London: Her Majesty's Stationery Office).

Cannon, C.M. (1978): 'International trade, concentration and competition in UK consumer goods markets', *Oxford Economic Papers*, **30**, 130–37.

Central Statistical Office (1979): *Standard Industrial Classification (revised) 1980* (London: Her Majesty's Stationery Office).

Clarke, R. (1985): *Industrial Economics* (Oxford: Basil Blackwell).

Cowling, K. (1978): *Monopolies and Mergers Policy: A View on the Green Paper*, Economic Research Paper no. 139, Warwick University.

Hart, P.E. and R. Clarke (1980): *Concentration in British Industry: 1935–75* (Cambridge: Cambridge University Press).

Henley, A. (1991): *Industrial Deconcentration in UK Manufacturing since 1980*, Discussion Paper 91/6, University of Kent.

Kumar, M.S. (1985): 'International trade and industrial concentration', *Oxford Economic Papers*, **37**, 125–33.

Sellwood, R. (1975): 'New statistical series analysing commodities imported and exported according to the industries of which they are principal products', *Economic Trends*, **256**, February, v–vii.

Utton, M.A. (1982): 'Domestic concentration and international trade', *Oxford Economic Papers*, **34**, 479–97.

Wells, J.D. and J.C. Imber (1977): 'The home and export performance of United Kingdom industries', *Economic Trends*, **286**, August, 78–81.

8. Market Concentration and Merger Policy

Michael Utton

8.1 INTRODUCTION

The inclusion of mergers within the framework of anti-trust policy has tended to lag far behind controls on single-firm market dominance or overt collusion. In the US effective control only became possible in 1950 following an amendment to the Clayton Act originally passed in 1914. In the European Community (EC), although it was recognized in 1973 that special provisions were required, they were not made effective until 1990. Similarly, in the UK it took the first postwar boom in merger activity in the late 1950s and early 1960s to persuade the authorities to expand the scope of the Monopolies Commission in 1965 to include merger enquiries.

A number of reasons help to explain this comparatively late development of merger policy, not least that initially the problems of monopoly and collusive behaviour appear most urgent. Once those are in place the difficulties posed by large mergers are thrown into sharper relief. When it is realized how intractable are the problems posed by existing positions of market dominance, merger control is seen as a means of blocking the creation of new ones. Similarly, some control is required to prevent firms which have had their previous collusive arrangements disturbed by anti-trust action from seeking more durable arrangements through consolidation.

In the EC, and to a lesser extent earlier in the UK, a further factor has been the reluctance of some governments to allow control over large mergers to pass exclusively to anti-trust authorities and away from those in charge of industrial policy. Since mergers can transform market structures very rapidly they have frequently been seen as a means of creating 'national champions' large enough to compete on equal terms with major foreign competitors. Within the EC some members which had not experienced significant merger waves considered themselves at a disadvantage *vis-à-vis* those that had. To incorporate mergers into anti-trust policy before they had had time to catch up might have put them at a permanent disadvantage.

If the weight of evidence had suggested that on the whole there were both private and social gains from mergers, the case for introducing controls would clearly be weakened. After all, since the multi-firm amalgamations at the turn of the century, promoters had invariably claimed that both investors and public would benefit from the creation of larger, more efficient enterprises. In the last 20 years a great many studies have addressed the question of whether, on average, mergers produce net benefits. The results are admirably surveyed in Hughes (1989) and Scherer and Ross (1990). Although clearly some mergers prove to be outstanding successes, the general impression created by the studies, using different techniques and data from a number of countries, is that they tend to have either neutral or negative effects. There is no strong evidence that, on average, they are beneficial. Thus studies using profitability to assess pre- and post-merger performance tend to suggest that it either deteriorates or at best remains unchanged following merger. The longer the period studied post-merger the less favourable the results become. In studies using data on share price movements during the acquisition period, the evidence suggests that whereas shareholders in acquired companies gain, shareholders in acquiring companies either make no gain or some loss, on average. Again, the longer the time period considered after merger, the less likely are the merged firms to show an improved performance. The pattern is largely repeated in those studies which have tracked the market shares of merged companies. Thus in a study by Mueller (1985) companies not involved in sizeable mergers were more likely to retain their market share in the long term than were companies that were acquired.

On the whole, therefore, there may be some short-term gains to shareholders in acquired companies but there is considerable doubt about the long-term benefits. The nature of the data used in many of the empirical studies means that private rather than public performance is measured. Improved post-merger profitability may mainly reflect enhanced market power rather than, say, reduced production costs. Hence there are sufficient empirical and theoretical grounds for placing mergers at the centre of anti-trust policy.

It is generally agreed that an effective merger policy creates particular problems for the policy-maker. In the case of both monopoly and collusion the authorities have past data to use in the cases. The recent market conduct by a dominant enterprise may be a reasonable guide to their future conduct in the absence of any major change in the market structure. Discovered evidence of collusion between firms may make action under Article 85 of the Treaty of Rome relatively straightforward. In contrast, a proposed merger between sizeable enterprises forces the anti-trust authority to make predictions about the effect on market power and, possibly, the scope for cost reductions. It is the essentially hypothetical nature of merger enquiries that makes the analysis at once both more difficult and fascinating.

Section 8.2 discusses the main analytical difficulties that arise in merger policy analysis, focusing particularly on market definition and the assessment of entry barriers. It also discusses the use of different concentration measures in this context. Section 8.3 considers in some detail the introduction by the EC of the new merger regulation and compares it to the approach adopted in the US since the introduction of the revised and more rigorous Department of Justice Guidelines in 1982. The main emphasis is on preliminary screening procedures. It has been widely recognized, especially in Europe, that a major requirement of an effective merger policy is speed. Many mergers yielding private benefits without simultaneously increasing market power may be frustrated by a long drawn-out preliminary investigation. The method of filtering out for further investigation those mergers where the dangers to competition seem greatest is therefore of the utmost importance. A brief conclusion is given in section 8.4.

8.2 HORIZONTAL MERGERS AND THE POLICY PROBLEM

The sole concern in this chapter is with the horizontal mergers which are likely to have an effect on market power. We shall not therefore discuss the rather different issues raised by conglomerate mergers, and although some vertical mergers raise market power issues, they will not be considered here; for a recent review see Perry (1989).

Possession of market power allows a firm to maintain prices persistently above competitive levels. In the present context, therefore, a central question is whether the proposed merger creates or enhances the opportunity for raising prices and profits. The complexities lying behind this seemingly simple question were recognized long ago by Stigler (1950) but have recently received a considerable amount of formal theoretical treatment.

A starting point is the observation that in a symmetric Cournot model of oligopoly, prices and profits per firm are higher the smaller the number of firms. A reduction in the number of firms following merger, therefore, appears to offer the prospect of increased profits. With characteristic insight, Stigler noted that, with relatively few firms in the industry, the major difficulty in forming a merger is that it is more profitable to be outside than to be a participant: 'Hence the promoter of a merger is likely to receive much encouragement from each firm – almost every encouragement, in fact, except participation' (Stigler, 1950, pp. 25–6). The merged firm would want to reduce its output and sell it at a higher price, but non-participants could then expand output and take advantage of the higher price. Only part of the increased profits that result from the merger thus actually accrues to the participants. Indeed, because of this reaction by non-participants, mergers which increase the profitability of the industry need not be privately profitable.

The model analysed by Salant *et al.* (1983) is in effect a limiting case of this type of outcome. Using a symmetric Cournot model where the firms have linear demand curves and constant costs, they show that, although industry profits increase following merger, the profits of the merged firm can be less than those of the pre-merger profits of the participating firms. The only exception is in the case where duopolists merge to form a monopoly. They concluded that merger is thus generally unprofitable in Cournot oligopoly.

However, as Perry and Porter (1985) have argued, the result depends on a very restricted view of how a merger may affect the structure of the industry and therefore severely underestimates the profit incentives for merger. The Salant *et al.* model treats the merged firm as no different from the others remaining in the industry. In the post-merger equilibrium all firms make the same contribution to total industry output. Instead of having access to the combined productive capacity of the participants, the merged firm 'forgoes the production and profits of one of the two original firms' (Perry and Porter, 1985, p. 219). The outcome, however, is counter-intuitive. If a merger occurs in an industry of equally sized firms, we expect the new structure to consist of n-2 'old' firms and one 'new' larger firm (Jacquemin and Slade, 1989, p. 435). Subsequent contributors, by providing for this size effect, indicate that the results of the Salant *et al.* model can be reversed. Thus, in a market for differentiated products supplied by price-setting oligopolists, Deneckere and Davidson (1985) show that when all firms follow a post-merger price increase they can all enjoy increased profits. Again, where the presence of a fixed factor allows a combined firm to produce at lower cost than a small firm, there is a distinct profit incentive for merger (Perry and Porter, 1985).

Clearly, the cases where disparities in size are likely to arise post-merger are those that will concern our anti-trust authority. Against this background three issues have received particular attention: what constitutes the relevant market; what is the effect on market concentration; and how difficult is it to enter the market?

As far as market definition is concerned, two main aspects must be addressed: the relevant products and the relevant geographic area. For products both demand – and supply – side substitutions are important. The more familiar concept is probably demand-side substitution: products with high cross-elasticities of demand are close substitutes. The price levels of one are constrained by those of the other. In practice, the concept is of limited direct use because reliable estimates of cross-elasticities are not readily available or easily calculable (especially in the time available in many merger enquiries). Even if they were available for particular products, it is not clear where the cut-off point would be. Thus it is possible to envisage a range of cross-elasticities relating to a number of candidate products for inclusion in the market. Ultimately the boundary will be based on a judgement of what constitutes a high enough cross-elasticity value.

In the absence of reliable cross-elasticity estimates, indirect evidence of consumers' willingness to switch between products may be taken as an indication of the availability of close substitutes which should therefore be included in the 'market' for policy purposes. The problem with this interpretation has been discussed at least since the famous Cellophane case in the US.[1] It is known from basic economic analysis that a profit-maximizing monopolist will operate on an elastic portion of the demand curve. At the monopoly price, therefore, consumers will attempt to substitute away from the product. Such substitutions, however, are a reflection of the use of market power, not an indication of its absence. The relevant question from the point of view of correctly defining the market is what products are perceived by consumers as close substitutes when the price is at a competitive level. In most merger enquiries one or both firms involved are likely already to have a degree of market power which the merger may enhance. In these circumstances it is misleading to place too much emphasis on evidence of consumer readiness to switch between products as an indication that they should therefore be included in the same market.

If anything, the question of supply-side substitution is more complicated. In principle, if small increases in the price of a product A would cause producers of another product to retool or adjust their equipment to supply that product, then they should be included as part of the relevant market on the ground that they clearly constrain the ability of producers of A to raise their prices. Even though current output from some firms may be no substitute in demand terms, the flexibility of the equipment may mean that it should be included in the market for purposes of analysing the effects of a merger. Conceptually there may be little difference whether such capacity is treated as part of the existing market or whether it is regarded as new entry, although in practice it may be appropriate to confine entry to entirely new capacity.

For policy purposes the relevant market may extend to part of a country or region, the whole of a country or a large part of the world. Indeed, for some products the whole of the world may constitute one market. A major objective of the EC is to ensure that as far as possible artificial constraints on trading are removed so that markets are as wide as possible. The presence of extensive intra-Community trade alongside domestic production implies that the market extends beyond national boundaries. Imports from outside the Community may also lead to the same conclusion, to the extent that they constrain the prices of domestic producers. There is some agreement, however, that imports should not be treated in exactly the same way as domestic output for antitrust purposes (see, for example, the symposium introduced by Salop, 1987). Not only may they be subject to sudden changes in government policy on quotas but, more important, they may also be vulnerable to the vagaries of the exchange rate. As the EC moves towards monetary union the latter point loses its force but it will remain for imports from outside the Community.

Supply-side substitution takes on special importance when the geographic limits of the market are considered. If it is technologically possible to adjust capacity to the production of another product in response to small price changes, and if shipment costs are low in relation to final values, then, in principle, all overseas capacity should be treated as part of the relevant market. The discretion that domestic firms have over prices is constrained by the presence of this productive capacity. At least this is the view of Landes and Posner (1981) in cases where significant imports already take place. For reasons given in the previous paragraph others are more cautious in what they would include in supply side substitution (for example, Schmalensee, 1982).

Once the considerable problems of market definition have been resolved, the calculation of market shares and the impact of the proposed merger on concentration is largely a matter of arithmetic. The proponents of the merger will favour a wider definition of the market; this would mean a smaller post-merger market share. Underpinning such calculations is the principle that the higher the level of concentration in the market, *ceteris paribus*, the stronger the likelihood that tacit collusion will allow prices to be maintained above competitive levels. The fact that it is possible to show in some models of oligopoly a direct relationship between price-cost margins and the Herfindahl index of concentration has persuaded many that the index should be formally incorporated into merger policy.[2] This point is taken up in more detail in section 8.3 below. For the moment, note that its relevance may not be as strong in this context as some enthusiasts have suggested. The models from which the result is derived involve firms aware of the interdependence of their decision-making, even if in the simplest case they choose to ignore it. However, many mergers which an anti-trust authority may wish to challenge, especially in the US, may involve firms of quite modest size. In fact, given the severity of past merger decisions by the Supreme Court, the acquired firm may be small enough to have no influence over the pre-merger behaviour of the acquiring firm. In such cases a more appropriate model may be that involving a dominant firm and a competitive fringe. In a market structure of this kind, Saving (1970) has shown that there is a direct relationship between the mark-up of price over cost and the n-firm concentration ratio (that is, the share of the largest n-firms in total market sales).

The lesson to be learned from this is not that one index is necessarily superior to another but, as Peter Hart (1971) some time ago reminded his readers, the important point is to choose the measure most appropriate for the question in hand. In a merger enquiry the obvious starting point is with the market shares of the firms directly and indirectly involved. Other firms in the market and anti-trust authorities have a legitimate interest in the possible indirect consequences of a merger: firms because they may wish to take defensive action if the merger is allowed (and this may involve further acquisitions), authorities precisely because they may decide that permitting the current proposal may trigger others which may rapidly transform the structure of the market.

The third issue which has taken on much greater significance in recent discussions of merger policy has been the condition of entry to the market. Although it has long been known that the exercise of market power ultimately rests on the presence of some barrier preventing the entry of additional firms to the market, entry conditions have not traditionally been given the systematic attention in actual enquiries that their significance warrants. Compared, say, with market concentration, it is not possible to measure entry conditions using a simple index. Any assessment has to remain largely subjective and therefore may tend to reflect differing views about the ultimate sources of barriers to entry (cf. Gribbin and Utton, 1986; Littlechild, 1989).

Entry and exit conditions have been the centre of attention in the profound theoretical developments in industrial economics that have been taking place over the past decade or so (Baumol *et al.*, 1982). As far as merger policy is concerned, the main contribution of the theory of contestable markets has probably been to emphasize the significance of sunk costs. In a market where a potential entrant is confident that it can replicate the production and distribution capacity of existing firms and achieve the same cost levels, it may still be deterred by the knowledge that a substantial portion of the total costs are irrecoverable should its attempted entry fail.

The same point also helps to inform the continuing debate about what actually constitutes a barrier to entry. Stigler's (1968) view that costs must be *differentially* higher for an entrant compared to an incumbent in order to be a genuine entry barrier led to a detailed reappraisal of those sources which had hitherto been accepted; that is, product differentiation, economies of scale, and absolute cost advantages, such as a patent. As far as product differentiation is concerned, it could now be argued that entrant firms may not only have to incur differentially higher advertising costs to dislodge the incumbent with its established brands and consumer loyalties but practically all such costs would be sunk and thus amount to a barrier to exit from the market in the event of failure.

For Stigler, economies of scale did not constitute an entry barrier because in principle such economies were also available to potential entrants. What another part of the recent theoretical development has emphasized, however, is that an incumbent firm may be able to rely on scale economies for its own strategic advantage and deter entry. In particular, where scale economies are significant in relation to market demand and where costs at suboptimal scales rise substantially above the minimum, a potential entrant may be deterred by the prospect that its own output added to that of the incumbent will drive prices down below costs. Rather than face the prospect of losses, the firm therefore stays out of the market. There may thus be a degree of ambiguity surrounding a merger which promises to generate additional economies of scale. Costs for the merged firm may be reduced but entry conditions may worsen, giving it greater control over prices. Partly for this reason the idea that economies of scale should offer a defence of mergers is often treated very cautiously, and only accepted if convincing evidence is offered that the economies are not attainable in any other way, for example, by internal growth (Fisher, 1987). This point is explored further in the next section.

More recently, Gilbert has suggested that a barrier to entry should be viewed as 'a rent that is derived from incumbency' (Gilbert, 1989, p. 478). A variety of factors including those identified by Bain and Stigler may yield an advantage to existing firms allowing their rents to persist. The emphasis in this definition is thus on factors which prevent the mobility of capital. A perfectly contestable market ensures that entrants can imitate exactly the production and distribution conditions of incumbents but all expenditures incurred are potentially reversible. All firms in such a market behave as if they faced perfectly elastic demand curves, and this can serve as the definition of a market where there is a complete absence of entry barriers (p. 479).

In a first-best world the removal of entry or mobility barriers would lead to a welfare improvement. The real world, however, does not yield first-best solutions. In the world where merger policy is thought necessary, impediments arising from technology and consumer preferences need not lead to reduced efficiency. As von Weizsäcker (1980) recognized, there is a variety of circumstances in which restraints on entry may actually improve welfare. An example is the Chamberlinian large-group case where product differentiation and free entry result in a zero profit equilibrium. The lack of entry barriers can then lead to an excessive number of products as measured by total economic surplus, and welfare may actually be improved by making entry more difficult. Recognition of such cases led von Weizsäcker to modify Stigler's definition of entry barriers as follows: 'A cost of producing which must be borne by a firm which seeks to enter an industry but is not borne by firms already in the industry *and which implies a distortion in the allocation of resources from the social point of view*' (von Weizsäcker, 1980, p. 400, emphasis added). With its particular stress on welfare effects the definition is thus especially appropriate for policy discussions.

8.3   MERGER POLICIES

The issues discussed in the previous section are all likely to play an important part in any horizontal merger challenged by an anti-trust authority. However, at any time only a small subset out of the total of all horizontal mergers will be of direct concern. The vast majority have no significant effect on the market. Even amongst those that initially appear to raise public policy issues, only some, on closer inspection, will be challenged. With limited resources available for anti-trust, therefore, an efficient policy requires an effective screening procedure so that only those likely to have substantially adverse market power consequences are targeted. It is significant that the characteristics of an effective screening procedure have recently been much discussed in connection with both EC and US merger policies. In this section we compare the two and see whether the new EC policy has anything to learn from the longer-established US approach.

The merger regulation that was finally accepted in December 1989, to become effective from September 1990, complements the two main articles of the Treaty of Rome that deal respectively with restrictive agreements (article 85) and single-firm market dominance (article 86).[3] Although both articles had been invoked in earlier cases to deal with problems arising from mergers it was widely recognized that these procedures were unwieldy and restricted, and that special provisions were required, particularly in view of the increased merger activity from firms both within the EC and those outside wishing to make acquisitions as the timetable for the completion of the internal market reached its conclusion.[4]

The regulation is aimed initially at only the very largest mergers and those which also have a genuinely international dimension. Thus to qualify for scrutiny by the European Commission the firms involved in the merger must have a world-wide turnover of ECU 5 billion or more (approximately £4 billion) and each firm involved must have EC turnover in excess of ECU 250 million (approximately £200 million) and do less than two-thirds of their business in one EC member country. The thresholds are to be reviewed within four years. Two important exceptions to these turnover thresholds can be made. First, where a member feels that a merger has a significant effect on competition in a properly defined market within its boundaries the Commission can allow it to be dealt with by the national jurisdiction.[5] Secondly, where the above thresholds are not met by a merger but where nevertheless a member state considers that it may have a significant impact within its borders, it can request an investigation by the Commission. This part of the procedure was included for the benefit of smaller member states which did not have their own well-developed merger policy.

By using turnover figures in these thresholds, unrelated to a particular market, the Commission can in principle investigate all types of mergers (vertical and conglomerate as well as horizontal). However, only those mergers which create or strengthen a dominant position, and which as a result are likely to impede competition in the EC or a significant part of it, will be prohibited. In making its assessment the Commission has to take account of a whole list of factors, encompassing those discussed in the previous section: thus under article 2 of the regulation the Commission has to take into account:

(a)   the need to preserve and develop effective competition within the Common Market in view of, among other things, the structure of all the markets concerned and the actual or potential competition from undertakings located either within or without the Community;

(b)   the market position of the undertakings concerned and their economic and financial power, the opportunities available to suppliers and users, their access to suppliers or markets, any legal or other barriers to entry, supply or demand trends for the relevant goods or services, the interests of the intermediate and ultimate consumers, and the development of technical and economic progress provided that it is to the consumers' advantage and does not form an obstacle to competition.

The regulation lays down a strict timetable for completing an enquiry. The parties to mergers of this size have to notify the Commission within one week of their bid or acquisition of control. Thereafter, the procedure can fall into two stages, a preliminary or screening stage which lasts one month in which the Commission has to determine whether or not the merger raises serious doubts about its compatibility with the Common Market. Some mergers meeting the turnover criteria but judged not to create a dominant position can thus be cleared within one month of their announcement (examples in this category include Digital–Philips, Delta–Pan American and BP–Petromed). In other cases meeting the criteria, where there is sufficient doubt about the likely consequences, the second stage can be used. This involves a full enquiry lasting a maximum of four months at the end of which the Commission has to give its decision on whether the merger is permitted or prohibited (examples of cases fully investigated but allowed are Tetra Pak–Alfa-Laval, and Varta–Bosch; so far one case, Aerospatiale-Alenia–de Havilland, has been prohibited). Appeals against decisions by the Commission can be made to the European Court. As with actions under articles 85 and 86 the Commission has wide remedial powers. It can, for example, order divestiture, impose conditions on the merger, and impose fines for breaches of the regulation.[6]

The very limited time available between notification and completion of the first- or second-stage enquiries plus the complexities of the issues involved thus place a heavy burden on the screening procedure and subsequent analysis by the merger secretariat. The screening proposals published by Jacquemin and his colleagues in 1989, although they are not official (in the sense of the US *Merger Guidelines*, discussed below), probably give a good idea of the procedure used by the secretariat at the first stage of their enquiries (Jacquemin *et al.*, 1989).[7] They also provide an interesting contrast with the US approach.

At the preliminary screening stage they focus on four market characteristics which they then use to provide a classification of mergers according to their likely effects on competition and efficiency. The four characteristics are: market demand growth; level of import penetration; extent of scale economies; and what they call 'technological content'. In the context of the developing EC they explain the importance of these indicators in the following terms. In markets where demand is growing, prospective profitability is likely to be good and entry barriers relatively low. Such markets are likely to encourage and accommodate new entry.

Mergers are thus unlikely to have a serious impact on competition. Similarly, in markets open to international competition, both from within the EC and from other countries, the danger that a merger will adversely affect competition is less than in markets effectively closed to international trade. To have this effect the imports must be genuinely competitive with those of the existing producers and not controlled by them. In the case of significant economies of scale the authors recognize their double-edged nature: they may contribute to barriers to entry and thus have a negative effect on competition; but they may also imply that only very large organizations can achieve the lowest costs. The authors take the view that only where an important part of total costs are sunk is the 'barrier' effect likely to be significant. They imply that in most instances this is not the case and therefore 'the existence of economies of scale will be regarded here as an argument in favour of concentration' (Jacquemin *et al.*, 1989, p. 25). Given the ambiguous evidence of the effect of mergers on performance referred to in the first part of this chapter, the authors' position is questionable but should perhaps be taken in conjunction with their interpretation of the fourth characteristic, 'technological content'. They have in mind here high technology industries where they consider that mergers between European firms may be justified by the very high research and development expenditures and risks involved in innovation. They envisage that the pooling of resources would allow firms to be more ambitious and improve 'their ability to translate their research into positions of international competitive advantage'. Although they are well aware of the need to protect competition within the EC in order to maintain performance, the interpretation of the third and fourth characteristics (economies of scale and technology content) carries more than a hint of the influence of industrial rather than competition policy, that is, that mergers may be a means of promoting 'national champions' capable of competing on equal terms with the largest US and Japanese firms.

However, putting these four characteristics together in different combinations they propose a preliminary screening procedure for mergers along the lines summarized in Table 8.1, which is adapted from their paper. Mergers which fall within the regulation according to the turnover criteria, but which are classified to categories II and III, would thus be likely to receive clearance within a month: they are unlikely to have a significant negative effect on competition but may generate some efficiency gains (category III). Those classified in categories I and IV are the difficult cases and are likely to require the more detailed stage two investigation. Both categories suggest that the mergers may reduce competition, but in case IV there is also the prospect of efficiency gains. It is noteworthy that in the final version of the regulation (although not in the version addressed by Jacquemin and his colleagues in their paper) there is no direct mention of an efficiency defence of a merger. Formally, therefore, a merger which creates or strengthens a dominant position and so impedes competition within the EC cannot be 'saved' by a demonstration that it would result in significant offsetting economies. Mergers falling in categories I and IV would thus be treated in the same way. The cases given in the table would be those most likely to concern the Merger Task Force. Other categories that can be distinguished using the four variables (for example, strong demand growth, below average import

Table 8.1   Preliminary screening procedure for large horizontal mergers in the EC

I *Mergers offering little prospect of efficiency gains but may endanger competition*	IV *Mergers offering prospect of efficiency gains but may endanger competition*
• weak demand growth • below-average import penetration • insignificant scale economies • low technology content	• weak demand growth • below-average import penetration • substantial scale economies • high technology content
II *Merger offering little prospect of efficiency gains and little danger of reduced competition*	III *Merger offering prospect of efficiency gains and little danger of reduced competition*
• strong demand growth • above-average import penetration • insignificant scale economies • low technology content	• strong demand growth • above-average import penetration • substantial scale economies • high technology content

Source: Adapted from Jacquemin *et al.*, (1989).

penetration, insignificant scale economies and low technology content) would be much less likely to raise significant policy questions.

If the procedure is to be applied speedily at the first stage, much of the basic information (on demand growth, import penetration and economies of scale) would have to be prepared in advance so that a particular merger proposal could then be slotted into the appropriate category. In their paper Jacquemin *et al.* give a considerable amount of detailed illustration of how this can be approached. They appreciate that some of the information may not be very precise but argue that it is probably adequate for preliminary screening purposes. Finer definitions can be introduced for second-stage enquiries. A particular problem they recognize is the industrial framework used for defining the four categories in Table 8.1. Although 120 separate industries are distinguished in the system used, many of these do not correspond at all closely to the relevant 'market' for anti-trust purposes. The identification of the market which, as argued in section 8.2, is regarded as one of the three key features of a correct analysis is thus not directly addressed in their preliminary screening procedure. The same point applies to the other issues discussed, market concentration and entry conditions. However, given that the purpose of the first stage is simply to distinguish those mergers warranting further detailed enquiry from those that do not, detailed measurement of the effect of the merger on concentration is not required. The philosophy behind the procedure is that the much more precise analysis can be deployed for those mergers in categories I and IV which are filtered into the second stage. More to the point, it can be argued that, indirectly at least, possibly the most significant issue in merger enquiries – entry conditions – is addressed by the variables used in Table 8.1. Markets with strong demand growth are likely to attract and sustain new entrants. Existing firms' main concern will be to meet the expanding demand rather than to frustrate the growth of entrants. Similarly, domestic firms already facing substantial competition from imports will be aware that any significant price increase on their part is likely to erode further their market share.

Taken in conjunction with the emphasis on high technology, therefore, the screening procedure's main concern is with the dynamics rather than the statics of market structure. In this important respect we may contrast the position with that in the US. Since the early 1980s the US Department of Justice has used a set of well-defined *Merger Guidelines* to screen sizeable mergers.[8] The *Guidelines* essentially involve a five-point procedure (Salop, 1987). The relevant anti-trust market is defined for the purpose of determining competitive effects. Secondly, concentration pre- and post-merger is calculated, using the Herfindahl index. Thirdly, the likelihood of entry is evaluated. Fourthly, any other competitive factors likely to facilitate collusion are considered. Finally, efficiency effects, primarily cost savings, are evaluated. The outcome of the analysis of these points will govern whether the merger is to be challenged in the courts. In view of the discussion in section 8.2 above, the first two points deserve some comment.

Instead of approaching the complex question of market definition by looking at market data on actual product substitution, the Department proceeds as follows: the relevant anti-trust market is defined as

> a product or group of products and geographic area in which it is sold such that a hypothetical profit maximizing firm . . . that was the only present and future seller of those products in that area would impose a 'small but significant and nontransitory' increase in price above prevailing or likely future levels'. (*Merger Guidelines* (1984))

In trying to pin down the elusive gap in the chain of substitutes, the Department has in principle, therefore, to consider all possible substitutes in demand and supply. As a starting point for market definition in merger cases the approach has received some highly distinguished support by focusing clearly on potential market power (see, for example, the papers by Fisher, Schmalensee and White in the symposium introduced by Salop, 1987). The approach emphasizes potential rather than actual competition. To this extent it reflects the recent theoretical developments referred to above. It is still a matter of some dispute, however, whether the empirical evidence indicates that actual rather than potential competition provides a stronger constraint on the price-raising abilities of dominant firms (Shepherd, 1984). In addition, taken literally the market definition may be prey to the Cellophane fallacy referred to above. In the merger cases considered, price is already likely to be above the competitive level. Hence, by gearing the market definition to *further* potential price increases, the Department may include products which at competitive prices consumers would not treat as substitutes.

Within the market so defined, the effect of the merger on concentration is then measured using the Herfindahl index scaled for convenience between zero and 10 000. These calculations may prove crucial to the decision on whether or not to challenge the merger. Thus if the post-merger index remains below 1000 (approximately equivalent to a four-firm concentration ratio of 50 per cent; White, 1987) the merger will not be challenged whatever the other market characteristics. Mergers resulting in an index between 1000 and 1800 (that is, a concentration ratio between approximately 50 and 70 per cent) will only be challenged if the index is increased by at least 100 points. For mergers raising the index to

1800 or more the criteria are more complex. For example, mergers increasing the index by at least 50 points and where entry conditions are judged to be difficult will probably be challenged. Where the index is raised by at least 100 points, then the merger will almost certainly be challenged. The assessment of entry conditions is thus likely to be especially important in the sensitive range above 1800. Whether this apparent precision of measurement is of value in advance to firms planning mergers depends, of course, on whether their interpretation of the market coincides with that of the Department. Previous experience suggests that they are likely to err on the side of optimism when interpreting market size which would work in their favour, whereas the Department may tend to start with too narrow a definition.

A highly important innovation in the 1984 *Guidelines* is to allow an efficiency defence even for those mergers which might result in increased market power and prices. Although Williamson (1968) has long argued in favour of such a provision it is still regarded with a good deal of scepticism. Fisher (1987), for example, argues strongly that claims *ex ante* of the cost reductions that a merger will bring are easily made and often too readily believed. He therefore would place the onus of demonstrating how the cost reductions would be made on the proponents of the merger and the evidence would have to be very convincing (p. 36–7). Nevertheless, the provision is now embodied in the US *Guidelines* whereas no comparable defence is allowed under the EC regulation.

Although there is a wide measure of agreement that the US *Guidelines* offer an improvement over the previous procedure, there is still concern that the apparent precision, particularly in relation to market definition and concentration measurement, may result in a far too mechanical application of the criteria. The fact that the concentration index is measured on a numerical scale and that the static effect of the merger on that scale can be calculated exactly, tends to give it an aura of scientific precision, and therefore significance, disproportionate to its actual effect. In general, given that the *Guidelines* are supposed to provide a screening device prior to a fuller enquiry for those mergers that are challenged, their practical application may be too inflexible and rigid. The evidence assembled for the preliminary scrutiny may be regarded as sufficient for any subsequent court action, whereas in fact a much more detailed analysis of the particular circumstances of the case is called for:

> The Guidelines are not a substitute for serious analysis, and the Department of Justice staff has tended to focus narrowly on issues of market definition and concentration measures as though such issues were dispositive. That is a mistake. In the present (and likely future) state of knowledge, serious analysis

of market power and oligopoly cannot be subsumed in a few spuriously precise measurements.
(Fisher, 1987, p. 39)

There is also controversy about how closely in practice the authorities have followed the *Guidelines*. Two distinguished legal observers, for example, quoting the substantial drop in the proportion of mergers challenged in the 1980s concluded: 'So far as we can ascertain, the merger policy by the present Administration departs widely from its professed standards and relies heavily on factors not shown to be reliable predictors of industry behaviour' (Krattenmaker and Pitofsky, 1988, p. 228). In a more recent paper, Coate and McChesney have been able to examine this and related claims in much more detail. They had access to the files on 70 merger investigations by the Federal Trade Commission between 1982 and 1986. As a result of their statistical analysis they concluded that 'merger challenges from the mid-1980s provide evidence that for the most part the merger guidelines have not been applied as written' (Coate and McChesney, 1992, p. 291). In particular, their analysis suggested that concentration *alone* was used not to establish a presumption of guilt, but rather to determine which cases required further investigations. The concentration effect was a necessary but not a sufficient condition for a merger challenge and a similar result held for entry barriers. However, they found no evidence to support another complaint from critics (such as Lande, 1988) that the new efficiency defence had overshadowed other more traditional concerns. The impression created by their investigation is thus that US policy has tended to follow the spirit if not the letter of the *Guidelines* and, in particular, has been consistent with economic theory.

As far as the much newer EC policy is concerned, the Director of the Merger Task Force, writing about the first year of the policy, emphasized that the critical test applied to mergers meeting the size thresholds was their impact on competition. Given the wording of article 2(3), this is the only feasible interpretation. Thus:

if the operation creates a dominant position which significantly impedes competition 'it *shall* be declared incompatible with the common market'. The existence of the word 'shall' here seems very important. If the Regulation envisaged the possibility for the Commission to undertake a competition-based analysis and then commence an industry/social policy balancing test to see whether the operation may nonetheless be approved, the wording would surely be different, and would, at least, have permitted some discretion on the part of the Commission.
(Overbury, 1991, p. 83)

The author adds that in none of the cases considered in the first year of the operation of the policy do the terms 'efficiency' or 'benefit to the economy' appear. The decisions were taken solely on competition grounds. The expectation by some authors, therefore, that in practice mergers offering the prospect of substantial economies may be viewed more favourably, has not so far been borne out (see, for example, George and Jacquemin, 1990). Furthermore, it was clear in the only case so far blocked by the Commission (Aerospatiale/Alenia and de Havilland, 1991) that 'industrial policy' considerations played no part in the decision, apparently to the considerable annoyance of the French and Italian governments.[9]

The relatively flexible system proposed for the EC allows for the speedy clearance of many sizeable mergers which are unlikely to create anti-competitive positions of dominance, according to Table 8.1. This leaves the way clear for the more detailed examination of those relatively few cases which raise serious competitive issues. At this stage the problems of market definition, the effect of concentration and entry conditions have to be addressed directly in order to determine the impact on market power. It is too early yet to determine whether the Commission will have any greater success in this respect than the Department of Justice.[10] What also remains to be seen is whether, despite the actual wording of the regulation, the Commission is swayed in favour of those merger proposals for which there is strong evidence of potential reductions in cost.

8.4   CONCLUSION

The special importance of merger policy has finally been recognized by the EC after many years of disagreement. However, as the US experience shows, the key questions that a merger enquiry has to address are highly complex. For this reason it is desirable that attention is focused clearly on those mergers where the threat to competition seems greatest. An efficient filtering system is thus required to ensure that in the limited preliminary enquiry time available, those posing a minimal threat can be cleared. It was argued in section 8.3 above that the approach embodied in the US *Guidelines*, although an advance over the previous system, may be unduly rigid and mechanistic with a rather static view of the market. In contrast, the approach at this preliminary stage proposed for the EC appears more flexible, with a focus on market change. For those mergers which proceed to the more detailed enquiry stage, the Commission is thus unencumbered with prior details of market measurement and data on potential increases in concentration.

Rather ironically, in view of the prolonged discussion of the issue, whereas the US authorities may now accept an efficiency defence of a proposed merger, the Commission, at least in principle, cannot. The influence of this factor, however, will probably be felt at the preliminary screening stage, when the potential for scale economies is likely to be viewed positively as long as other factors (such as demand growth and openness to import competition) are also favourable.

NOTES

1. *United States* v. *E.I. du Pont de Nemours & Co.*, 351 US 377 (1956).
2. The Herfindahl index is equal to the sum of the squared shares of all firms in the market. The relationship between it and the price–cost margin is demonstrated in Cowling and Waterson (1976).
3. Council Regulation No. 4064/89.
4. *BAT and R.J. Reynolds* v. *Commission* (142 and 156/84) [1988] 4 CMLR 24. *Europemballage and Continental Can* v. *Commission* (6/72) [1973] ECR 215: CMLR 199.
5. Similarly, permission can be allowed where legitimate national interests arise in areas such as security or plurality of the media.
6. See Regulation 4064/89, articles 8 and 14.
7. Professor Jacquemin was economic adviser and his co-authors were administrators in the Directorate General for Economic and Financial Affairs at the time the article was written.
8. The modern *Merger Guidelines* were introduced in 1982 and slightly modified in 1984. Our references are to the 1984 *Guidelines*. A further elaboration, focusing particularly on the assessment of entry conditions, was published in April 1992.
9. *Financial Times*, 8 October 1991.
10. The controversy that has surrounded the market definition used in the case of the first merger to be blocked by the Commission (Aerospatiale/Alenia and de Havilland) is not encouraging. The Commission appears to give very great weight to the opinion of existing manufacturers and customers as to what constitutes the relevant market. What manufacturers legitimately see as their 'market' for planning purposes may bear little relation to the relevant anti-trust product market. In particular, in the context of a merger, the relevant question of whether aircraft with different seating capacities would become substitutes if their relative prices changed as a result of market power does not appear to have been addressed (Aerospatiale/Alenia and de Havilland, *Common Market Law Reports*, 1992, p. M6).

REFERENCES

Baumol, S.J., J. Panzar and R. Willig (1982): *Contestable Markets and the Theory of Industry Structure* (New York: Harcourt Brace Jovanovich).

Coate, M.B. and F.S. McChesney (1992): 'Empirical evidence on FTC enforcement of the Merger Guidelines', *Economy Inquiry*, **30**, 277–93.

Cowling, K. and M. Waterson (1976): 'Price cost margins and market structure', *Economica*, **43**, 267–74.

Deneckere, R. and C. Davidson (1985): 'Incentives to join coalitions with Bertrand competition', *Rand Journal of Economics*, **16**, 473–86.

Fisher, F.M. (1987): 'Horizontal mergers: triage and treatment', *Journal of Economic Perspectives*, **1** (2), 23–40.

George, K.D. and A. Jacquemin (1990): 'Competition policy in the European Community', in *Competition Policy in Europe and North America: Economic Issues and Institutions*, ed. W.S. Comanor, A. Jacquemin and J.A. Ordover (London: Harewood Academic Publishers) pp. 206–45.

Gilbert, R.J (1989): 'Mobility barriers and the value of incumbency', in *Handbook of Industrial Organisation*, vol. I, ed. R. Schmalensee and R. Willig (Amsterdam: North-Holland) pp. 475–535.

Gribbin, J.D. and M.A. Utton (1986): 'The treatment of dominant firms in UK competition legislation', in *Mainstreams in Industrial Organisation*, Book II, ed. H.W. Jong and W.G. Shepherd (Dordrecht: Martinus Nijhoff) pp. 243–72.

Hart, P.E. (1971): 'Entropy and other measures of concentration', *Journal of the Royal Statistical Society*, Series A, **134** (1), 73–85.

Hughes, A. (1989): 'The impact of mergers: a survey of empirical evidence for the UK', in *Mergers and Merger Policy*, ed. J.A. Fairburn and J.A. Kay (Oxford: Oxford University Press) pp. 30–98.

Jacquemin, A. and M. Slade (1989): 'Cartels, collusion and horizontal mergers', in *Handbook of Industrial Organisation*, vol. I, ed. R. Schmalensee and R. Willig (Amsterdam: North-Holland) pp. 415–73.

Jacquemin, A., P. Buigues and F. Ilzkovitz (1989): 'Horizontal mergers and competition policy in the European Community', *European Economy*, May, 11–95.

Krattenmaker, T.G. and R. Pitofsky (1988): 'Antitrust merger policy and the Reagan administration', *Antitrust Bulletin*, **33**, Summer, 211–32.

Lande, R.H. (1988): 'The rise and (coming) fall of efficiency on the rules of antitrust', *Antitrust Bulletin*, **33**, Fall, 429–65.

Landes, W.M. and R.A. Posner (1981): 'Market power in antitrust cases', *Harvard Law Review*, **94**, 937–96.

Littlechild, S.C. (1989): 'Myths and merger policy', in *Mergers and Merger Policy*, ed. J.A. Fairburn and F.A. Kay (Oxford: Oxford University Press) pp. 301–21.

Merger Guidelines (1984), issued by the Justice Department, *Antitrust and Trade Regulation Report*, 14 June.

Mueller, D.C. (1985): 'Mergers and market share', *Review of Economics and Statistics*, **67**, 259–67.

Overbury, C. (1991): 'First experiences of European merger control', *European Law Review*, **16**, 79–88.

Perry, M.K. (1989): 'Vertical integration: determinants and effects', in *Handbook of Industrial Organisation*, vol. I, ed. R. Schmalensee and R.D. Willig (Amsterdam: North-Holland) pp. 185–255.

—— and R.H. Porter (1985): 'Oligopoly and the incentive for horizontal merger', *American Economic Review*, **75** (1), 219–27.

'Re the Concentration between Aerospatiale SNI and Alenia-Aeritalia E. Selenia Spa and de Havilland', *Common Market Law Reports*, January 1992, M2–M35.

Salant, S.W., S. Switzer and R.J. Reynolds (1983): 'Losses from horizontal merger: the effects of an exogenous change in industry structure on Cournot–Nash equilibrium', *Quarterly Journal of Economics*, **98** (2), 185–99.

Salop, S.C. (1987): 'Symposium on mergers and antitrust', *Journal of Economic Perspectives*, **1** (2), 3–11.

Saving, T.R. (1970): 'Concentration ratios and the degree of monopoly', *International Economic Review*, **11** (1), 139–46.

Scherer, F.M. and D. Ross (1990): *Industrial Market Structure and Economic Performance* (Boston, MA: Houghton Mifflin).

Schmalensee, R. (1982): 'Another look at market power', *Harvard Law Review*, **95**, 1789–1816.

—— (1987): 'Horizontal merger policy: problems and changes', *Journal of Economic Perspectives*, **1** (2), 41–54.

Shepherd, W.G. (1984): 'Contestability vs. competition', *American Economic Review*, **74**, 572–87.

Stigler, G.J. (1950): 'Monopoly and oligopoly by merger', *American Economic Review*, Papers and Proceedings, **40** (2), 23–34.

—— (1968): *The Organisation of Industry* (Homewood, IL: Irwin).

von Weizsäcker, C. (1980): 'A welfare analysis of barriers to entry', *Bell Journal of Economics*, **11**, 399–420.

White, L.J. (1987): 'Antitrust and merger policy: a review and critique', *Journal of Economic Perspectives*, **1** (2), 13–22.

Williamson, O.E. (1968): 'Economies as an antitrust defense', *American Economic Review*, **58**, 18–31.

9. Merger Appraisal Under the EC Merger Control Regulation

Eleanor J. Morgan[1]

9.1 INTRODUCTION

The lack of a specific merger regulation at European Community level was, for many years, an important weakness in EC competition policy. It had been established through case law that article 85 of the Treaty of Rome, which deals with restrictive practices, and article 86, dealing with the abuse of dominant positions, could be applied to mergers. However, it was generally agreed that both had serious drawbacks as instruments of merger control (see Banks, 1988; Bishop, 1990).

The first proposal for an EC merger regulation was submitted by the European Commission to the Council of Ministers in July 1973. There was a long struggle to gain acceptance from all the member states but eventually, after 16 years of discussion and as a result of various political compromises, the new system of Community-wide regulation was adopted in December 1989. The two major stumbling blocks in the negotiations were divergent views about the extent to which non-competition effects should be included in the appraisal of mergers and the size of mergers to be included in the scope of the legislation. The regulation finally adopted is based on a competition test and gives the Commission prime responsibility for mergers involving the very largest firms.[2]

The regulation, which falls under the Competition Directorate of the European Commission, established a system of compulsory pre-notification for 'concentrations with a Community dimension'. The Commission's approach to transactions notified under the regulation can be divided into three steps. First, it establishes whether the notified operation is a concentration. Concentrations are defined to include mergers, takeovers and certain types of joint ventures.[3] Secondly, it determines whether the transaction has a 'Community dimension' in terms of turnover thresholds. These are due for review in 1993, but in the initial phase mergers are subject to the EC regulation when the total world-wide turnover of all firms concerned exceeds ECU 5 billion (then £3.5 billion) and total turnover within the Community of any two of them, taken individually, exceeds ECU 250 million. However, if each of the firms concerned realizes two-thirds of its total Community turnover within one and the same member state, the transaction is excluded. As a third step, the Commission investigates whether the merger is compatible with the Common Market.

This chapter focuses on the third step in the Commission's approach, namely, the application of the appraisal criteria to mergers within the scope of the regulation.[4] The merger control was introduced on 21 September 1990, so it has been in effect for 18 months at the time of writing. The cases provide useful insights into the way in which the Commission's approach to merger appraisal is evolving, especially as all the various types of decision allowed for in the regulation have now been adopted.

An introduction to the relevant legislative framework is given in section 9.2. Section 9.3 provides an overview of the decisions, and then examines how mergers have been appraised in practice in terms of market definitions, the application of the competition test and the operation of the exemption clauses. Conclusions are drawn in section 9.4.

9.2   THE LEGISLATIVE FRAMEWORK

The regulation is based on a neutral stance, with no presumption for or against mergers. Each case is assessed individually in terms of its likely effects on competition. This represents an intermediate position between the two main approaches to merger control which are usually distinguished, namely cost–benefit assessment and the harsher structuralist approach (see George and Jacquemin, 1992). Appraisal is carried out on the basis of article 2(3) of the regulation, which states that 'a concentration which creates or strengthens a dominant position as a result of which effective competition would be significantly impeded in the Common Market or in a substantial part of it shall be declared incompatible with the Common Market'.[5]

Several criteria are specified which the Commission must take into account in its assessment, although it is not restricted to these alone. The first is the most general and cites 'the need to preserve and develop effective competition within the Common Market, in view of, among other things, the structure of all the markets concerned and the actual or potential competition from undertakings located either within or without the Community'. Specific factors affecting the assessment of dominance are then mentioned, including the market position of the undertakings concerned and their economic and financial power, the opportunities available to suppliers and users, their access to supplies or markets, barriers to entry and supply and demand trends. The final criterion is 'the development of technical and economic progress, provided that it is to the consumers' advantage and does not form an obstacle to competition'.

The list of criteria is unsystematic and allows the Commission considerable discretion in its treatment of mergers. No guidelines were published to indicate how the criteria would be applied but the approach is becoming clearer as the case law evolves. In addition, companies may obtain confidential guidance on likely competition problems raised by particular proposals through informal pre-notification discussions.

The economic effects of mergers in the EC and possible policy approaches have been well covered previously (see, for example, Jacquemin, Buigues and Ilzkovitz, 1989) and both Langeheine (1991) and Lever (1991) contain helpful early discussions of the likely interpretation of the appraisal criteria from a legal perspective. This section continues by identifying the main sources of uncertainty about how mergers would be assessed in practice under the regulation before turning to the evidence provided by the recent decisions.

The framework for appraisal owes much to policy towards the abuse of dominant positions developed under article 86 and appears to be based on the view that dominant positions, rather than oligopoly structures, are the main threat to competition. The regulation makes no reference to concentration but rather to 'market position', 'economic and financial power' and the 'structure of the market affected'. This is despite the Commission's statement in 1986 that one of the main aims of the merger regulation proposed at the time was to prevent situations resulting in stable collusions among oligopolists (see Venit, 1991). It remained to be seen whether the Commission would try to tackle oligopoly problems in the EC through the merger regulation.

The regulation gives little indication of the weight to be attached to the different factors in the assessment. A central question in the European context is whether to allow the creation or strengthening of a dominant position if it is likely to be eroded in time by increased competitive pressure. Markets within Europe are integrating rapidly and becoming more contestable with the harmonization of regulations, the reform of public procurement and the progressive removal of other non-tariff barriers as part of the single market programme. It may, however, take a considerable time for this competitive pressure to threaten dominant positions, and mergers themselves may occur as a defensive reaction to the possible erosion of market share. It was clear from the outset that the Commission's approach to defining geographical markets and assessing the dynamics of competition would be particularly important aspects of merger appraisal, especially in the transitional phase.

Uncertainties also surrounded the likely treatment of efficiency gains resulting from mergers. Unlike the draft proposal, which allowed the efficiency gains from mergers to be traded off against the welfare losses due to decreased competition, the last criterion suggests little scope for efficiency arguments. The member states eventually agreed that anti-competitive mergers in the EC should not be cleared on the basis of possible gains in firms' international strength. However, the wording of the initial criterion is rather ambiguous and the recitals to the regulation suggest the possibility of a wider role for non-competition considerations.

Concern has been expressed that, irrespective of the wording of the regulation, there is a danger of 'back-door' intervention and internal compromise allowing non-competition considerations to surface in the Commission's decisions (see Jacquemin, 1990, for example). This is because, unlike the decision-making structure in Germany and the UK, the Commission is both an administrative and a political body. It is made up of 17 Commissioners who are political appointees, some of whom have responsibility for industrial, social or regional policy. It was feared that this might bring the risk of Community, or even national, industrial policy and politics influencing the deliberations.

The Competition Commissioner, Sir Leon Brittan, made a clear commitment to the competition test when the regulation was introduced (Brittan, 1990). He is responsible for deciding whether to open full proceedings on individual cases; but once proceedings have been opened the final decision is taken by the Commission. If broader issues are to play a part, they are most likely to intrude at this stage. There are, however, two safeguard mechanisms. The first is the Community's system of judicial review. The second is an Advisory Committee, established under the regulation, which consists of representatives of all the member states; this has to be consulted before proceedings are finalized and the Commission is required to take the 'utmost account' of the Advisory Committee's opinion in reaching a final decision.

One of the aims of the merger regulation was to provide a 'one-stop' merger control and, in principle, transactions of Community dimensions fall within the exclusive jurisdiction of the European Commission. There are two main exceptions. The first, in article 9, allows member states to intervene in transactions which have anti-competitive effects within a 'distinct market'. If the Commission agrees to refer the case, it will be decided under national legislation. The other exception, article 21(3), recognizes that the regulation is principally concerned with competition policy and allows member states to take appropriate measures to protect 'legitimate' non-competition interests (public security, plurality of the media and prudential rules or, with the agreement of the Commission, other legitimate interests).

Both exemptions were the result of political compromise, a response, in the first case, to pressure from Germany and, in the second, to UK demands. These exceptions result in a system of dual control, with the possibility of some mergers of Community dimensions being assessed under national laws (see Bright, 1991). The exceptions are at the discretion of the Commission; their importance and the jurisdictional uncertainties they create can only be assessed in the light of experience.

9.3   THE APPRAISAL IN PRACTICE

An Overview of the Cases

It was estimated that the Commission would have to deal with about 50 mergers a year and this has proved reasonably accurate, with 88 notifications in the first 18 months. Only 22 of these concerned companies from the same member state and roughly half were joint ventures. Administrative procedures within the newly created Mergers Task Force (which carries out the investigations) are streamlined and firms are required to provide a considerable amount of information on notification. Time-scales for decisions are short; they provide for initial scrutiny within one month to see if the merger has a 'Community dimension' and, if so, whether it raises serious doubts about compatibility with the Common Market. If there are serious doubts requiring full proceedings to be opened, a further decision must be reached within four months. Failure to meet the deadlines results in automatic clearance, but so far all the deadlines have been met.

Decisions have now been reached in 79 cases. Eight notifications were found to be outside the scope of the regulation so investigation was terminated. Of the cases with a Community dimension, 65 have been cleared within one month. Decisions have been taken on the basis of full proceedings in five cases and only one of these has been blocked (*ATR–de Havilland*) although clearance was subject to conditions in three cases. In addition, the first case has recently been referred back to the national authorities (*Tarmac–Steetley*) on the basis of concern about dominance in a distinct market. The individual cases are listed in the appendix, with dates notifications were received and decisions as at 20 March 1992.

Details of the decisions resulting from full proceedings have been published in the *Official Journal*, namely *Alcatel–Telettra*, *Magneti Marelli–CEAc*, *Tetra Pak–Alfa-Laval*, *Varta–Bosch* and *ATR–de Havilland*.[6] Other unpublished decisions, apart from the most recent, have been obtained from the Commission.[7] The decisions are relatively short compared with other European competition cases and the coverage does not always seem to reflect the importance of the case.[8] It is not clear how far these differences in length reflect the relative depth of the investigations or simply are due to different reporting styles within the Task Force.

The next section examines how the appraisal criteria have been applied to concentrations with a Community dimension. Within the confines of a single chapter the approach is necessarily summary and selective. The review focuses on evidence relating to the issues raised in the previous section and the examples cited generally relate to cases where full proceedings were opened.

Market Definition

The term 'dominance' is not defined in the regulation, but the Commission's interpretation reflects the body of case law built up under article 86 which regulates the abuse of dominant positions (Brittan, 1991). For example, in the *Hoffman-La Roche* case:

> the dominant position . . . relates to a position of economic strength enjoyed by an undertaking which enables it to prevent effective competition being maintained on a relevant market by affording it the power to behave to an appreciable extent independently of its competitors, customers and ultimately of the consumers.[9]

The first necessity, as in article 86 cases, is to define the relevant market. This has both a product and a territorial dimension. According to the notification form, a relevant product market 'comprises all those products and/or services which are regarded as interchangeable or substitutable by the consumer, by reason of their products' characteristics, prices and their intended use'.[10] In practice, relatively narrow product-market definitions have been adopted and these have usually been based on demand substitutability and the structure of demand. Definitions of product markets seem to have raised comparatively few problems and this may partly reflect the very small number of contested mergers which have been considered. Choice between possible alternative definitions has typically been avoided if it is clearly irrelevant to the outcome of the case.

Formal estimation of cross-price elasticities plays little part in the analysis, although an interesting attempt at quantification is provided in *Tetra Pak–Alfa-Laval*. The market was limited to aseptic packaging in cartons as 75 per cent of the respondents to a Commission survey said that a price increase of more than 20 per cent would be needed for them to switch to other aseptic packaging or non-aseptic packaging.

As well as demand substitution, the structure of demand has also played an important part in product definition. For example, in two cases involving starter batteries (*Magneti Marelli–CEAc* and *Varta–Bosch*) the distinction between the original and replacement equipment markets was based not on differences in the products or their end uses but, instead, on the different competitive conditions in the two markets which were seen as requiring different policies on the part of the producers. The approach was particularly controversial in *Varta–Bosch*: the main suppliers in each of the markets were the same so they were clearly capable of adapting to the different requirements of the two market segments, and the parties argued that the distinction was unjustified, a view supported by a minority of the Advisory Committee.[11]

Occasionally, supply-side characteristics have been considered. This was not surprising in *VIAG–Continental Can*, as neglect of supply factors in the earlier *Continental Can* case, the only merger to be dealt with formally under article 86, had led to the decision by the Court of Justice against the merger being overturned.[12] In *ATR–de Havilland*, three distinct markets for regional turboprop aircraft were distinguished by seat size: 20–39, 40–59 and over 60 seats. The parties claimed this was too restrictive, but the Commission supported its definition by reference to the clustering of aircraft seat sizes around 30, 50 and 65 seats as well as to the results of enquiries among competitors and customers. The Commission also cited the considerable time it would take for established manufacturers to develop competing products in higher segments as additional evidence on the supply side. The evidence in this controversial case is discussed in more detail later in the chapter.

In defining a market's territorial scope, the Commission has tended to determine the geographical market that is likely to be affected by the merger before considering whether that market is in fact the relevant one. The notification form indicates that the factors which will be considered in assessing this include:

> the nature and characteristics of the products or services concerned, the existence of entry barriers or consumer preferences, appreciable differences between the undertakings' market shares between neighbouring areas, or substantial price differences.[13]

In practice, it is not always clear what weight will attach to different features, and defining the territorial scope of markets has been particularly problematic. This is because, although markets in Europe are integrating rapidly, many still show signs of being national in scope. During the transitional phase in the run-up to the single market, possible changes in geographic scope have to be assessed at some stage in the analysis to see whether dominance in the existing market is likely to be eroded and, if so, how soon.

The Community market has already been regarded as the relevant one in some cases (for example, aseptic carton packaging in *Tetra Pak–Alfa-Laval*); exceptionally the market has been defined as global (for example, *ATR–de Havilland*) and competition in both the world and the EC market then assessed. Although the development of the internal market is likely to result in the EC or the world increasingly being regarded as the relevant market, the approach to market definition has been deliberately cautious (see Brittan, 1991; Overbury, 1991). It has tended to be based on current competitive conditions rather than likely developments in the near future and these have usually been dealt with as part of the subsequent appraisal of the merger. This approach does not seem to have made a substantive difference to the results so far, although it can be seen as a way of scrutinizing the build-up of strong positions in national markets to ensure that mergers do not pre-empt the possibility of more competitive markets in future.

The Commission's approach to defining market area can be illustrated with reference to *Magneti Marelli–CEAc*, a case which centred on the French market. There are no legal barriers preventing the import and sale of batteries in France, so the reference market was not limited to the national market on those grounds. Instead, the definition was based on variations in price in the different parts of the EC and the very disparate market shares held by European manufacturers in the various countries. These were attributed to the lack of cross-border distribution and marketing networks, brand loyalty and the variety of customer requirements in the different markets. It was felt that these features, together with the high market shares, deterred new entrants and made imports into the French market unlikely. The parties disagreed that France formed a distinct geographical market but the Advisory Committee supported the Commission's view.[14]

Some markets are likely to remain local or national because of the nature of the activity and they have been treated as such. In *Promodes–Dirsa*, a merger of two groups with retail activities in Spain, the market was considered local, as in the more recent German retailing merger, *Spar–Dansk Supermarked*. In the latter case, the market was defined in terms of travel time, with other stores within a 20-minute car journey considered to form part of the same market. Transport costs may continue to limit the scope of some markets despite improvements in infrastructure, as in *VIAG-Continental Can*, where the national market was considered relevant.

Dominance and Effective Competition

Once the market has been defined, the Commission investigates whether a dominant position has been created or strengthened by the merger. It is not clear from the regulation whether the requirement to show a dominant position has been created or strengthened 'as a result of which effective competition would be significantly impeded' is to be interpreted as a single test of dominance, as in article 86, or whether the effective competition requirement constitutes an additional legal test (see Venit, 1990; Langeheine, 1991). In practice, the decisions do not usually deal with these aspects separately and it was not until the *ATR–de Havilland* decision in October 1991 that the Commission dealt explicitly with effective competition as a separate test requiring a dynamic assessment of dominance. Although this two-step approach may have been a new departure from a legal perspective, the assessment of changing competitive conditions had formed part of previous investigations; however, the emphasis on dynamic competition resulted in a more detailed treatment of potential entry in *ATR–de Havilland* than seen in the earlier cases.

In assessing dominance, the market shares of the merging companies are quantified as a first step. There is a presumption in the recitals to the regulation that combined shares of less than 25 per cent will normally raise no serious concerns and the Commission has shown itself willing to dispense with detailed analysis in such cases. These arise because the reference criteria are based on the size of the firms involved rather than the size or market share represented by the transaction itself. Where a high market share exists, there is no presumption that it will lead to a dominant position and, instead, this depends on the analysis of the other features of the case.

The size and importance of the remaining competitors plays a key part in determining whether actual competition will be sufficiently strong to prevent the merging companies acting independently. The existence of companies with similar shares to the merged firm is regarded as an indicator of their ability to influence its behaviour and prevent independence of action, an approach which has some empirical support (see Kwoka and Ravenscraft, 1986). This strength is assessed in terms of relative financial position and practical ability to increase sales, as well as relative market shares.

The approach is evident in *Renault–Volvo*, the first case the Commission considered, where the main reason for clearing the merger in the truck market was the existence of other well-established suppliers with their own distribution and service networks. This was seen as making it 'unlikely that Renault and Volvo will have the power to behave to an appreciable extent independently of these competitors or gain an appreciable influence on the determination of prices without losing market share'.[15] This was a complex case involving both the bus and truck market and, in view of the very high market shares created in some markets (for example, Renault accounted for nearly 70 per cent of the bus market in France and Volvo held 64 per cent in the UK), it seems surprising that this transaction was cleared after initial scrutiny.

There has been considerable controversy in the literature about the degree of active competition which can be expected among firms in tightly oligopolistic markets. The traditional view, stemming from work by Bain (1951), was that collusive pricing behaviour is more likely in highly concentrated industries, resulting in higher profitability to the detriment of the consumer. Attempts to test for a relationship between concentration and profitability have had mixed results and, more recently, the difficulties that oligopolists face in co-ordinating their behaviour have been stressed. Although dominant firm structures may pose a greater threat to competition than tight oligopolies, there is some evidence to suggest the possibility of tacit collusion rather than active competition with market leaders in such situations (see, for example, Utton, 1986).

Under the merger regulation, dominance has been treated as characteristic of a single firm. This is reflected in the merger decisions; they mention concentration of the market and the implications of oligopolistic structures only exceptionally. However, mergers which reduce competition in tightly oligopolistic markets have caused concern. For example, the possibility of co-ordinated behaviour was referred to in *Varta–Bosch* in considering the replacement battery market in Spain, where the market share of the new entity would have been 44.5 per cent. The Commission noted that 'The existence of an equally strong competitor, Tudor SA, could lead for several reasons to alignment of the behaviour of both competitors'.[16] There were no other large firms in the Spanish market to counter this but, after an oral hearing (of which no details are given), the Commission dropped its objections. One can only speculate that this may have been because of the difficulty of dealing with the problem under the existing case law.

In future, it seems likely that the interpretation of the regulation's scope may be extended to the creation or strengthening of strong oligopolies in mature markets with high entry barriers. The most likely route towards achieving this within the existing framework would be to extend the interpretation of dominance to multi-firm or joint dominance. An indication that this interpretation is being considered is given by the following extract from a speech by the Competition Commissioner in October 1991:

> It is my belief that the concept of dominance in Article 2 of the Regulation covers oligopolistic dominance. If a merger or acquisition creates or reinforces a market structure on which price collusion or price parallelism between companies is highly likely, that concentration should be considered incompatible with common market.
> (Brittan, 1991)

The Commission has already made several attempts to introduce the concept of joint dominance in other aspects of competition policy. Most notably, it was applied under article 86 in *Italian Flat Glass* where three members of a tight oligopoly who had allegedly engaged in a price fixing and quota cartel were, as a result of this, also held to have abused a jointly held dominant position. However, the producers appealed to the Court of First Instance which found in their favour and annulled the decision (in its judgment of 10 March 1992). The Commission's arguments were not well developed and, as the article 86 joint-dominance finding was an adjunct of proceedings under article 85, it was affected by the Court judgment against the latter. Although not establishing a useful precedent, the case is unlikely to deter the Commission from acting against collective dominance in future when it finds a case that appears sufficiently strong to survive legal challenge. Even if the concept of collective dominance is accepted in dealing with European mergers, it will still give less scope for dealing with oligopoly problems under the regulation than the UK or German legislation.

Market definition, the calculation of market shares and the position of actual competitors typically receive most attention in the decisions, but other features mentioned in the appraisal criteria can play a significant part in the assessment. Rather than taking each of them separately, their treatment is best discussed with reference to particular cases. Some of the decisions have raised concerns about the role of non-competition considerations but they have all ostensibly been taken on competition grounds and references to efficiency considerations, benefits to the economy or economic progress are very rare. In fact, little information is generally given about cost structures, although this would help in assessing entry barriers. In view of the importance now attached to entry barriers as a determinant of monopoly power in the industrial economics literature and the significance of their role in merger policy elsewhere (for example the United States), one would expect more systematic analysis of this aspect to be presented in decisions on large European mergers, particularly those in which full proceedings have been opened.

Proceedings were opened in *Alcatel–Telettra* because of the high combined market shares created by the acquisition of control in Telettra by Alcatel. This affected the Spanish telecommunication line transmission market, where the merged firm would have an 81 per cent share, and the microwave equipment market (83 per cent). Firms established in other European markets, such as Siemens, claimed there were barriers to competition; they pointed out that the directive on public procurement will not apply to Spain until 1996 and that Telefonica, the Spanish telecommunications operator and main buyer, traditionally purchased from local suppliers and also held a 10 per cent stake in Telettra and 21 per cent of Alcatel. Despite the high market shares, the Commission cleared the merger largely on the strength of potential competition and the power of the major buyer, although the vertical links with Telefonica were seen as posing a possible barrier to new entry.

In order to obtain clearance, Alcatel agreed to buy the shares of Telefonica held in Alcatel and Telettra, thereby severing the financial links which may have given the two companies privileged market access. In addition, Telefonica promised to open the market to other providers of transmission equipment, agreeing to clarify its procedures for technical approval and to ensure that an industrial presence in Spain was no longer a decisive factor in awarding contracts, although back-up support in the country would still be necessary. On this basis, it was argued that the two main actual competitors would be able to increase their supply in the Spanish market and companies established elsewhere in Europe would face no significant barrier to new entry. This decision appears to have been reached on competition grounds alone and gave an early indication of the willingness of the Commission to accept undertakings as the basis for clearance.

Two companies based outside the EC were investigated in *Tetra Pak–Alfa-Laval*. This case concerned the proposed aquisition by Tetra Pak of Switzerland, the largest manufacturer of liquid packaging machines in Europe, of Alfa-Laval of Sweden, a major producer of dairy and food processing equipment. Tetra Pak already had over 90 per cent of the market for aseptic carton packaging machines and its dominance was already being investigated under article 86, so the decision to investigate this merger was not unexpected. Unlike the article 86 investigation which resulted in a heavy fine, this transaction was cleared without conditions.

The ability of the enlarged firm to provide a full range of both processing and packaging machinery was not expected to create an undue advantage over competitors as the two types of machines were regarded as distinct in both technical and commercial terms. In addition, it was felt unlikely that the merger would affect potential entry into Tetra Pak's markets, although the likelihood of entry by Alfa Laval in the absence of the merger was not specifically discussed in the decision. So far, eleven decisions have involved non-EC firms alone and this is the only one in which full proceedings have been opened, so the Commission's powers if findings are adverse in such cases have still to be tested.

In the two cases concerning the market for starter batteries where proceedings were opened (*Magneti Marelli–CEAc* and *Varta–Bosch*) the original equipment market was separated from the replacement battery market and individual countries were taken as the geographical market, as discussed earlier. The decision on the aquisition of Alcatel's battery operation, CEAc, by Magneti Marelli, a subsidiary of Fiat, focused on the French market, where the new enterprise would have a 60 per cent share. This was seen as creating a dominant position, owing to the gap in relation to its nearest large competitor which had a 40 per cent share, its financial strength and its greater access to the relatively mature French market which was thought unlikely to attract intense competition. Fiat agreed to reduce its shareholding in Magneti Marelli's French subsidiary to 10 per cent within an agreed period and not to increase it again without the Commission's agreement (as well as reducing its representation on the board). This concession meant that the two largest French firms in the starter battery market were no longer regarded as merging and the transaction was cleared.

Having examined this case, the decision to examine *Varta–Bosch*, a concentrative joint venture between two German companies in the starter battery market, was predictable. The Commission rejected the parties' view that the EC was the relevant market and focused on the proposed joint venture's 40 per cent share of the German market. The transaction was approved after Varta agreed to end its co-operative links with Deta–Mareg, which had a market share of 10 per cent, and to ensure no overlapping board membership. These obligations did not have to be met until 1993. Another important factor in clearance was the acquisition of the German battery manufacturer, Sonnenschein by Fiat–Magneti Marelli, which would become Varta–Bosch's second largest competitor. The Commission concluded: 'as a result, it is now at least doubtful if a market share of 44 per cent and the current lead over the next competitor is sufficient to prove a dominant position'.

This decision seems to raise more questions than conceded by the

Commission and the wording of the decision is unusually hesitant. The preliminary draft decision did not find favour with the Advisory Committee although the decision was not altered. A minority challenged the basis of the case: they viewed the acquisition of Sonnenschein by Fiat as suggesting a European rather than a national market, while a majority felt the decision was too lenient because the structural changes would be insufficient to alter the dominant position of the proposed joint venture.[17]

The published opinion does not give the reasons for this conclusion. However, the presence of entry barriers limiting potential competition seems an important feature of this market, and this received scant attention in the decision. The Commission simply notes the existence of market-related barriers as evidenced by the difficulty of establishing a significant market presence in any of the five target member states without acquiring a national company or an existing plant, and it refers to Tudor's unsuccessful attempt to enter the German market on its own.

Whatever the defects of the analyses, these first cases appear to have been decided on competition grounds and suggest a relatively lenient approach, especially in view of the Commission's readiness to accept compromise solutions rather than banning anti-competitive transactions outright. At the beginning of the second year, the fifth full case (*ATR – de Havilland*) showed that the Regulation would be used to prohibit mergers and rekindled the controversy about the role of industrial policy in merger decisions. In view of the likely importance of this case in the evolution of EC merger control, it will be examined in greater detail.

A previous merger in the aerospace industry, between Aerospatiale of France and Messerschmitt-Bolkow-Blohm (MBB) had been permitted after initial scrutiny. This case raises some concerns about the role of industrial policy: the proposed joint venture would have 52 per cent of the civil helicopter market, a considerable lead over its closest rival which was a US company. The merger was cleared after initial scrutiny largely on the basis of the EC producers' views that cuts in US military spending would lead to more intense competition in the civilian market. However, no evidence is presented to substantiate these claims. It is possible that full proceedings may have been avoided to prevent a full-scale discussion of the non-competition issues which this merger would have been likely to provoke.

The only merger to be banned to date concerned the bid by two state-owned aircraft manufacturers, Aerospatiale of France and Alenia of Italy, for de Havilland which was a Canadian division of Boeing. Through their joint venture, ATR, the bidders were the world and leading European manufacturer of regional turboprop (commuter) aircraft, and de Havilland was second largest in both markets. In its analysis of the likely effects on competition, the Commission divided the industry into three separate markets according to seat capacity – 20–39 seats, 40–59 seats and 60–70 seats, as discussed earlier. The Commission found ATR's position in both the world and EC markets would be strengthened in a number of ways if the merger was allowed to proceed. The only existing competitive overlap between the parties was in the 40–59 seat market where the merger would result in de Havilland being eliminated as one of ATR's main competitors, raising ATR's share of the world market in this capacity range from 45 per cent to 64 per cent (72 per cent in the EC) and increasing its lead over Fokker and Saab. De Havilland did not compete in the top segment of the industry but had plans to introduce a new, larger aircraft; so acquisition by ATR could be seen as eliminating a potential competitor in the faster-growing 60–70 seat market where ATR's world share was 76 per cent (74 per cent in the EC). The acquisition of de Havilland would give a 25 per cent share of the world market in the smallest size segment where it was not previously represented and the widening of its product base would mean that ATR would be the only commuter plane manufacturer providing a comprehensive product range. This was regarded as a significant marketing advantage because individual airlines tend to buy different-sized aircraft for their fleet as a whole. In earlier cases, the Commission had shown itself willing to accept substantially higher post-merger market shares because of other industry features which were regarded as limiting monopoly power. In this case, the Commission took the view that a dominant position would be created in both the EC and the world as the high market shares of the joint venture would not be counterbalanced by the remaining competitors or the bargaining power of buyers.

The Commission's assessment of the way in which competition might develop if the joint venture were allowed played an important part in its decision to prohibit the merger by establishing that besides the effect on dominance, competition would be 'significantly impeded'. New entry was seen as unlikely, partly because of the maturity of the market and its expected downturn by the time new entrants would be able to enter. This is in contrast to a fairly relaxed attitude taken by the Commission in other cases towards high shares in growing, high-technology markets where strong positions were regarded as raising no 'serious doubts' because they were likely to be transient (for example *Digital–Kienzle* and *Digital– Philips*). A very firm stance was taken in the *ATR–de Havilland* case regarding possible efficiency and marketing gains. These were viewed as detrimental to the consumers because of the likely effect on industrial structure; existing competitors were expected to find it harder to compete and to lose share, perhaps being driven out of the industry completely.

It is difficult to see how the joint venture could have been restructured to avoid these charges and it was prohibited as incompatible with the Common Market.[18] The decision to block the *ATR–de Havilland* transaction provides the first evidence of the Commission's willingness to use the regulation to prevent a merger that would greatly reduce competition. This decision attracted widespread criticism. Some of the criticisms concerned the narrowness of the product-market definition and the possibility that the potential power of the joint venture had been exaggerated. The product definition according to seat capacity was challenged by ATR and by a minority of the Commission who considered that the resulting high market shares were misleading.[19] However, an examination of the detailed evidence presented in the full text of the decision tends to support the Commission's view.

It appears that the range of commuter aircraft is not evenly spread throughout all seat sizes between 20 and 70; instead, there are distinct clusters of aircraft around 30 seats, 50 seats and 65 seats. The main factor determining an airline's fleet requirement is the number of seats required to suit its routes, so buyers focus on the choice within a particular capacity range and demand substitutability between them is generally limited. Supply-side substitutability is also limited; for example, the Commission found that it would take more than 3–4 years for existing manufacturers to switch production from producing 30-seat to 50-seat aircraft. Having defined the required capacity, the relative cost of acquiring the aircraft is only one factor in buyers' choice; direct operating costs, technical and other aircraft features are important too.

In any case, the market definition adopted does not appear to have been crucial to the outcome of this enquiry. Considerations other than the immediate impact on market position played an important part in the decision and, even if the commuter aircraft industry had been taken as a whole, market share would still have been significantly raised by the merger. For example, figures based on the number of firm orders, weighted by the standard number of seats, show the combined world market share post-merger would be 50 per cent (ATR 29 per cent and de Havilland 21 per cent), more than two-and-a-half times that of Saab, its nearest competitor, and the EC share would be 65 per cent (ATR 49 per cent and de Havilland 16 per cent). Alternative measures of capacity give similar results.

The main objection to the *ATR–de Havilland* decision was not concerned with potential weaknesses in the analysis of competition but with industrial policy aspects of the merger which it was felt had been given insufficient weight. A minority of the Commission seems to have favoured the merger as a means of building up the European aerospace industry, despite the anti-competitive effects. The Italian and French ministers were unwilling to accept the Commissioners' majority view and demanded a re-examination of the case. The Commission refused this, stating that any appeal must be to the European Court. The European Parliament acknowledged that the decision accorded with the regulation, but called for the regulation to be amended to take account of industrial, regional and other non-competition issues. The powers of the Commissioner to decide whether to initiate full proceedings were also called into question by the Commissioner with responsibility for industrial policy, Mr Martin Bangemann. This challenge was successfully resisted, with virtually unchanged procedures approved until the end of 1992, when the term of the current Commission expires. It remains to be seen whether the Commission can continue to fend off the renewed calls for a broader-based analysis of merger cases.

The Main Exemptions

The scope for the national authorities to deal with mergers with a Community dimension is still relatively untested, although initial experience suggests that the Commission will take a firm stance on possible referrals. No exceptions have been made under article 21(3) and the Commission has made it clear to the UK authorities that one possible non-competition concern, the state ownership of a bidder, will not be considered valid grounds for referral. Only one of the three requests made under article 9 (concern about competition in a distinct market) has been granted.

This was a request by the UK authorities to examine *Tarmac–Steetley*, a joint venture in the building materials industry. The Commission agreed to refer the effects on bricks and clay tiles to the UK Monopolies and Mergers Commission. The request would have been very hard to refuse in view of the high market shares created and the absence of international competition. Indeed, the brick market was the example usually cited as suitable for exemption when article 9 was being debated initially. However, the proposed joint venture was subsequently abandoned and proceedings terminated as a result of the successful bid for Steetley by Redland, which avoided a reference to the Monopolies and Mergers Commission by making divestment undertakings.

The Commission opened proceedings itself in *Varta–Bosch* to investigate the effects on competition in the German market rather than agreeing to a request to refer it back. In *Alcatel–AEG Kabel*, the Commission rejected the German *Bundeskartellamt*'s view that the proposed merger caused concern in two of the five markets affected, telecommunication cables and power cables, about competition in a distinct market and again cleared the merger after initial scrutiny. In this decision, the telecommunications market was treated by the Commission as Community-wide because more open procurement policies had already been established and technical standards harmonized. AEG's business was primarily in Germany and, under this wider definition of the market, AEG had only a 3 per cent share, which would increase to 18 per cent post-merger. In contrast, the market for power cables was seen as national due to differences in technical standards and low levels of international trade so the controversy centred on this market.

German law contains a presumption against mergers where the three firm concentration levels would be over 50 per cent; in this case concentration increased from 48 per cent to 58 per cent as a result of the merger. However, the Commission ruled that there had been effective competition in the supply of power cables prior to the merger due to the strength of the major buyers. A price fall of about 20 per cent in the previous decade was cited in evidence, although the significance of this is difficult to assess in the absence of information about costs or relative performance elsewhere. The bargaining power of buyers and imminent changes in procurement procedures were also seen as safeguarding the position in future. The countervailing power of buyers had been an important consideration in clearing other mergers (such as *Renault–Volvo*) but little evidence is typically presented to show how strongly it is actually exercised, so it is possible that this constraint on the sellers' power may be more apparent than real. The tension between the Commission and the German authorities in the treatment of *Alcatel–AEG Kabel* highlights the potential conflicts in approach due to the differences in merger control under EC and national laws. The Commission may try, in time, to deal with oligopoly problems under the regulation, as discussed earlier, but it is likely to want a more clear-cut case than this to use as a test case.

Although the Commission has been reluctant to refer mergers back to the national authorities, the existence of the exceptions detracts from the attempt to establish a 'one-stop shop' under the regulation. Where firms fear the possibility of member state intervention, they tend to consult with the national authorities to see if they are likely to request a referral; so in practice they often deal with two authorities in the initial stages. National competition authorities may also wish to review cases to see if there is any need to take action. In the UK, for example, the guidance booklet prepared by the Office of Fair Trading (1991) suggests that UK companies should notify the OFT of any merger proposals which fall within the scope of EC legislation, and this has been the practice. In addition, the recent Select Committee on Takeovers and Mergers (House of Commons, 1991) recommended that the UK government should 'press vigorously' for jurisdiction over mergers within the exceptions of the European control.

Many cross-border mergers are still dealt with under the very varied national regulations of the member countries because they fall below the high thresholds that the Commission accepted initially in order to get agreement to the regulation. There are plans to extend coverage by reducing the thresholds from ECU 5 billion to 2 billion and from ECU 250 million to 75 million respectively when they are reviewed in 1993. Although a change can be made by majority vote of the Commission it is likely to be resisted by the member states with well-established merger controls of their own, especially if the Commission is regarded as having allowed industrial policy considerations or political expediency to influence its decisions during the initial period.

9.4 CONCLUSION

The lack of specific provisions to deal with mergers at Community level was a serious gap in EC competition policy and the adoption of the new regulation was generally welcomed. At the same time, a number of concerns were expressed about its likely operation, many of which centred on the actual appraisal of mergers. In particular, it was feared that the timescales would prove too tight, that the exemption clauses would result in uncertainties about jurisdiction, leading to national authorities vying with the Commission for control, and that the Commissioners would be influenced by broader considerations as much as by the competition test underpinning the regulation. In addition, the appraisal criteria gave the Commission a good deal of discretion, and there were concerns about how strictly they would be applied.

The regulation has now been in operation for just 18 months. This is a relatively short time in which to reach any firm conclusions about performance, especially as policy is still evolving. Procedurally the regulation appears to have been successful, with all 79 decisions to date reached within the time-scales allowed. The exemptions are relatively untested; only one case out of three article 9 requests has been referred back to the authorities, suggesting the continued reluctance of the Commission to cede power. Uncertainties about jurisdiction remain and companies often consult initally both nationally and in Brussels.

There are still uncertainties about the way in which the appraisal criteria will be applied in individual cases and the conditions which will lead to full proceedings. In particular, the treatment of tight oligopolies remains unresolved, although it seems likely that the interpretation of the regulation will be extended in the future to include joint dominance. Although other features have played an important part in the decisions, the emphasis in many of the investigations to date appears to have been on establishing market definitions and calculating market shares and the strength of existing competitors. The economic analysis would be strengthened by more detailed treatment of entry barriers to aid the dynamic assessment of competition, as in the *ATR– de Havilland* case.

In the first year, the regulation operated smoothly and in a fairly uncontentious way. The approach appeared fairly lenient and the Commission was prepared to accept undertakings from firms to remove anti-competitive features of their transactions as a precondition for clearance rather than ban them outright. In view of the strength with which the case for an effective merger control at Community level had been advocated, it is surprising how few of the small number of mergers falling within its scope were fully investigated and that none of these mergers were actually prohibited.

The prohibition in the *ATR – de Havilland* case at the beginning of the second year showed that the regulation has some force against anti-competitive mergers. It also brought to the surface the underlying tension caused by differing views of the aims of competition policy – whether to ensure competitive market structures as the best guarantee of international competitiveness or to allow the build-up of large European firms. This basic difference in approach had delayed the adoption of the merger regulation in the first place and the compromises necessary to reach agreement were reflected in its rather ambiguous wording.

Some of the mergers on the scale considered under the regulation are bound to raise equally or even more-sensitive issues in future. The Commission has already been put under intense pressure to allow broader considerations to influence merger policy and this may prove difficult to resist. Unless the Commission does manage to keep to the competition test, there is likely to be very strong opposition to further extension in the scope of the regulation from countries with competition-based national merger controls.

APPENDIX: EC MERGER CONTROL REGULATION DECISIONS

Decisions to 20:03:92

(A) Outside Scope of Regulation

Date Notified	Parties	Date of 6(a) decision
08.11.90	Arjomari-Prioux–Wiggins Teape	10.12.90
04.01.91	Baxter-Nestlé–Salvia	06.02.91
22.05.91	Apollinaris–Schweppes	24.06.91
21.06.91	Elf–Enterprise	22.07.91
30.10.91	Cereol–Continentale Italiana	03.12.91
27.11.91	Mediobanca–Generali	19.12.91
27.11.91	Sunrise	13.01.92
16.01.92	BSN-Nestlé–Cokoladovy	17.02.92

(B) No Serious Doubts Raised

Date Notified	Parties	Date of 6(b) decision
05.10.90	Renault–Volvo	07.11.90[a]
19.10.90	AG–AMEV	21.11.90
21.12.90	Dresdner Bank–Banque Nationale	04.02.91
30.10.90	ICI–Tioxide	28.11.90
15.11.90	Promodes–Dirsa	17.12.90
20.11.90	Cargill–Unilever	20.12.90
26.11.90	Mitsubishi–Union Carbide	04.01.91
03.12.90	Matsushita–MCA	10.01.91
07.12.90	AT&T–NCR	18.01.91
03.01.91	Digital–Kienzle	22.02.91
07.01.91	Fiat Geotech–Ford New Holland	08.02.91
21.01.91	Asko–Omni	21.02.91
23.01.91	Aerospatiale–MBB	25.02.91
06.02.91	Kyowa–Saitama Banks	07.03.91
22.02.91	Otto–Grattan	21.03.91
22.03.91	Usinor–ASD	29.04.91
22.03.91	Elf–Ertoil	29.04.91
25.03.91	Redoute–Empire Stores	25.04.91
09.04.91	Asko–Jacobs–ADIA	16.05.91

25.04.91	ConAgra–IDEA	30.05.91
29.04.91	RVI–VBC–Heuliez	03.06.91
30.04.91	VIAG–Continental Can	06.06.91
03.05.91	Sanofi–Sterling Drug	10.06.91
13.05.91	Elf–Occidental	13.06.91
16.05.91	Elf–BC–CEPSA	18.06.91
21.05.91	Pechiney–Usinor-Sacilor	24.06.91
27.05.91	Nissan–Nissan	28.06.91
28.05.91	Dräger–IBM–HMP	28.06.91
10.06.91	Lyonnaise des Eaux Dumez–Brochier	11.07.91
14.06.91	ICL–Nokia Data	17.07.91
18.06.91	EDS–SD-Scicon	19.07.91
28.06.91	BP–Petromed	29.07.91
04.07.91	Eridania–ISI	30.07.91
18.07.91	Kelt–American Express and 7 others	20.08.91
24.07.91	BNP–Dresdner Bank	26.08.91
30.07.91	Digital–Philips	02.09.91
07.08.91	ABC–Generale des Eaux–Canal+ –W.H. Smith TV	10.09.91
09.08.91	Delta Air Lines–Pan Am	13.09.91
22.08.91	Mannesmann–Boge	20.09.91
12.09.91	Metallgesellschaft–Feldmühle	14.10.91
16.09.91	Paribas–MTH–MBH	17.10.91
20.09.91	Thomson–Pilkington	23.10.91
23.09.91	BankAmerica–Security Pacific	24.10.91
07.10.91	UAP–TransAtlantic–Sun Life	11.11.91
07.10.91	Metallgesellschaft–Safic-Alcan	11.11.91
28.10.91	TNT–Canada Post and 4 others	02.12.91
06.11.91	Alcatel–AEG Kabel	18.12.91
06.11.91	Lucas–Eaton	10.12.91
12.11.91	Mannesmann–VDO	13.12.91
15.11.91	Eurocom–RSCG	18.12.91
19.11.91	Ingersoll Rand–Dresser	18.12.91
19.11.91	Repsol-Petromed–CAMPSA	19.12.91
19.11.91	Viag–EB	19.12.91
19.11.91	Courtaulds–SNIA	19.12.91
19.11.91	Gambogi–COGEI	19.12.91
29.11.91	Saab–Ericsson Space	13.01.92
05.12.91	Volvo–Atlas	14.01.92
10.12.91	Inchcape–IEP	21.01.92
11.12.91	Ericsson–Kolbe	22.01.92
16.12.91	Schweizer Ruck–ELVIA	14.01.92

20.12.91	Spar–Dansk Supermarked	03.02.92
20.12.91	Tarmac–Steetley	12.02.92[b]
06.01.92	Grand Metropolitan–Cinzano	07.02.92
10.01.92	James River–Rayne	13.02.92
22.01.92	Torraspapel–Sarrio	24.02.92
30.01.92	Ifint–Exor	02.03.92

(C) Full proceedings

Date Notified	Parties	Proceedings opened 6(1)c cleared 8(2)
11.12.90	Magneti Marelli–CEAc	21.01.91 30.05.91[c]
11.12.90	Alcatel–Telettra	21.01.91 12.04.91[c]
18.02.91	Tetra Pak–Alfa-Laval	19.03.91 19.07.91
25.02.91	Varta–Bosch	12.04.91 31.07.91[c]

		Proceedings opened 9(1)c banned 8(3)
13.05.91	Aerospatiale-Alenia– de Havilland	12.06.91 02.10.91

[a] part cleared under 6(a)
[b] article 9 referral
[c] cleared subject to undertakings

Cases Outstanding

14.11.91	Wagons Lits–Accor	16.12.91[d]
20.02.92	Henkel–Nobel	
25.02.92	Nestlé–Source Perrier	
05.03.92	Asscurazieni–Banco Central Hispano-americano	
11.03.92	Flachglas–VEGLA	
16.03.92	Banesto–Totta	
17.03.92	BSN–Exor	
20.03.92	Thorn-EMI–Virgin Music	
20.03.92	Eureko–Centraal Beheer–Topdanmark–WASA	

[d] Proceedings opened

NOTES

1. I wish to thank Graham Atkinson of the Office of Fair Trading for his encouragement in the early stages of this work, and the School of Management, University of Bath, for a grant to support research into European competition policy.
2. Council Regulation (EEC) No. 4064/89 of 21 December 1989, *Official Journal*, L395/ 1, 1989.
3. For simplicity, the term 'merger' is used throughout to refer to all concentrations, unless otherwise specified.
4. For a good overview of the complex legal issues involved in the first two steps, see Reynolds (1991); Siragusa and Subiotto (1991); and Venit (1990). These also contain useful commentaries on the substantive appraisal from a legal perspective; the first two references consider the early cases.
5. Under the new European Economic Area Agreement, the scope of the regulation will not change, but in assessing compatibility the Commission will need to look at the effect within the Community and in any substantial part of the EEA as well.
6. *Alcatel–Telettra* (1991), *Official Journal* [in future referred to as *OJ*], L122,. 48–55 *Magnetti Marelli–CEAc* (1991), *OJ*, L222, 38–41. *Tetra Pak–Alfa-Laval* (1991), *OJ*, L290, 35–43. *Varta–Bosch* (1991), *OJ*, L320, 26–34. *ATR–de Havilland* (1991), *OJ*, L334, 42–61.
7. Most of the unpublished decisions were available in English.
8. In *Metallgesellschaft–Alcan*, for example, the world latex market was dealt with in one page, despite the relatively high market share involved.
9. Case 85/76 *Hoffman-La Roche* v. *Commission*, 3 CMLR 211 (1979).
10. Form CO, section 5.
11. Opinion of the Advisory Committee, *Varta–Bosch* (1991), *OJ*, C302, 6.
12. Case 6/72, Judgment of 21 February 1973.
13. See note 10.
14. See note 6.
15. *Renault–Volvo* (1991) unpublished decision. Extract from paragraph 14.
16. See note 5.
17. See note 10.
18. De Havilland was subsequently acquired in January 1992 by Bombardier (51 per cent) and the Ontario Government (49 per cent).
19. Opinion of the Advisory Committee, *ATR–de Havilland* (1991), *OJ*, C314, 7.

REFERENCES

Banks, K. (1988); 'Mergers and partial mergers under EEC law', in *United States and Common Market Antitrust and Trade Laws*, ed. B. Hawk (New York: Matthew Bender) 373–427.

Bain, J.S. (1951): 'Relation of profit rate to industry concentration: American manufacturing 1936–1940', *Quarterly Journal of Economics*, **65**, 243–64.

Bishop, M. (1990): 'European or national? The EEC's new merger regulation', in *Continental Mergers are Different: Strategy and Policy for 1992*, ed. J.A. Fairburn and J. Kay (London: London Business School Centre for Business Strategy Report) 105–33.

Bright, C. (1991): 'The European merger control legislation: do member states still have an independent role in merger control? Part 1', *European Competition Law Review*, **4**, 139–47; Part 2, *European Competition Law Review*, **5**, 184–93.

Brittan, Sir L. (1990): 'The law and policy of merger control in the EEC', *European Law Review*, October, **15**, 351–7.

—— (1991): 'Competition Policy and Mergers', *Address to the Centre for European Policy Studies*, Brussels, 28 October (mimeo).

Council Regulation (EEC) No. 4064/89 of 21 December 1989 on the Control of Concentrations between Undertakings, *Official Journal* (1989) L395/1.

George, K.D. and A.P. Jacquemin (1992): 'Dominant firms and mergers', *Economic Journal*, **102** (410) 148–57.

House of Commons Trade and Industry Committee (1991): *Takeovers and Mergers, First Report* (London: Her Majesty's Stationery Office).

Jacquemin, A.P. (1990): 'Mergers and European policy', in *Mergers and Competition Policy in the European Community*, ed. P.H. Admiraal (Oxford: Basil Blackwell) 3–38.

——, P. Buigues and F. Ilzkovitz (1989): 'Horizontal mergers and competition policy in the European Community', *European Economy*, **40**, May, 1–95.

Kwoka, J.E. and D.J. Ravenscraft (1986): 'Cooperation v. rivalry: price cost margins by line of business', *Economica*, **53**, 351–63.

Langeheine, B. (1991): 'Substantive review under the EEC merger regulation', in *International Mergers and Joint Ventures*, ed. B. Hawk (New York: Transnational Juris Publications) 481–502.

Lever, J. (1991): 'Substantive review under the EEC merger regulation: a private perspective', in *International Mergers and Joint Ventures*, ed. B. Hawk (New York: Transnational Juris Publications) 503–17.

Office of Fair Trading (1991): *Mergers: A Guide to the Proceedings under the Fair Trading Act, 1973* (London: Her Majesty's Stationery Office).

Overbury, C. (1991): 'First experiences of European merger control', *European Law Review*, **16**, 79–88.

Reynolds, M.J. (1991): 'The first year of enforcement under the EEC merger regulation – a private view', unpublished address to the Fordham Corporate Law Institute, New York, October (mimeo).

Siragusa, M. and R. Subiotto (1991): 'The EEC merger control regulation: the Commission's evolving case law', *Common Market Law Review*, **28**, 877–934.

Utton, M.A. (1986): *Profits and the Stability of Monopoly, National Institute of Economic and Social Research Occasional Papers* no. 38 (Cambridge: Cambridge University Press).

Venit, J. (1990): 'The "merger" control regulation: Europe comes of age . . . or Caliban's dinner', *Common Market Law Review*, **27**, 7–50.

—— (1991): 'The evaluation of concentrations under regulation 4064/89: the nature of the beast', in *International Mergers and Joint Ventures*, ed. B. Hawk (New York: Transnational Juris Publications) 519–60.

10. Corporate Research and Development Strategies: The Influence of Firm, Industry and Country Factors on the Decentralization of R&D

Mark Casson and Satwinder Singh[1]

10.1 INTRODUCTION

This chapter analyses survey data on large corporations to compare two different approaches to the decentralization of research and development (R&D). *Internationalization* is an approach in which overseas laboratories are given a small and usually subordinate role in corporate research activity; whereas *globalization* involves a greater commitment to overseas research based on a systematic division of labour between laboratories in different countries. The evidence suggests that internationalization is usually motivated by the need to support established overseas production and marketing operations. Globalization evolves from internationalization in those industries where global marketing strategies and internationally rationalized production are appropriate – principally chemicals, pharmaceuticals and engineering.

The first part of the paper (sections 10.1–10.5) shows how the concept of globalization has evolved as a strategic response to changes in the policy environment, and to increasing pressure from corporate shareholders to raise the private returns from R&D. The discussion ranges widely, to include factors such as Japanese competition, shortening product life-cycles and the influence of mergers and acquisitions on the organization of R&D. The second part (sections 10.6–10.9) presents some new statistical results which corroborate and amplify results obtained from earlier studies. They suggest that firm-level, industry-level and parent-country factors are all important in the growth of overseas R&D. Parent-country factors are particularly relevant to government policy-makers. Relative to US and Northern European firms, UK firms feel that they derive little advantage from their indigenous science base. This is associated with a weighting of UK overseas research towards low-technology industries, noted in earlier studies. Southern European firms seem to invest abroad when as 'national champions' they feel obliged to keep up with the leading international competitors in their industries. This suggests that both science policy and industrial policy in the parent country are potentially important influences on corporate attitudes to overseas R&D.

The final part (section 10.10) speculates on the future of overseas R&D. In the light of the preceding discussion, it identifies three factors which are likely to govern the spread of globalized R&D: trade policy, telecommunications, and organizational restructuring in multinational firms.

It is argued that the globalization of R&D will become more important during the 1990s because the emergence of regional trading blocs will require global innovations to draw on local knowledge and scientific expertise in each of the major blocs. Improvements in telecommunications are also likely to remove some of the existing obstacles to the geographical decentralization of research. Finally, the limitations posed by large-firm bureaucracy are likely to be addressed by greater use of scientists as internal entrepreneurs, maintaining responsibility for their projects from the drawing-board through to the market-place. Despite the growth in global R&D, however, it is likely to remain a large-firm phenomenon.

10.2 GLOBALIZATION IN HISTORICAL PERSPECTIVE

The postwar period has witnessed significant advances in international economic integration. In the 1950s and 1960s the liberalization of trade under GATT rules was a major driving force. In the 1960s and 1970s the development of the eurobond markets facilitated the financing of foreign investments – particularly by US companies. As a result, domestic firms in many countries faced new sources of competition from imports and from the local operations of foreign-owned firms. During the 1980s deregulation and privatization opened up further sectors – such as utilities and defence industries – to foreign competition. Japanese competition was particularly devastating – at first in motor vehicles but subsequently in consumer electronics, machine tools, optical instruments and so on.

Competition eroded the profits from secure home markets which used to be the basis for long-term funding of R&D. Firms were forced to re-examine their research commitments. Either research productivity was improved, so that innovation was sustained on smaller profit margins, or the firm's products became increasingly obsolete as research budgets were cut, leading to a vicious circle of profit decline culminating in takeover or bankruptcy.

Four main methods of raising research productivity have been used. The first is to develop products for a global market rather than a national one. By thinking in terms of global market share rather than national market share the firm can spread fixed development costs over a larger number of units. The growth of travel and tourism and the spread of satellite broadcasting has encouraged firms to develop heavily advertised global brands targeted on young, middle-income consumers. The second approach is to do less basic research, where private returns are more difficult to appropriate, and concentrate on 'near-market' development instead. The third is to collaborate with a partner firm, particularly in pre-competitive development work. Finally, the firm can simultaneously cut costs and shorten lead times by improving the efficiency with which research is organized within the company.

All these methods have been tried, and all have implications for overseas R&D. But, as indicated above, the implications tend to differ according to the type of research involved. For present purposes, it is convenient to divide R&D into four main categories: basic research; generic development; adaptive development; and technical support.

Basic research is a rather difficult concept to define. Some R&D managers publicly deny that they carry out any basic research, simply because they believe that shareholders do not approve of expenditure of this kind. Yet some of the research that they classify as development might well be regarded as basic in the sense that highly qualified researchers are addressing fundamental issues – for example, in developing pharmaceutical products it is usually necessary to improve understanding of the biological mechanisms that the product is intended to control.

The difference between basic industrial research and university research lies in its problem-centred nature and the emphasis on the output of patents and the commercialization of the results. Problem-orientation is even more conspicuous in development work, of course. A distinction is often drawn between product and process development, but the research described in this chapter suggests that this is not as crucial as it might seem. A more relevant distinction is between generic and adaptive development. Generic development is exemplified by the formulation of a new drug; adaptive development might involve investigating different ways of administering the drug – injections, tablets and so on – tailored to local production conditions and standards of health care.

Technical support involves quality control (applied to both inputs and outputs) and the fine-tuning of production equipment to reduce the incidence of breakdown, wear-and-tear and so on. Like adaptive development, technical support involves strong linkages to local operations. Thus, as a firm internationalizes its production operations, those aspects of R&D will tend to be internationalized too.

By contrast, basic research and generic development are instruments of overall corporate strategy. Within the firm, their strongest linkages are likely to be with headquarters. Their links to local production and markets will generally be mediated through adaptive research (see Casson, 1991).

10.3 THE IMPLICATIONS OF GLOBAL STRATEGY FOR PRODUCT DEVELOPMENT

As a project moves from the research to the development stage it quickly becomes more expensive. Moreover, as it moves 'closer to the market', commercial appraisal becomes more stringent. Whilst all projects are promising when they first move into the development stage, many of them will be 'killed off' as they run into unforeseen difficulties. The successful R&D manager will kill off projects that face major difficulties before enormous costs have been incurred in attempting to overcome them (the consequences of failing to do this are only too apparent when politicians or military leaders take these decisions – as in the defence industry).

The traditional approach to product development is captured by the product-cycle theory (Vernon, 1966, 1979) where the product is first developed for a sophisticated home market and then adapted later for overseas markets. This approach has a number of weaknesses.

First, there is a tendency to use domestic customers as 'guinea-pigs'. Not only do they pay a premium price for a novel product, but they help the manufacturer to 'de-bug' the product as well. Customers impatient with the inconveniences of product failure will revert to mature products which are both cheaper and more reliable.

A second problem is that the lag between the product launches in home and overseas markets provides an opportunity for competitors to imitate the product. The Japanese were particularly effective during the 1970s at imitating new products launched in advanced Western markets and then entering third-country markets ahead of the innovator.

Finally, it is inefficient to design a product which will eventually be produced and marketed globally with just the requirements of the home market in mind. Costs of adapting the design to foreign tastes and to less-developed off-shore production locations can be reduced by taking these considerations into account at the outset.

All these objections can be addressed by a global approach in which a standardized product is simultaneously introduced into all leading markets. Where appropriate, the product will have a modular design to facilitate rationalization of assembly and component production. This also allows low-cost differentiation through permutation of components. It is important that the product is perfected before it is introduced for otherwise warranty problems following a global launch will be excessive.

In a global strategy home country laboratories no longer occupy a privileged position. To begin with, the advantages of being close to the customer to carry out warranty work is of limited significance if the product is 'right first time'. It is still useful to be close to the customer for design and trial marketing, but this can now be done in any of the leading markets (and preferably in all of them). In this sense large, wealthy and sophisticated markets such as the US, Germany and Japan attract development work carried out by firms based in smaller countries. There are exceptions, of course: many drugs are still tested in small countries which have good state health and welfare services.

Secondly, because competition in the home market (as well as foreign markets) comes from foreign firms pursuing global strategies, it is important for each firm to have access to the very best scientists. These scientists are often clustered around leading universities, working under the guidance of a few distinguished researchers. Scientific specialists with family commitments are often geographically immobile. They prefer the 'deep' professional labour markets associated with major regional agglomerations of research activity because of the difficulty they would otherwise encounter in finding another employer. If the scientists will not move to the firm then the firm must move to the scientists, and hence laboratories are attracted to centres of major research excellence (Cantwell, 1989, 1991). The status of the home laboratory within the company may be reduced as a result.

10.4   THE ORGANIZATION OF GLOBAL R&D

While global launching gives the innovator the same lead in foreign markets that he has in the home market, it cannot eliminate the problem of imitation altogether. Imitators, too, can adopt a global strategy. To keep ahead of the imitator continuous improvement is required. This encourages an emphasis on incremental rather than discrete innovation, with correspondingly shorter lead times for development work.

The desire to shorten lead times encourages parallel research in different countries. Some research projects are amenable to a division of labour in which constituent projects are hived off and allocated to different laboratories. Even more ambitious is the idea of exploiting differences in time zones to work at a project night and day in laboratories on opposite sides of the world.

Parallel research in various locations can be organized in several ways. In one approach, a particular laboratory is given overall responsibility for the project from start to completion (as with world product mandates). Evidence from interviews suggests that such responsibility can be highly motivating for the team members involved. It may stretch the team unduly, though, because specialized competences required at particular stages of development may not be available. This can be solved by secondment of personnel or new recruitment, although the social integration of a new team member may take some time.

An alternative approach is to switch projects between laboratories as they progress through the stages of development. This exploits differences in local comparative advantage, with laboratories close to major universities, say, carrying out the basic research and laboratories close to the major markets designing the product and getting it into production. A potential difficulty with this approach is that no-one feels that they 'own' the project. Effort may be reduced as no one takes responsibility for the project. There may also be communication problems between the laboratories. These may be solved by transferring key staff to the new laboratory, although there is always the risk that their advice will be ignored on the grounds that the idea was 'not invented here'.

A more radical approach is to empower internal entrepreneurs to manage the project from start to finish and allow them, rather than their bosses, to decide whether the project should be shifted between laboratories. Entrepreneurs become internal subcontractors to the firm, and laboratory managers become internal subcontractors to the entrepreneurs. Only the decision on project finance remains centralized, with senior managers acting as venture capitalists on behalf of their shareholders, deciding which projects to back, and fixing the duration of internal loans (Buckley and Casson, 1992).

The relevance of this more radical approach stems from the high organizational costs associated with global R&D. There are several disadvantages of global R&D to be offset against the advantages indicated above. First, much of the key information used in research is tacit and so requires face-to-face communication. The distance between different laboratories is therefore a major obstacle. Jet travel is a poor method of reconciling the face-to-face requirement with the distance constraint, because putting scientists on planes takes them away from the laboratory bench (and may also reduce their productivity by interfering with their personal lives). Using managers as intermediaries between laboratories is a poor substitute because they may misunderstand the information if they are unfamiliar with the specialists' professional culture.

Cultural problems can lead not only to misunderstandings but to suspicion and distrust. Where laboratories behave as tight-knit communities, each laboratory may be suspicious of its internal rivals. This is particularly likely where the multiplicity of laboratories is the legacy of mergers and acquisition activity, since there is no corporate culture shared by all the personnel. Furthermore, anxieties about post-merger rationalization may cause inflexible defensive strategies to be employed. As a result, international research co-ordinators may be faced with major internal political problems which require considerable diplomacy to resolve.

Co-ordination problems are not only disadvantages of a global research strategy. In some industries research is a capital-intensive activity with a high minimum efficient scale; in the oil industry, for example, engine test beds involve very large fixed costs. The replication of facilities is therefore problematic except in the very largest firms. Sometimes it is feasible to rent out the facilities to other firms or to finance them on a joint-venture basis, but this is not always the case.

Concern over secrecy may also be a factor: confidential information could leak out through overseas laboratories which are not under the close supervision of the parent firm. Despite continuing concern over industrial espionage, however, it appears that firms do not perceive such differential risk in respect of overseas laboratories (Pearce and Singh, 1992).

10.5   IMPLICATIONS OF REGIONAL TRADING BLOCS

The significance of the globalization of markets was much exaggerated in the 1980s. It is now apparent that the forces of economic integration are likely to be much stronger within regional trading blocs than between them. Globalization does not mean the end of adaptive R & D; it will still have a significant role. But instead of adapting a generic product to a national market the firm will adapt it to a regional market instead.

The enlargement of the European Community and the emergence of the North American Free Trade Area is likely to encourage the rationalization of adaptive research facilities within these areas. At the same time, the threat of higher common external tariffs and other protectionist devices will encourage firms pursuing global market share to invest behind the tariff walls if they have not already done so; a factor of particular relevance to Japanese firms (and to firms from other South-East Asian countries too). To support their local operations they will need to establish adaptive development and technical support laboratories.

New investors will be able to choose many different national locations for their new facilities. Established investors, too, will have opportunities to rationalize, although they will not be so footloose as the new entrants. Because political integration is less advanced than economic integration, traditional national rivalries within the trading blocs can still play an important role in competition to host R & D facilities. For example, within Europe it is possible to channel grants for regional development into subsidizing buildings and infrastructure for foreign R & D operations. Tax breaks can be made conditional or to satisfy local value-added requirements, and the high political status of advanced technology means that considerable weight may be given to the value of local R & D – even though this is usually just of an adaptive kind. Finally, governments can use their purchasing power and regulatory authority to influence location decisions – as when the local testing of drugs is made a condition for local market access in spite of overwhelming evidence on safety generated in other countries.

10.6   GLOBALIZATION AND CROSS-INVESTMENT

Evidence suggests that global research strategies are mainly confined to the very largest multinational enterprises, and in particular to those which are significantly engaged in basic research. The evidence comes from a survey of the world's multinationals carried out in 1989 and reported in detail elsewhere (Casson, 1991; Pearce and Singh, 1992).

A population of 914 corporate research laboratories was first identified, mainly owned by Fortune 500 industrial enterprises (Pearce and Singh, 1991, pp. 185–8). These comprised 561 home-country laboratories and 353 foreign laboratories. Some enterprises had several laboratories in their home country. On the other hand, many had only one major domestic laboratory and no overseas laboratories at all.

The US is absolutely dominant where research is concerned: 463 of the laboratories were located in the US, some 282 being owned by US firms. The 181 foreign-owned laboratories in the US are matched by 124 US-owned laboratories overseas. Thus US foreign dependence, as measured by the percentage of all local laboratories which are foreign owned (39 per cent) exceeds US internationalization, as measured by the percentage of all US-owned laboratories which are located abroad (30 per cent).

Ownership of overseas research laboratories within the chosen population is concentrated in just 12 countries. The foreign dependence and internationalization ratios of these countries are given in Figure 10.1. Enterprises from countries other than these 12 have only domestic

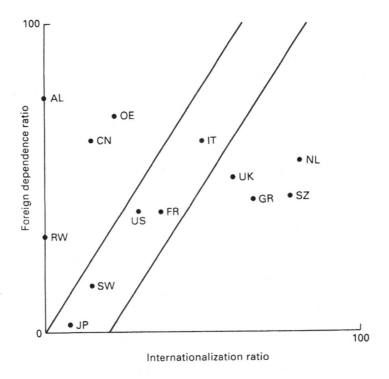

Note: The diagonal band encloses those countries for which foreign dependence and internationalization are approximately equal.

Figure 10.1   Foreign dependence and internationalization, based on the frequency distribution of laboratories

research laboratories, so the internationalization ratio for the rest of the world is zero. The rest-of-the-world foreign dependence ratio is positive, because the rest-of-the-world hosts foreign-owned laboratories, but fairly small, because rest-of-the-world countries are not particularly attractive as locations, so that domestically owned laboratories predominate there.

The overall pattern of globalization is one of cross-investment, with four countries – Switzerland, Netherlands, Germany and the UK – sourcing rather than hosting overseas laboratories, and three countries – Australia, Canada and the 'Other European' group (Austria, Belgium, Finland, Norway) – doing the reverse. It is interesting that small countries tend to exhibit strong net positions, whereas larger countries – notably US, Japan, France and Italy – tend to be in balance. The main exceptions are Germany – a large country that is relatively internationalized – and Sweden – a small country that is in balance.

Small countries exhibit net positions of both kinds, so the difference between large and small countries cannot easily be explained by the natural openness of small countries, since they should then score highly on both foreign dependence and internationalization, and not on one at the expense of the other. This argument may have some validity, however, in predicting the relatively low pair of ratios for Japan and the US. Even here, however, more specific explanations are more appropriate, especially in the case of Japan where, for historical reasons, both internationalization and foreign dependence are extremely low.

10.7 THE PROPENSITY TO UNDERTAKE OVERSEAS RESEARCH

The main part of the study was based on responses to questionnaires (sent separately to parent and subsidiary companies). These were combined with a variety of other corporate data in a regression analysis. Because many of the dependent variables are categorical, logit and probit regressions were run (Amemiya, 1981, 1985) as well as ordinary least squares (OLS), but the inferences were negligibly different and so only the OLS results are reported here.

Previous publications based on this survey have concentrated on the responses from the subsidiary companies, with much of the information from the parents being used for corroboration only. This reflected policy interest in how subsidiaries in different countries perceived their local environment, and how well they integrated into the firm as a whole. The emphasis in this paper on global strategies *per se* suggests that the parent's perspective is the most relevant, and so the regression results focus exclusively on their responses.

The results are based on 163 parent responses, a response rate of 26.2 per cent. Because some respondents did not answer particular questions, however, the number of observations used in each regression is variable. Regressions which combine data from more than one source also involve fewer observations, because of difficulties in matching the data accurately. In particular, firms engaged in major mergers and acquisitions will be under-represented in regressions of this kind.

The propensity to internationalize R&D is measured by two variables, both based on the number of overseas countries in which research is done, as reported in the questionnaires. The first is a zero–one variable which determines whether a firm undertakes overseas R&D at all, and the second is the logarithm of the number of countries involved. It might seem more desirable to use the number of overseas laboratories rather than the number of countries, but unfortunately this information is not reliable, particularly for large companies which have several laboratories in each country.

A number of potential influences on the propensity to research abroad were identified, based upon the costs and benefits involved. The first was the obstacle to international diversification of research posed by the minimum efficient scale of an R&D facility (Hirschey and Caves, 1981). Minimum efficient scale was proxied by the size of the parent laboratory, as measured by the logarithm of total employment in the laboratory (as reported by respondents). The greater the employment in the parent laboratory, the smaller should be the propensity to carry out research overseas.

Ideally, minimum efficient scale should be matched against the research needs of the firm, as proxied by its expenditure on R&D. Unfortunately, reliable information on this is available for only a small number of firms and so to avoid losing too many degrees of freedom it was not used. It is possible that research needs could be proxied by the size of the firm. In this case, size of firm would be positively associated with the propensity to undertake overseas R&D. On the other hand, organizational diseconomies in large firms could actually constrain the internationalization of their research. Information on firm size, as measured by the logarithm of sales, is readily available from a separate source (Casson, Pearce and Singh, 1992). The sign of the coefficient on firm size should indicate whether research needs or organizational diseconomies are the major influence on the internationalization of research.

Turning to the benefits of overseas research, an attempt was made to test whether the benefits are greater for basic research or for adaptation and technical support (taking generic development as a control). If the benefits of subcontracting basic research are important, then a commitment to basic research (as expressed in parent firm responses) should increase the propensity to undertake overseas research. Conversely, if the benefits of adaptation and technical support are significant, then a measure of the internationalization of the firm's production should carry a positive coefficient. Internationalization of production was measured by the proportion of the firm's output generated overseas, obtained from a separate source (Dunning and Pearce, 1985).

The only other firm-specific variable used was the age of the parent laboratory (again in logarithmic form). The introduction of this variable makes it possible to test the view that the globalization of R&D is part of an evolutionary process which begins with the establishment of a parent R&D facility.

Firm-specific factors are not the only factors likely to influence global R&D, however. International business research provides numerous instances of the importance of industry- and location-specific factors (Dunning, 1988). A number of instances have already been given of significant differences between industries in both the nature and the strategic importance of R&D, and it is unlikely that the firm-specific variables mentioned above capture all the relevant effects (Håkanson, 1992). To test the importance of industry factors, different industry groups were identified using a new classification which is a significant improvement in the relatively crude classification used in earlier published reports of this research (Casson, 1991).

There are various reasons why country factors may be important in the R&D strategies of parent firms. Countries such as the UK are highly internationalized because of the cultural legacy of empire, whereas others, notably Japan, are not. This affects the accumulated experience, and hence the perceived risk, of overseas R&D. In the previous studies it has proved difficult, however, to identify meaningful country effects, and so in this chapter a modified strategy has been used. Countries have been classified into six major groups – US, Japan, UK, Northern Europe, Southern Europe and rest-of-the-world – designed to reflect significant cultural and historical differences. In particular, the division of continental European countries between north and south is intended to reflect the difference between the individualistic Protestant countries of the north and the more collectivist Roman Catholic countries of the south. The same distinction is sometimes expressed in terms of 'Anglo-Saxon' and 'Latin' countries, or in terms of the Mediterranean countries and the rest (Laurent, 1983).

To test for 'openness' effects, a subset of small countries was defined comprising the UK, Austria, Belgium and the Scandinavian countries. Theory suggests that parent firms located in these countries should have an above-average propensity to engage in overseas R&D. This is because a given degree of geographical diversification is more likely to generate international diversification when the home country is small.

Regression results for the two measures of the overseas research propensity are reported in Table 10.1. Each regression was estimated in full, and adjusted using a stepwise procedure in which the least significant variable was dropped until all the remaining variables were significant at the 10 per cent level. The main inferences are based on the full regressions, as econometric theory requires; the results of the stepwise regressions are shown for interest; they summarize the kind of effects that are observed in the coefficients of the significant variables as insignificant variables are removed. The 'significance' of the remaining variables cannot, of course, be given a rigorous interpretation because of the extensive data-mining that is involved.

It is convenient to begin with the binary regression which distinguishes only whether a firm researches overseas or not. It can be seen that the size of the firm is of no significance in the binary regression, once other factors are controlled for. Although the zero-order correlation between size and overseas research propensity (not shown) is positive and significant at 10 per cent – confirming that global R&D is a 'large-firm' phenomenon even within this severely truncated sample of very large firms – the partial correlation is insignificant, indicating that it is the other attributes of size that are important. The results leave no doubt as to what the key attribute is: it is overseas production. Large firms undertake overseas R&D because they generate a high proportion of their output overseas.

The positive sign of the coefficient on size of laboratory (which is significant only in the stepwise regression) indicates that, contrary to the hypothesis presented above, a large size of parent laboratory encourages overseas research. This suggests that either considerations of minimum efficient scale are unimportant or, more likely, that size of laboratory proxies something else instead. The first possibility can be quickly ruled out. Table 10.2 summarizes the responses of 21 firms which reported that they had considered overseas R&D and rejected the idea. It shows that economies of scale are the dominant consideration, achieving a score of 2.22 on a scale of importance running from one to three. The results also confirm the importance of the overall internationalization of the firm as an influence on its overseas research propensity. Notice also that problems of communication at a distance are of fairly modest importance, except in the office equipment industry – a paradoxical result, given that the products of this industry are supposed to help solve communication problems.

*Table 10.1   Regression analysis of propensity to undertake overseas
              research*

Regression number	1.1	1.2	1.3	1.4
Type	Full	Step-wise	Full	Step-wise
Dependent variable	Binary	Binary	No. countries	No. countries
Intercept	−0.71	−0.85[b]	0.02	−1.24[b]
	(0.69)	(0.41)	(0.98)	(0.54)
Parent country				
UK	0.06		−0.02	
	(0.16)		(0.22)	
US	0.77[a]	0.59[a]	−0.61	
	(0.40)	(0.32)	(0.57)	
Japan	0.77[a]	0.68[b]	−0.75	
	(0.42)	(0.34)	(0.60)	
S. Europe	1.40[c]	1.15[c]	0.11	
	(0.50)	(0.43)	(0.72)	
Rest of world	0.17		−0.34	
	(0.24)		(0.34)	
Small country	0.84[b]	0.64[a]	−0.40	
	(0.40)	(0.33)	(0.58)	
Industry				
Pharmaceuticals	0.27		0.84[c]	0.80[c]
	(0.21)		(0.31)	(0.23)
Office equipment	−0.44	−0.57[a]	−0.27	
	(0.35)	(0.31)	(0.50)	
Scientific	0.59		0.99	
instruments	(0.52)		(0.74)	
Aircraft	−0.05		−0.31	
	(0.25)		(0.36)	
Chemicals	0.35[b]	0.21[a]	0.41	0.42[b]
	(0.17)	(0.13)	(0.25)	(0.18)
Petroleum	0.20		−0.01	
	(0.27)		(0.38)	
Electrical	0.15		0.60[b]	0.70[c]
engineering	(0.18)		(0.25)	(0.18)
Mechanical	0.20		0.60[b]	0.61[b]
engineering	(0.22)		(0.32)	(0.25)
Motor vehicles	0.30		0.21	
	(0.26)		(0.38)	
Textiles and	0.16		−0.10	
clothing	(0.40)		(0.57)	
Paper and pulp	−0.10		−0.28	
	(0.26)		(0.37)	
Non-metallic	−0.31	−0.46[a]	−0.46	
minerals	(0.30)	(0.26)	(0.43)	
Food, drink and	0.08		0.04	
tobacco	(0.21)		(0.30	

Printing, publishing, rubber and other manufacturing	−0.03 (0.30)		0.18 (0.43)	
Firm-specific				
Size of firm	−0.01 (0.07)		0.13 (0.10)	0.16[b] (0.06)
Overseas production	0.65[b] (0.28)	0.87[c] (0.23)	0.78[a] (0.39)	1.11[c] (0.28)
Age of laboratory	−0.08 (0.08)		−0.02 (0.11)	
Size of laboratory	0.08 (0.05)	0.09[b] (0.03)	−0.05 (0.07)	
Basic research	0.09 (0.12)		0.18 (0.17)	
F (country)	1.59		0.84	
F (industry)	1.00		1.89[b]	
F (total)	2.02[b]	5.33[c]	2.48[c]	9.04[c]
No. observations	98	98	98	98
R^2	0.41	0.35	0.46	0.37

Notes:
Standard errors are shown in brackets.
[a]   10 per cent significance
[b]   5 per cent significance
[c]   1 per cent significance
Control country is N. European group. Control industry is metals.

Table 10.2   Reasons for rejecting overseas R&D after consideration

Reason	Average rating	Industries where it is particularly significant
Economies of scale require centralized research	2.22	Chemicals
Overseas markets are not distinctive	1.91	
Overseas markets are small	1.90	
Home country expertise is superior	1.81	
Communication problems related to distance	1.77	Office equipment
Security of research requires home country control	1.45	Aircraft Chemicals Mechanical engineering

Note: Ratings are on a scale 1 (not important) to 3 (very important). No locations are of particular significance. All significant industry effects are positive.

The most probable explanation of the positive coefficient on the size of the parent laboratory is that when controlling for size of firm and overseas production, size of the parent laboratory proxies the firm's commitment to R&D. This interpretation is compatible with the positive (though insignificant) coefficient on the basic research variable, since it is very likely that firms committed to R&D will have parent laboratories that attach high priority to basic research. This view is also supported by regressions involving the subsample of firms for which R&D expenditure data is available (not shown) in which a positive coefficient on expenditure is obtained (although because of the small number of degrees of freedom, none of the explanatory variables appears significant).

If the role of commitment to research is accepted, then it is perhaps surprising to find that firms with older parent laboratories, which might be expected to have the strongest tradition of research and hence the greatest commitment to it, tend to be less internationalized than others. The explanation may be that the commitment factor is picked up mainly by the other variables mentioned above, and that the age of the laboratory represents instead a tendency to centralize research in what has become a politically powerful parent laboratory.

All the preceding results are conditioned on the parent country and the industry. The small country openness effect appears positive and significant, as expected, but there is also a positive Southern European effect which is rather surprising. This is accounted for by large French and Italian firms investing not only in Europe but also in the US and as far afield as Brazil. These firms are the 'national champions' in their industries – the cultural factors alluded to earlier seem to be important only in so far as national industrial policies that favour such firms may reflect a collectivist approach to industrial organization in these countries.

When discussing industry effects it is useful to compare directly the results of the two sets of regressions. This is because the industries in which there is a significant propensity to establish some laboratories overseas differ quite markedly from those where there is a propensity to establish a lot of laboratories overseas in different countries. Chemicals is the only industry where both propensities are significantly above the norm. It is the second measure of overseas research which is most relevant in the context of global strategies, and the results indicate that in addition to chemicals, pharmaceuticals, electrical engineering and mechanical engineering are the 'global' industries. Results from previous studies (confirmed by the results in section 10.8 below) indicate that pharmaceutical research is rather different from the others, in that it is more orientated towards basic research which taps into local centres of excellence and is correspondingly more detached from adaptive work related to production sites overseas.

The fact that industry variables take over much of the explanatory power from firm- and location-specific variables in this second set of regressions suggests that globalization – in the sense of a strategic commitment to world-wide research – is a rather different phenomenon from ordinary internationalization – in the sense of having one or two laboratories in a different country. Thus the general commitment to research, which underlies internationalization, translates into globalization more readily in some industries than in others. What is more, these industries all involve the application of sophisticated science to the production of goods which are marketed on the basis of technical superiority rather than adaptation to local needs. These are industries, in other words, which are not only high-technology, but are the high-technology industries to which the marketing concept of globalization really applies.

If globalization of R&D is part of a general globalization strategy affecting production and marketing too, then it would seem that only the very largest firms would be in a position to pursue this strategy. This may be why the partial impact of size is significant in the second set of regressions: it is a proxy for the capability to implement a truly global corporate strategy.

10.8   THE CO-ORDINATION OF OVERSEAS RESEARCH

This section examines whether the factors that influence the overseas research propensity also influence the way that research is co-ordinated. The answer is that they do – but only to a limited extent. Industry factors are particularly important in deciding how research is organized, but the influence of industry on organization, once an overseas laboratory has been established, is different from its influence on whether a laboratory should be established in the first place.

Two main dimensions of organization have been selected as being particularly relevant to global R&D. The first is the frequency of interaction between parent and overseas laboratories, reflecting the degree of systematic co-ordination in day-to-day affairs. The second is the strength of the leadership exercised by the parent laboratory in setting the research agenda for the whole group. Respondents were asked to rate the importance of both systematic co-ordination and parent leadership on a scale from one (unimportant) to three (very important). These two

Table 10.3   Factors influencing the co-ordination of overseas research

Regression number Dependent variable	3.1 Frequency of interaction	3.2 Strength of parent leadership
Intercept	2.16	4.42[c]
	(1.66)	(0.94)
Parent country		
UK	−0.99[b]	0.33
	(0.38)	(0.22)
US	−0.29	−0.65
	(0.87)	(0.58)
Japan	0.03	−0.64
	(0.95)	(0.59)
S. Europe	−0.23	−0.42
	(0.96)	(0.69)
Rest of world	−1.30	−0.25
	(0.95)	(0.49)
Small country	0.55	−0.68
	(0.84)	(0.58)
Industry		
Pharmaceuticals	−0.38	0.60[a]
	(0.46)	(0.30)
Office equipment	−0.04	0.15
	(0.78)	(0.46)
Scientific instruments	1.22	0.57
	(0.85)	(0.67)
Aircraft	—	0.25
		(0.34)
Chemicals	−0.04	0.13
	(0.43)	(0.24)
Petroleum	−0.20	−0.36
	(0.62)	(0.38)
Electrical engineering	−0.72	−0.12
	(0.47)	(0.24)
Mechanical engineering	−0.01	0.02
	(0.51)	(0.30)
Motor vehicles	−0.36	0.08
	(0.53)	(0.35)
Textiles and clothing	—	0.15
		(0.66)
Paper and pulp	—	0.03
		(0.39)
Non-metallic minerals	—	−0.27
		(0.62)
Food, drink and tobacco	0.79	0.32
	(0.61)	(0.29)

Printing, publishing, rubber and other manufacturing	-1.67^a (0.86)	0.37 (0.51)
Firm-specific		
Size of firm	-0.09 (0.15)	-0.23^b (0.09)
Overseas production	-2.11^c (0.74)	0.52 (0.39)
Age of laboratory	0.41^b (0.19)	-0.06 (0.10)
Size of laboratory	-0.05 (0.13)	0.06 (0.07)
Basic research	0.36 (0.25)	0.14 (0.16)
F (country)	1.48	0.91
F (industry)	1.32	0.81
F (total)	1.48	1.38
No. observations	47	87
R^2	0.54	0.36
Mean	1.54	1.96

Note: Control country is N. European group. Control industry is metals.

dimensions, though distinct, are clearly related, and the relationship between them is indicated by the results reported in Table 10.3.

It could be argued that frequent interaction and strong leadership are substitutes. Frequent interaction may involve intrusive attempts at day-to-day supervision of subsidiaries that the parent laboratory does not trust. In this context the use of leadership would indicate an attempt to create a climate of trust within the firm which makes intrusive monitoring unnecessary.

The evidence suggests that there is a weak trade-off of the kind suggested, with firm-specific factors such as overseas production and the age of the parent laboratory playing an important role. Extensive overseas production appears to weaken the frequency of interaction. This could partly be explained by the greater communication costs involved. The most likely reason, though, is that overseas laboratories are locally integrated with the overseas production and marketing operations rather than with other laboratories in the group. They are engaged in adaptive work rather than in an integrated programme of basic research. This interpretation of the significance of overseas production is supported by the positive coefficients for both frequency of interaction and strength of parent leadership which are associated with basic research. Although insignificant, these coefficients suggest that co-ordination involving basic research is particularly important because both instruments of co-ordination are used.

The fact that older laboratories co-ordinate group activities through frequent interaction rather than research leadership is consistent with the view expressed earlier that older laboratories enjoy more political power within the firm. By insisting on frequent interaction they can inhibit other laboratories from developing an autonomous research agenda of their own. Given this power they need not rely on exercising leadership as well.

These regressions were also run with the number of countries in which laboratories are based as an additional independent variable, to test the impact of geographical diversity on co-ordination methods. It was hypothesized that greater diversity would reduce the frequency of interaction and encourage reliance on strong leadership, but the results indicated that, if anything, the opposite was the case. Although the coefficients on the additional variable were insignificant, their signs suggest that interaction becomes stronger and parental leadership weaker as diversity grows. This suggests that the management of diversity requires formal systems of co-ordination *within which the parent laboratory no longer occupies a privileged position*. In other words, parent laboratories are most influential where there are only one or two other countries in which research is based; their power diminishes as the geographical diversity of research increases.

It was noted in the previous studies that the pharmaceutical industry is unusual in the duration, cost and complexity of its research projects. The long-term horizons involved explain why there is less-frequent inter-action and more reliance on leadership in this industry than in most others.

Finally, it should be noted that UK parent laboratories interact significantly less frequently with their overseas laboratories than do others; this tendency probably reflects the culturally specific attitude of leaving researchers to 'go away and get on with it' – a strategy which at its best avoids unwanted interference, and at its worst can marginalize the researchers concerned and allow project delays to go unnoticed.

10.9 FACTORS GOVERNING THE GROWTH OF THE PARENT LABORATORY

During the 1980s the importance of central laboratories under-taking basic research declined. Economies of scope in basic research which could be exploited within the firm turned out to be smaller than expected. The problems of managing highly diversified firms became increasingly apparent, and as the divisions of these firms sought to 'get closer to their customers' so they demanded research that was more relevant to their short-term needs. Central laboratories were turned from cost centres into profit centres, acting as contract suppliers to the divisions (and in some cases to external customers too). If they were unlucky, they might be entirely 'captured' by one of the key divisions or even shut down altogether. As a result, the parent laboratories in this study are not necessarily central laboratories in the traditional sense; some of them are just 'first amongst equals' in a network of laboratories.

These phenomena have been described in detail in Casson (1991) and Pearce and Singh (1992), but the question of how the fate of parent laboratories depends on factors specific to these laboratories, rather than on general global trends, has not been examined previously. This can be done using respondents' ratings of various factors impinging on the performance of their laboratories.

The most interesting point to emerge in this respect concerns UK firms; they stood out from the others in four separate ways (see Table 10.4). Managers of UK parent laboratories considered that local research traditions were of little influence on the laboratory's work; that the local environment and its technological infrastructure was of little significance to them; that the wage rates of scientific professionals were particularly important; and that overseas research was driven very much by the need to 'keep up' with the technological competence of other firms. This can reasonably be interpreted as reflecting a rather negative view of the UK 'science base', with cheap scientific labour being the main advantage of a UK location. This interpretation is confirmed by responses to other questions concerned with the motivations for overseas research, where UK firms considered that access to cheap scientific labour was a significantly less important motive for their overseas research than it was for other firms.

These results confirm the responses obtained from foreign firms' laboratories based in the UK, namely that a major attraction of the UK to foreign firms is its cheap scientific labour. But while foreign subsidiaries were on the whole satisfied with the UK environment, UK parents were clearly not. One explanation may be that foreign-owned firms are more footloose, so that if they do not like the UK environment they simply move elsewhere, whereas parent firms are 'locked in' to a greater degree. Thus the sample captures fewer dissatisfied subsidiaries than it does dissatisfied parent firms. Given the large number of overseas laboratories that have been attracted to the UK in the postwar period, it seems that there must be problems in the UK which particularly afflict parent firms. Given that parent laboratories are on average larger than subsidiary

Table 10.4   Factors in the growth of the parent laboratory

Regression number	4.1	4.2	4.3	4.4	4.5
	Distinctive local	Helpful local	Favourable wage	Concern to 'keep	Reaction to rivals'
Dependent variable	tradition	environment	rates	up'	R&D
Intercept	0.38	1.73[a]	0.06	2.26[b]	−0.37
	(1.21)	(0.99)	(0.96)	(0.94)	(0.98)
Parent country					
UK	−0.56[a]	−0.93[a]	0.48[b]	0.41[a]	0.27
	(0.30)	(0.24)	(0.23)	(0.22)	(0.24)
US	−0.51	−0.30	0.38	0.62	1.14[a]
	(0.70)	(0.58)	(0.56)	(0.55)	(0.57)
Japan	−0.30	−0.23	0.35	0.39	0.70
	(0.73)	(0.60)	(0.58)	(0.57)	(0.60)
S. Europe	−0.60	−0.34	−0.04	1.06	0.63
	(0.87)	(0.72)	(0.81)	(0.68)	(0.71)
Rest of world	−0.28	−0.41	0.16	0.44	0.18
	(0.44)	(0.35)	(0.34)	(0.33)	(0.35)
Small country	0.02	0.24	0.30	0.40	1.11[a]
	(0.70)	(0.58)	(0.56)	(0.55)	(0.58)
Industry					
Pharmaceuticals	0.30	−0.01	0.27	−0.22	−0.13
	(0.38)	(0.31)	(0.30)	(0.30)	(0.31)
Office equipment	0.94	−0.13	0.22	0.38	0.06
	(0.61)	(0.50)	(0.48)	(0.48)	(0.50)
Scientific	1.34	1.00	−0.04	−0.31	−1.45[a]
instruments	(0.89)	(0.74)	(0.71)	(0.70)	(0.73)
Aircraft	0.83	−0.51	0.15	0.35	−0.34
	(0.43)	(0.36)	(0.34)	(0.34)	(0.36)
Chemicals	0.49	−0.04	0.17	0.11	−0.35
	(0.31)	(0.25)	(0.25)	(0.24)	(0.25)
Petroleum	−0.45	0.07	−0.10	−0.56	−0.61
	(0.46)	(0.38)	(0.37)	(0.36)	(0.38)
Electrical	−0.04	−0.16	0.08	0.11	−0.05
engineering	(0.32)	(0.26)	(0.26)	(0.24)	(0.26)
Mechanical	−0.02	0.08	0.46	−0.02	0.18
engineering	(0.40)	(0.33)	(0.32)	(0.31)	(0.32)
Motor vehicles	−0.14	0.08	−0.39	0.32	0.39
	(0.51)	(0.33)	(0.40)	(0.36)	(0.42)
Textiles and	−0.61	0.62	0.26	0.15	0.09
clothing	(0.69)	(0.57)	(0.55)	(0.54)	(0.57)
Paper and pulp	−0.22	−0.27	−0.20	0.54	−0.19
	(0.51)	(0.37)	(0.36)	(0.36)	(0.37)
Non-metallic	−0.26	−0.51	−0.41	0.27	−0.33
minerals	(0.60)	(0.49)	(0.47)	(0.41)	(0.49)
Food, drink and	0.57	0.26	0.02	0.07	−0.23
tobacco	(0.37)	(0.30)	(0.29)	(0.29)	(0.30)

Printing, publishing, rubber and other manufacturing	−0.55 (0.52)	−0.83 (0.43)	−0.23 (0.41)	0.50 (0.41)	−0.50 (0.42)
Firm-specific					
Size of firm	0.14 (0.12)	−0.03 (0.10)	0.03 (0.10)	−0.10 (0.09)	0.20[b] (0.99)
Overseas production	−0.51 (0.51)	−0.29 (0.41)	−0.33 (0.40)	−0.05 (0.37)	−0.82[b] (0.41)
Age of laboratory	0.03 (0.13)	−0.09 (0.11)	0.13 (0.10)	−0.03 (0.10)	−0.13 (0.11)
Size of laboratory	0.07 (0.09)	0.20[c] (0.07)	0.03 (0.07)	0.09 (0.07)	0.02 (0.07)
Basic research	−0.10 (0.21)	−0.30[a] (0.17)	−0.03 (0.56)	−0.00 (0.16)	0.02 (0.17)
F (country)	0.79	2.96[b]	1.00	1.27	1.35
F (industry)	1.44	1.10	0.56	0.92	0.90
F (total)	1.29	2.11[c]	0.64	0.99	0.90
No. observations	93	95	93	98	95
R^2	0.32	0.43	0.19	0.25	0.24
Mean	1.70	1.85	1.35	2.56	1.68

Note: Control country is N. European group. Control industry is metals. All the dependent variables are measured on a scale from one (unimportant) to three (very important).

laboratories and more orientated to basic research, it is presumably something to do with the restricted 'science base' of the country, or perhaps the unwillingness of the government to 'champion' its major research-orientated firms.

There is already concern that the growth of continental European markets relative to the UK market will switch not only production but also adaptive research out of the UK. The apparent dissatisfaction of parent laboratories with their UK base may mean that eventually even basic research will move out as well. Indeed, some firms may go so far as to switch their headquarters operations to the Continent. The European headquarters of some foreign firms have already made this switch and their UK rivals may be forced to follow suit with their global headquarters if they are to retain their competitive position in the long run.

10.10 FUTURE DEVELOPMENTS

What, then, is the future of global R&D strategies? A number of scenarios are possible, but just one of them will be considered here. It has three key aspects.

First, it may be assumed that advances in information technology – and teleconferencing in particular – will help to reconcile the conflicting demands for face-to-face communications and for collaboration at a distance. This is despite the fact that video-conferencing is likely to remain significantly more expensive than voice-only communication, not only because of the greater demands on transmission facilities but because of the specialist media skills necessary to set up and direct a conference. On the other hand, it is almost certain to be cheaper than jet travel – particularly when the human stress on researchers and their co-ordinators is taken into account.

Cameras can be placed not only in the office but in the laboratory too. It is already possible to produce video reports on key experiments, but the opportunity to 'go live' and to interact with others whilst performing an experiment is likely to provide added benefits. Like many other innovations, video-conferencing may not only solve the problems which are the immediate stimulus for it but open up new horizons, so that people begin to wonder how they ever managed to do without it in the past.

Secondly, economic integration is likely to proceed faster within the major trading blocs than it does between them. This seems to have been a common pattern in the past and it is likely to be repeated in the future. Within these integrated blocs scientific labour is likely to become more mobile than before as legal obstacles to movement are reduced. Because of the advantages of agglomeration noted earlier – in particular, greater depth of specialist labour markets – one region is likely to emerge as a major centre of R&D within each trading bloc. From the standpoint of national interests, it is a crucial issue where the centre of each region will be. Competition within Europe is particularly intense, with Germany and France both making significant attempts to erode the postwar lead of the UK.

Both economic theory and geographical evidence suggest that R&D facilities will encircle a major commercial centre, being based in outer suburban areas or along motorway corridors emanating from the centre – up to, say, two hours journey time away (Hall *et al.*, 1987). R&D facilities are likely to be some distance from the centre because they are more space-intensive than office facilities and so cannot compete effectively for space where rents are high. At the same time R&D facilities require good access to the centre in order to co-ordinate with marketing and financial functions located there.

Proximity to the national metropolis is particularly important for the major laboratories of domestic firms which are carrying out generic research. It is less important for foreign firms, since their headquarters are in any case elsewhere. The increasing availability of science parks linked to some of the major universities will make it more viable to hive off basic research as a separate function and locate it on a university site. Some types of basic research may be sufficiently routine (for example, debugging scientific software) that they can be carried out remote from any centre, whether a university or not. On this basis the use of freelance research consultants working from home or from small laboratories may well increase in order to reduce the salary costs of such research.

While labour mobility within blocs may increase, mobility between blocs may decrease because of political obstacles. This means that firms wishing to access distinctive scientific capabilities in a foreign bloc will have to consider investing there, even if they have previously rejected the idea. This incentive will be strengthened by the facts that obstacles to trade will encourage local production and that persistent cultural and geographical differences may require adaptation of the product to local conditions within each bloc. Furthermore, increasing political concern over the local research content of production may result in substantial subsidies for investment in research facilities (or, equivalently, substantial penalties for failing to invest). As a result, it is likely that major firms will wish to have at least one research facility in each of the major blocs.

In some cases they may opt for a single multi-purpose facility, but evidence suggests that trying to mix functions as diverse as basic research and technical support is unsatisfactory (Casson *et al.*, 1991). Thus firms may have several laboratories in each of the major trading blocs, specializing in different kinds of research.

This leads naturally to the final issue, namely the growing sophistication of globalization strategies. It may be assumed that with growing awareness of the strategic issues involved in R&D and greater experience of implementation, managers will learn to appreciate more fully the different factors that apply to the location of different types of R&D. As a result, attempts to rationalize research activities are likely to gain momentum – particularly in the wake of mergers and acquisitions – thereby achieving greater internal clarity and transparency regarding the role of each laboratory.

Greater emphasis will also be placed on individual motivation, empowering the more entrepreneurial researchers to develop projects which they can see through from start to finish, provided that they can maintain the financial backing of senior management. By affording greater internal flexibility it should be possible to retain key researchers who might otherwise become frustrated with the bureaucracy and leave to set up their own firms. Firms which afford too much flexibility run the risk of losing sight of their core business areas, of course; but on the other hand, the core competences of the innovative firm reside very much in its recruitment, training and team-building practices; it is only natural that the exploitation of these should result in some unanticipated diversification from time to time.

It is interesting to note that half the respondents expected to see greater use of global research networks within their firms. Regression analysis (not shown) indicates that this trend is particularly significant in certain industries: pulp and paper (5 per cent significance); aircraft, motor vehicles and pharmaceuticals (10 per cent significance). It is also most significant in firms with the largest parent laboratories (1 per cent significance) and the greatest existing degree of globalization (5 per cent significance). This may be interpreted as showing that global networks are the emerging norm within an élite group of firms which already have a strong global orientation and strong commitment to research.

Overall, therefore, it seems likely that globalized R&D will become an established strategy for firms that are committed to building and marketing global market share in a polycentric world economy. There will probably be never more than a small number of such firms but they are likely to continue to exercise a disproportionately large influence on production and investment in innovative industries.

The prospects for local economic growth within the major trading blocs will depend on the relative success of regions in attracting these firms' key research facilities. Regions which in the past have successfully attracted foreign manufacturing and distributive investment will not necessarily be so successful in attracting foreign R&D, since rather different environmental qualities are required. If supranational government becomes stronger, at the expense of the nation state, then intranational local governments may well acquire greater autonomy and be able to compete amongst themselves to attract research facilities on a more level 'playing field'. It is therefore quite possible that in the long run it will be the relative performance of these local government strategies – involving tax concessions, infrastructure investments, support for universities and so on – which will determine where the major R&D agglomerations of the future are based.

NOTE

1. The data were collected as part of a research project financed by the UK Economic and Social Research Council and carried out at the University of Reading, 1988–9. The questionnaire was designed by Bob Pearce, one of the co-directors of the project, and the authors are grateful to him for his continued help and advice. He also kindly made

available his database on 792 of the world's largest firms. The other members of the project team were John Cantwell and John Dunning. The authors are grateful to Michael Waterson for his comments on an earlier draft.

REFERENCES

Amemiya, T. (1981): 'Qualitative response models: a survey', *Journal of Economic Literature*, **19**, 1483–1536.

—— (1985): *Advanced Econometrics* (Oxford: Basil Blackwell).

Buckley, P.J. and M.C. Casson (1992): 'Organising for innovation: the multinational enterprise in the twenty-first century', in P.J. Buckley and M.C. Casson (eds), *Multinational Enterprises in the World Economy: Essays in Honour of John Dunning* (Aldershot: Edward Elgar).

Cantwell, J.A. (1989): *Technological Innovation and Multinational Corporations* (Oxford: Basil Blackwell).

—— (1991): 'The international agglomeration of R&D', in Casson (ed.) (1991). 104–32.

Casson, M.C. (ed.) (1991): *Global Research Strategy and International Competitiveness* (Oxford: Basil Blackwell).

Casson, M.C., R.D. Pearce and S. Singh (1991): 'A review of recent trends', in Casson (ed.) (1991) 250–71.

—— (1992): 'Global integration through the decentralisation of R&D', in M.C. Casson (ed.), *International Business and Global Integration* (London: Macmillan) 163–204.

Dunning, J.H. (1988): *Explaining International Production* (London: Unwin Hyman).

—— and R.D. Pearce (1985): *The World's Largest Industrial Enterprises, 1962–1983* (Aldershot: Gower Press).

Håkanson, L. (1992): 'Locational determinants of foreign R&D in Swedish multinationals', in O. Grandstrand, L. Håkanson and S. Sjölander (eds), *Technology, Management and International Business* (Chichester: John Wiley) 97–116.

Hall, P., M. Breheny, R. McQuaid and D. Hart (1987): *Western Sunrise: The Genesis and Growth of Britain's Major High Tech Corridor* (London: Allen & Unwin).

Hirschey, R.C. and R.E. Caves (1981): 'Internationalisation of research and transfer of technology by multinational enterprises', *Oxford Bulletin of Economics and Statistics*, **42**(2), 115–30.

Laurent, A. (1983): 'The cultural diversity of Western conceptions of management', *International Studies of Management and Organisation*, **13** (1–2), 75–96.

Pearce, R.D. and S. Singh (1991): 'The overseas laboratory', in Casson (ed.) (1991) 183–212.

—— (1992): *Globalizing Research and Development* (London. Macmillan).

Vernon, R. (1966): 'International investment and international trade in the product cycle', *Quarterly Journal of Economics*, **80**, 190–207.

—— (1979): 'The product cycle hypothesis in a new international environment', *Oxford Bulletin of Economics and Statistics*, **41**, 255–67.

11. Corporate Technological Specialization in International Industries

John Cantwell

11.1 INTRODUCTION

This chapter rests on the supposition that firms in the same industry differ (Nelson, 1991), in that they each have their own distinctive forms and areas of technological competence (Cantwell, 1991b). It is further supposed that the distinct competence of each firm is reflected in its pattern of technological specialization; that is, in the composition of its technological activity across various types of such activity relative to other companies in the same industry. The pattern of technological specialization of the leading firms in two key industries is measured quantitatively using data on the characteristics of the patents they are granted. Changes in the pattern of corporate technological specialization over time are thus examined statistically, through the application of methods that were pioneered by Peter Hart and Sig Prais (Hart and Prais, 1956; Hart, 1976).

Two central propositions are considered. The first is that technological competence tends to persist over time, given that the essential underlying skills and capabilities residing within a firm are the product of a cumulative and incremental learning process which cannot be readily imitated by others. The implication is that the pattern of technological specialization of a firm within its industry changes only gradually, although it is expected to evolve as a result of the continuation of the learning process that builds upon existing corporate competence. Variations across firms in the pace at which specialization changes can be examined statistically, as well as the overall pace of change.

The second proposition derives from the observation that the inter-relatedness between formerly quite separate branches of technology has been rising in recent times (Cantwell, 1989). This suggests that firms' degree of (concentration of) technological specialization will display a tendency to fall over time; that is, as a response to greater inter-relatedness the technological activities undertaken by firms tend to broaden out. However, it will be shown that changes in the actual composition of technological specialization – a shift away from one particular favoured activity and towards some other already favoured field – tend to work against this trend. The significance of this qualification can again be assessed statistically.

11.2 THE ORGANIZATION OF THE DATA

Technological activity is measured by a count of patents granted in the US over the period 1969 to 1986. In these data it is possible to identify separately the firm to which a patent is assigned and the type of technological activity with which the patent is associated. Each of these dimensions has been organized in a way which suits the purpose of the exercise. At the company level the objective is to establish which patents are granted to the world's largest industrial firms, the major players in modern international industries. To do so the patents granted to affiliates of the largest firms, including foreign affiliates in the case of multi-nationals, have been consolidated into the relevant corporate groups. This consolidation of US patenting by international corporate groups has been carried out for the world's largest 792 industrial firms, as measured by the value of their global sales in 1982. Together, these firms account for around 43 per cent of all patents granted in the US between 1969 and 1986.

Using information on the product distribution of their sales the same firms have also been allocated to their primary industry of output. Further details of this and the other characteristics of this group of firms are described by Dunning and Pearce (1985). The focus of attention in the current exercise is on firms in the chemicals and electrical equipment industries. These are the industries in which the greatest volume of science-related technological activity takes place, and firms in these industries are granted large numbers of patents accordingly. Of the 729 largest firms patenting in the US (leaving aside the 63 for which no record of patenting could be traced), just under a quarter are in the relevant industries; 101 companies in chemicals and pharmaceuticals, and 78 in electrical and computer equipment. Between them, these 179 companies accounted for nearly a half of all US patents granted to the world's largest firms during the period from 1969 to 1986.

The second dimension by which the patent data are organized is that they are grouped into common types of technological activity. This

Table 11.1   The major categories of patenting activity by firms in the chemicals and pharmaceuticals and the electrical and computer equipment industries

Sector	Chemicals and pharmaceuticals	Electrical and computer equipment
Food	x	
Inorganic chemicals	x	
Agricultural chemicals	x	
Chemical processes	x	x
Bleaching and dyeing	x	
Organic chemicals	x	x
Pharmaceuticals	x	
Metallurgical processes	x	x
Metal products	x	x
Chemical equipment	x	x
Metalworking equipment	x	x
Assembly equipment	x	x
Mining equipment		
Specialized machinery	x	x
General machinery	x	x
Power plants		
Nuclear systems		
Telecommunications		x
Image and sound equipment		x
Electrical systems		x
General electrical equipment	x	x
Semiconductors		x
Office equipment		x
Motor vehicles		
Aircraft		
Other transport equipment		
Textiles		
Rubber and plastic	x	
Non-metallic mineral products	x	x
Coal and petroleum products	x	
Photographic instruments	x	x
Other instruments	x	x
Others		

sectoral allocation of patents derives from the US patent class system, each patent having been classified by examiners at the US Patent Office. Similar patent classes or parts of classes that all relate to a certain underlying kind of technological activity are brought together. To illustrate, patents belonging to some of the subclasses that fall within US patent class 62, refrigeration, have been assigned to the broader category chemical processes, while those that fall under other subclasses within refrigeration have been allocated to general electrical equipment. In all, patents have been placed under one of 33 of these broader types of technological activity as listed in Table 11.1. Not all these categories of activity are important for firms in the chemicals and pharmaceuticals or the electrical and computer equipment industries. Due to the problems created by small numbers of patents, explained further below, the analysis is restricted to sectors in which over 500 US patents were granted to firms in the industry in question between 1969 and 1986. As shown in Table 11.1, this involves 20 sectors of technological activity in the chemicals and pharmaceuticals industry and 18 sectors in the electrical and computer equipment industry.

One advantage of using US patent data is that the US is the single largest national market, and it is therefore common for companies to patent there at around the same time or immediately after taking out a patent in the country of invention (Soete and Wyatt, 1983; Pavitt, 1988). The measure is improved by virtue of the fact that patents extended to the US by non-US firms are more likely to represent significant innovations than do purely domestic patents (Basberg, 1987). Indeed the reliability of this indicator is reinforced by considering only the largest firms, since larger firms follow stricter screening procedures than do smaller firms or individual inventors prior to embarking upon patent applications (Schmookler, 1966). Firms originating from different countries must also all meet the requirements of the official US patent assessment criteria; this helps to provide a common standard for comparison.

It is well known that there are interindustry differences in the propensity to patent (Scherer, 1983), intersectoral differences in the likelihood of patenting from various types of technological activity, and international differences in that US-based firms are more likely to patent in the US than are non-US firms. Interindustry variation in the propensity to patent does not present a problem here, as the analysis is conducted through drawing comparisons between firms in the same industry and not between firms from different industries. Intersectoral and interfirm differences in the propensity to patent are also controlled for in the form of the index that is constructed from the data. The index employed depicts the revealed technological advantage (RTA) of each firm with

respect to others in the same industry across a spectrum of types of
technological activity. A similar index has previously been used in
intercountry comparisons (Soete, 1987; Cantwell, 1989), and has not
often been applied as here to intraindustry, interfirm comparisons (but
see Patel and Pavitt, 1989, 1991, and Pavitt and Patel, 1990, for a related
method).

The RTA of a firm in a particular sector of technological activity is
given by the firm's share in that sector of US patents granted to companies
in the same industry, relative to the firm's overall share of all US patents
assigned to firms in the industry in question. Denoting as P_{ij} the number
of US patents granted in sector or activity i to firm j in a particular
industry, then the RTA index is defined as follows:

$$RTA_{ij} = (P_{ij} / \Sigma_j P_{ij}) / (\Sigma_i P_{ij} / \Sigma_{ij} P_{ij})$$

The index varies around unity, such that values greater than one suggest
that a firm is comparatively advantaged in the activity in question relative
to other firms in the same industry, while values less than one are
indicative of a position of comparative disadvantage. Table 11.2 shows
the values of the index calculated for the German company Bayer, which
was granted more US patents than any other firm in the chemical and
pharmaceutical industry between 1969 and 1986. The index is displayed
for the 20 sectors of technological activity over which the analysis is
organized for firms in the chemical industry. Relative to its major
international rivals, Bayer's greatest technological strengths lay in the
fields of bleaching and dyeing, assembly and material handling equipment, and photographic instruments. Bayer held a substantial share of
the patents granted to chemical firms across most fields of activity.
However, the figures in Table 11.2 illustrate (for example) that in 1977–
86 Bayer's share of patenting in bleaching and dyeing processes was 1.39
times its share of all patenting.

By examining relative shares rather than absolute numbers of patents,
the RTA index is normalized for intersectoral differences in the
propensity to patent (in the numerator), and for similar international
interfirm differences (in the denominator). Of course, there may still be
intersectoral variation in interfirm differences in the propensity to patent;
for instance, a company may be more likely to patent than its rivals in
most fields of activity, but in one particular sector it adopts a more
cautious approach than other firms. However, given that patenting
decisions are usually centrally controlled within firms for strategic
reasons (Etemad and Séguin Delude, 1985), it seems reasonable to
assume that this kind of intrafirm variance is systematically lower than the

Table 11.2 The RTA index for Bayer, relative to the other leading firms in the international chemicals and pharmaceuticals industry

Sector	1969–76	1977–86
Food	0.31	0.33
Inorganic chemicals	0.79	0.37
Agricultural chemicals	0.85	1.17
Chemical processes	0.57	0.66
Bleaching and dyeing	1.54	1.39
Organic chemicals	0.98	1.23
Pharmaceuticals	0.95	0.91
Metallurgical processes	0.23	0.31
Metal products	0.51	0.51
Chemical equipment	0.80	0.70
Metalworking equipment	0.48	0.45
Assembly equipment	1.66	1.85
Specialized machinery	0.60	0.77
General machinery	0.34	0.50
General electrical equipment	0.33	0.27
Rubber and plastic	0.75	1.37
Non-metallic mineral products	0.45	0.56
Coal and petroleum products	0.34	0.31
Photographic instruments	5.30	2.58
Other instruments	1.03	0.74

Source: US patent database held at the University of Reading, and compiled with the assistance of the US Patent Office.

more general intersectoral differences in the propensity to patent that run across firms. It can then be hypothesized that on relatively large numbers the propensity to patent of a given firm in any sector cannot be expected to have any systematic bias as compared to that firm's notional average propensity to patent and the notional average propensity to patent of all firms in that sector.

The assumption that the propensity to patent varies more systematically between firms and between sectors than within them relies on having a large number of patent counts. In addition, the use of the RTA index in linear regression analysis (which is explained in the next section) requires that the cross-sectoral RTA distributions for each firm are approximately normal. This again depends upon having a sufficient number of observations. In a comparable analysis of an RTA index (Cantwell, 1991a) it has been shown that with a distribution across 30 or so sectors of activity a minimum count of about 1000 patents is in general needed to construct an index that roughly conforms to a normal distribution. For this reason the regression analysis described below has been confined to the ten firms granted the largest numbers of US patents in each of the industries concerned. All these companies have at least 1000 patents within any individual period under examination, and they were granted at least 3500 patents during the 1969–86 period as a whole.

11.3 THE STATISTICAL METHODOLOGY

The RTA index described above measures the technological special-ization of firms across activities relative to other companies in the same industry. To examine changes in specialization over time, the RTA distribution for each firm is calculated for 1969–77 and 1978–86, as illustrated for Bayer in Table 11.2. In comparing these bivariate distributions for each firm the relevant statistical methodology is the Galtonian regression model. The application of this approach to economic problems was pioneered by Peter Hart and his colleagues, in the context of work on the size distribution of firms (Hart and Prais, 1956) and income distribution (Hart, 1976; Creedy, 1985). More recently, it has been applied to the analysis of cross-sectoral distributions of techno-logical activity of the kind described here, and to similar cross-country distributions (Cantwell, 1991a; 1991c). In this instance the correlation between the sectoral distribution of the RTA index at time t (1978–86) and at the earlier time $t-1$ (1969–77) is estimated through a simple cross-section regression of the form:

$$RTA_{it} = \alpha + \beta RTA_{it-1} + \varepsilon_{it} \qquad (11.1)$$

This is estimated for a particular firm in a chosen industry, where the subscript refers to the sector of technological activity i at time t. The standard assumption of this analysis is that the regression is linear and the residual ε_{it} is independent of RTA_{it-1}. This is valid if the cross-sectoral index approximately conforms to a bivariate normal distribution, which requirement is met if the index is constructed from an adequate number of patent counts as outlined above. The estimated regression line will pass through the point of means.

When $\beta=1$ the ranking of sectors on average remains unchanged (advantaged sectors of activity remain advantaged, while disadvantaged sectors remain disadvantaged), and they retain the same proportional position (sectors in which the firm has an advantage do not become any more advantaged, nor does the firm become any more disadvantaged in sectors in which it is already disadvantaged). Where $\beta > 1$ there is a proportional shift in which in its existing fields of advantage the firm tends to become still more advantaged, while in disavantaged sectors it is increasingly disadvantaged.

Where $\beta < 1$ the firm improves its position in disadvantaged sectors, but in advantaged fields it tends to slip back. This is what is termed 'regression towards the mean' (Galton, 1889, cited in Hart, 1976). Where this is a true representation of a perfect correlation with $0 < \beta < 1$ then the ranking of sectors is unchanged, but they come closer to one another. The magnitude of $(1-\beta)$ therefore measures the size of what is here called the 'regression effect', and the strength of this effect is estimated by $(1-\hat{\beta})$.

When $\beta < 0$ (the regression effect exceeds unity) the very ranking of sectors is reversed, contrary to the prediction that the pattern of corporate technological competence, and hence specialization, tends to persist over time. The expectation that $\hat{\beta} > 0$, such that the RTA index is positively correlated across two points in time, can be readily tested for each firm.

The test of whether β is significantly greater than zero is a test of the proposition that patterns of corporate technological specialization tend to persist over the period. However, this proposition also still allows for such specialization to evolve gradually over time, and where specialization tends to broaden out the rate at which it is changing can be measured by the size of the regression effect, estimated by $(1-\hat{\beta})$. A test of whether this kind of change in specialization is significant during the period in question is the test that $(1-\hat{\beta})$ is greater than zero, or in other words, the test of whether $\hat{\beta}$ is significantly less than one. This is quite a strict test of the significance of the regression effect. It implies that at the accepted level of significance the confidence interval that surrounds the point estimate of $\hat{\beta}$ falls entirely below unity. Yet a point estimate of $\hat{\beta}$ that lies some way below one (say, an estimate of 0.9 or lower) may be indicative of some positive regression effect, even if the standard error of the coefficient estimate is too large for the relevant t-test to be satisfied.

A positive regression effect is a necessary but not sufficient condition for the technological specialization of the firm to broaden out over time. To appreciate that the regression effect is not the only consideration in this respect, note that a firm's degree of technological specialization can be measured by the variance of its RTA index, which shows the extent of dispersion of the distribution around the mean. The procedure for estimating changes in the variance of a distribution over time follows from Hart (1976). Taking equation (11.1) above, if the variance of the RTA index at time t is denoted by σ_t^2 then:

$$\sigma_t^2 = \beta^2\sigma_{t-1}^2 + \sigma_\varepsilon^2 \qquad (11.2)$$

Now the square of the correlation coefficient (ρ^2) is given by:

$$\rho^2 = 1 - (\sigma_\varepsilon^2/\sigma_t^2) = (\sigma_t^2 - \sigma_\varepsilon^2)(1/\sigma_t^2) \qquad (11.3)$$

Combining equations (11.2) and (11.3) it follows that:

$$\sigma_t^2 - \sigma_\varepsilon^2 = \beta^2\sigma_{t-1}^2 = \rho^2\sigma_t^2 \qquad (11.4)$$

Equation (11.4) may be rewritten to show the relationship between the variance of the two distributions as follows:

$$\sigma_t^2/\sigma_{t-1}^2 = \beta^2/\rho^2 \qquad (11.5)$$

Hence the degree of technological specialization rises where $\beta^2>\rho^2$, and it falls where $\beta^2<\rho^2$. A high variance indicates a high or narrow degree of specialization, while a low variance shows that the firm has a broad range of technologically advantaged activities or a low degree of specialization. Using the estimated regression values, where R is the estimate of ρ, and for convenience of exposition supposing that $\hat{\beta}$ and R are both positive, the extent of specialization as measured by the estimated variance of the RTA index rises where $(\hat{\beta}/R)>1$, and it falls where $(\hat{\beta}/R)<1$. As a special case the estimated variance increases where the measured regression effect is negative ($\hat{\beta}>1$), since the maximum value of R is unity.

The estimate of the correlation coefficient, R, is a measure of the mobility of activities up and down the RTA distribution. A high value of R indicates that the relative importance of sectors of activity to the firm in question is little changed, while a low value indicates that specialization in some activities is moving closer together and others further apart, quite likely to the extent that the ranking of sectors changes. The magnitude of $(1-R)$ thus measures what is here described as the 'mobility effect'. It may be that, even where the regression effect is not significant according to the t-test of whether $\hat{\beta}$ falls below one, it is still strong enough to create a fall or a broadening out in the degree of technological specialization – that is, the condition $(\hat{\beta}/R)<1$ may still hold.

The test of the proposition that the degree of technological specialization of firms has tended to broaden out is thus provided by assessing the expectation that for most firms the regression results are likely to yield estimates such that $(\hat{\beta}/R)<1$. For this condition to be met for any firm it is necessary that the estimated regression effect is positive, since the maximum value of R is one. However, a positive estimated regression effect is not sufficient to ensure $(\hat{\beta}/R)<1$. To ensure $(\hat{\beta}/R)<1$ the estimated regression effect must outweigh the measured mobility effect; that is, $(1-\hat{\beta})>(1-R)$ and so $(\hat{\beta}/R)<1$. Even where the regression effect is not very strong, if it exceeds the size of the mobility effect the degree of technological specialization of the firm falls or becomes broader.

Another indicator that can be derived from the regression results relates the composition of technological specialization of the firm to its overall rate of innovation as measured by the rate of growth of its technological activity. The linkage is provided by the extent to which a firm is represented in the sectors of fastest (or slowest) growing technological activity. For any firm j in a selected industry, denote its share of patents associated with activity i by p_{ij}, its share of all patents granted to firms in its industry by a_j, and the mean value of its RTA index by M_j. That is, supposing there are altogether n sectors of technological activity:

$$\text{RTA}_{ij} = p_{ij}/a_j$$

$$M_j = \Sigma_i p_{ij}/na_j$$

The ratio of the mean value of RTA in an earlier period $t-1$ to that in the next period t is then given by:

$$M_{jt-1}/M_{jt} = (a_{jt}/a_{jt-1})/(\Sigma_i p_{ijt}/\Sigma_i p_{ijt-1}) \tag{11.6}$$

Now since the regression equation (11.1) must pass through the point of means it is also known that:

$$M_{jt} = \hat{\alpha} + \hat{\beta}M_{jt-1} \tag{11.7}$$

This may be rewritten:

$$M_{jt-1}/M_{jt} = (M_{jt} - \hat{\alpha})/(\hat{\beta}M_{jt}) \tag{11.8}$$

From equations (11.6) and (11.8) it follows that the higher is $(M_{jt} - \hat{\alpha})/\hat{\beta} M_{jt}$ the faster is the rise (or the slower is the decrease) in the firm's share of all patents (a_j) compared with its average share across sectors of activity at the chosen level of disaggregation $(\Sigma_i p_{ij}/n)$. It can be shown that this happens *either* because the firm in question is particularly advantaged in the fastest growing sectors of technological activity (it has a favourable pattern of specialization), *or* because of a strong mobility effect (a shift in the structure of sectoral shares and thus in the cross-sectoral pattern of RTA). At a country level in recent years Japan has had a favourable pattern of technological specialization in this sense, and this has contributed towards her faster overall rate of innovation by comparison with other industrialized countries (Cantwell, 1991a).

11.4   THE RESULTS

The results of the company regressions of the RTA index in 1978–86 on 1969–77 are reported in Tables 11.3 and 11.4 for the chemical and pharmaceutical and the electrical and computer equipment industries respectively. As explained above, for the purposes of these regressions the RTA distributions span 20 sectors of technological activity for firms in the chemicals and pharmaceuticals industry, and cover 18 sectors in the case of companies in the electrical and computer equipment industry.

Table 11.3   *The results of the company regressions of the RTA index in 1978–86 on the index in 1969–77, for firms in the chemicals and pharmaceuticals industry*

	$\hat{\alpha}$	$\hat{\beta}$	$t_{\beta 0}$	$t_{\beta 1}$	R
1. Bayer	0.408	0.470	7.24^b	-8.17^b	0.863
2. Dow Chemical	0.038	0.798	5.09^b	-1.29	0.768
3. Ciba-Geigy	-0.230	1.534	13.43^b	4.67^b	0.954
4. Hoechst	0.406	0.706	6.26^b	-2.61^a	0.828
5. BASF	0.253	0.706	5.15^b	-2.14^a	0.772
6. Monsanto	-0.584	1.303	7.52^b	1.75	0.871
7. ICI	0.559	0.455	2.38^a	-2.85^a	0.489
8. Union Carbide	0.273	0.851	10.74^b	-1.88	0.930
9. Fuji Photo Film	0.198	0.704	21.88^b	-9.20^b	0.982
10. 3M	-0.043	1.073	9.10^b	0.62	0.906

Notes:
[a]   Denotes $\hat{\beta}$ significantly different from zero or one at the 5% level
[b]   Denotes $\hat{\beta}$ significantly different from zero or one at the 1% level
Number of observations = 20.

The hypothesis that β is significantly greater than zero can be accepted for all 20 firms, against the alternative that the pattern of technological specialization of firms is not path dependent but is random ($\beta = 0$). The hypothesis is accepted at the 1 per cent level of significance for 18 firms,

Table 11.4   The results of the company regressions of the RTA index in 1978–86 on the index in 1969–77, for firms in the electrical and computer equipment industry

	$\hat{\alpha}$	$\hat{\beta}$	$t_{\beta 0}$	$t_{\beta 1}$	R
1. General Electric	−0.381	1.437	20.74[b]	6.31[b]	0.982
2. IBM	0.056	0.914	9.22[b]	−0.87	0.917
3. Westinghouse Electric	−0.044	1.111	7.11[b]	0.71	0.871
4. Hitachi	0.593	0.448	2.73[a]	−3.36[b]	0.564
5. Siemens	0.229	0.729	5.59[b]	−20.08	0.813
6. Xerox	0.039	0.938	20.75[b]	−1.37	0.982
7. Toshiba	0.290	0.660	3.14[b]	−1.62	0.617
8. Matsushita Electric Industries	0.236	0.784	5.94[b]	−1.64	0.830
9. Honeywell	0.153	0.835	9.47[b]	−1.87	0.921
10. Motorola	0.039	0.786	6.02[b]	−1.64	0.833

Notes:
[a]   Denotes $\hat{\beta}$ significantly different from zero or one at the 5% level
[b]   Denotes $\hat{\beta}$ significantly different from zero or one at the 1% level
Number of observations = 18.

and at the 5 per cent level for the remaining two, ICI and Hitachi. As explained above, in each industry the firms listed in Tables 11.3 and 11.4 are the ten largest in terms of the total number of US patents granted over the 1969–86 period as a whole, and they appear in descending order of size measured in this way.

While the test of the persistence of patterns of corporate specialization yields equally affirmative results in both industries, a difference between industries emerges when testing the strength of the regression effect. At the 5 per cent level of significance or above, the regression effect is estimated to be significant – that is, β is significantly less than one – for five companies in the chemical and pharmaceutical industry, but for only one company in electrical and computer equipment. According to this test, the regression effect is strongest in the chemicals case for Bayer and Fuji Photo Film, but it is also significant for Hoechst, BASF and ICI; while in electrical equipment it is only significant for Hitachi, which firm has the highest estimated mobility effect of any of the leading ten electrical and computer equipment producers. Taken together, the results of this test suggest that the composition of technological specialization has changed more for chemical firms than it has for electrical firms between the early 1970s and early 1980s.

However, as already outlined, this is not a good test of the proposition that the degree of corporate technological specialization has tended to become broader. The degree of specialization of a firm is measured as falling or broadening out where $(\hat{\beta}/R)<1$, or in other words, where the estimated regression effect outweighs the size of the equivalent indicator of the mobility effect. The results of this test are to be found in Tables 11.5 and 11.6 for the two industries respectively. In measuring trends in the breadth of specialization the results are again quite similar for the two industries; indeed, a trend towards broader technological specialization is even more evident in the electrical equipment industry than it is in chemicals. This trend is observed for six firms in chemicals and pharmaceuticals, and as many as seven companies in the electrical industry; overall, the condition $(\hat{\beta}/R)<1$ holds for 13 firms out of 20. Thus it seems reasonable to claim that there has been a general trend towards broader patterns of technological specialization at the corporate level, although the trend is not an overwhelming one.

Table 11.5   *Technological specialization indicators derived from the regression analysis for firms in the chemicals and pharmaceuticals industry*

		$\hat{\beta}/R$	$(1-R)$	$(M_t-\hat{\alpha})/M_t\hat{\beta}$
1.	Bayer	0.545	0.137	1.105
2.	Dow Chemical	1.039	0.232	1.196
3.	Ciba-Geigy	1.609	0.047	0.876
4.	Hoechst	0.853	0.172	0.879
5.	BASF	0.915	0.228	1.001
6.	Monsanto	1.496	0.129	1.174
7.	ICI	0.931	0.511	1.070
8.	Union Carbide	0.915	0.070	0.973
9.	Fuji Photo Film	0.717	0.018	1.191
10.	3M	1.184	0.094	0.963

The decomposition of this trend is worth noting. In the reported regressions the mobility effect appears to have been quite weak, at least as judged in this context by comparison with the estimated magnitude of the regression effect. Consequently, a significant estimated regression effect as defined above proved to be sufficient here for the measurement

Table 11.6   Technological specialization indicators derived from the
regression analysis for firms in the electrical and computer
industry

		$\hat{\beta}/R$	$(1-R)$	$(M_t-\hat{\alpha})/M_t\hat{\beta}$
1.	General Electric	1.463	0.018	0.905
2.	IBM	0.996	0.083	1.025
3.	Westinghouse Electric	1.275	0.129	0.943
4.	Hitachi	0.795	0.436	0.969
5.	Siemens	0.896	0.187	0.998
6.	Xerox	0.955	0.018	1.035
7.	Toshiba	1.070	0.383	1.060
8.	Matsushita Electric Industries	0.945	0.171	0.986
9.	Honeywell	0.906	0.079	0.963
10.	Motorola	0.944	0.167	1.202

of a broader degree of technological specialization, although this
consideration was of greater weight in the chemicals industry. The six
chemical firms for which $(\hat{\beta}/R)<1$ include the five companies for which
the estimated regression effect was significant, and other than those, just
Union Carbide. By contrast, of the equivalent seven electrical and
computer equipment producers, only Hitachi recorded an apparently
significant regression effect, but a further six firms – IBM, Siemens,
Xerox, Matsushita Electric Industries, Honeywell and Motorola – still
had an estimated regression effect that was strong enough to outweigh the
comparable measure of the mobility effect.

Although overall the estimated mobility effect was weak it clearly had
some impact for ICI and Hitachi, and it is necessary to take account of
such variations across firms in the magnitude of the mobility effect when
examining the indicator that relates the composition of corporate
technological specialization to overall innovative performance. In the
chemical and pharmaceutical industry the value of $(M_t-\hat{\alpha})/M_t\ \hat{\beta}$ was
highest for Dow Chemical and Fuji Photo Film. However, of these two
companies the mobility effect as estimated by $(1-R)$ was considerably
higher for Dow Chemical, and so of the two it seems safer to infer a
favourable pattern of technological specialization geared towards the
faster-growing fields of activity in the case of Fuji Photo Film. The
indicator $(M_t-\hat{\alpha})/M_t\ \hat{\beta}$ is more difficult to interpret among firms in the
electrical equipment industry. It is highest for Motorola and Toshiba, but

both these firms apparently experienced quite a high mobility effect by comparison with other companies in the same industry.

11.5 CONCLUSIONS

The results of this chapter are consistent with the view that the technological competence of firms tends to persist over time, where the distinctiveness of that competence is reflected in the specific structure of corporate technological specialization. They also suggest that the pattern of such competence gradually evolves, as would be expected to be the outcome of a process of firm-specific learning. The pace at which such evolutionary change has been taking place in recent years seems to have been greater in the chemical and pharmaceutical industry than it has in the electrical and computer equipment industry. One possible explanation of this finding is that technological opportunities have generally been greater in recent times in electrical and electronic-related fields, which has created a stronger incentive for chemical firms than electrical firms to broaden the spectrum of their technological activity beyond their areas of traditional focus.

However, the increase in technological interrelatedness between different types of activity has affected the largest firms in both industries. This has helped to ensure that the degree of technological specialization at a corporate level has tended to become broader among companies in the electrical and computer equipment industry as well as in chemicals. In neither industry have changes in the actual composition of technological specialization (the mobility effect) been strong enough to disturb the gradual trend towards a broader degree of corporate specialization. Yet this trend has not been universal, and exceptions are to be expected – where, for example, a company has specialized in a fairly fast-growing field of activity which becomes more isolated from some previously complementary activity and which has few potential spillover benefits in other areas, the firm may well adopt a strategy of increased specialization, at least in the first instance. A greater isolation of certain fields may itself be the consequence of a competitive process whereby the once complementary types of activity begin to develop mainly through new and better linkages with formerly separate branches of technology which are being used by other appropriately specialized firms as the basis for new and wider systems.

It is also of interest that the general broadening of corporate technological specialization runs counter to the reverse trend observed among countries over the same period (Cantwell, 1991a). Most of the major industrialized countries (13 out of 16) became more highly or narrowly specialized in their technological activity between the 1960s and the early 1980s. The trend towards greater locational specialization can be attributed to increased international competition (the rise in international trade as well as production), the expansion of the international division of labour within multinationals as they have reorganized their operations to meet this objective, and the increased significance of economies of agglomeration in technologically sophisticated activities. The combination of these trends implies that the management of the increased linkages between different types of technological activity is more and more the responsibility of large international firms.

REFERENCES

Basberg, B.L. (1987): 'Patents and the measurement of technological change: a survey of the literature', *Research Policy*, **16**, 131–41.

Cantwell, J.A. (1989): *Technological Innovation and Multinational Corporations* (Oxford: Basil Blackwell).

—— (1991a): 'Historical trends in international patterns of technological innovation', in J. Foreman-Peck (ed.), *New Perspectives on the Late Victorian Economy: Essays in Quantitative British Economic History, 1860–1914* (Cambridge: Cambridge University Press).

—— (1991b): 'The theory of technological competence and its application to international production', in D.G. McFetridge (ed.), *Foreign Investment, Technology and Economic Growth* (Calgary: University of Calgary Press).

—— (1991c): 'The international agglomeration of R&D', in M.C. Casson (ed.), *Global Research Strategy and International Competitiveness* (Oxford: Basil Blackwell).

Creedy, J. (1985): *Dynamics of Income Distribution* (Oxford: Basil Blackwell).

Dunning, J.H. and R.D. Pearce (1985): *The World's Largest Industrial Enterprises, 1962–1983* (Aldershot: Gower).

Etemad, H. and L. Séguin Delude (1985): 'The development of technology in MNEs: a cross-country and industry study', paper presented at the Round Table on International Technical Transfers in Advanced Countries: Multinational Firms and National Policies, University of Paris, Dauphine, September.

Hart, P.E. (1976): 'The dynamics of earnings, 1963–1973', *Economic Journal*, **86**, 541–65.

—— and S.J. Prais (1956): 'The analysis of business concentration: a statistical approach', *Journal of the Royal Statistical Society*, Series A, **119**, 150–81.

Nelson, R.R. (1991): 'Why do firms differ, and how does it matter?', *Strategic Management Journal*, **12**, 61–74.

Patel, P. and K.L.R. Pavitt (1989): 'A comparison of technological activities in West Germany and the United Kingdom', *National Westminister Bank Quarterly Review*, May, 27–42.

—— (1991): 'Europe's technological performance', in C. Freeman, M. Sharp and

W. Walker (eds.), *Technology and the Future of Europe: Global Competition and the Environment in the 1990s* (London: Frances Pinter).

Pavitt, K.L.R. (1988): 'Uses and abuses of patent statistics', in A. van Raan (ed.), *Handbook of Quantitative Studies of Science Policy* (Amsterdam: North-Holland).

Pavitt, K.L.R., and P. Patel (1990): 'Sources and directions of technological accumulation in France: a statistical comparison with FR Germany and the UK', *Technology Analysis and Strategic Management*, 2, 3–26.

Scherer, F.M. (1983): 'The propensity to patent', *International Journal of Industrial Organisation*, 1, 107–28.

Schmookler, J. (1966): *Invention and Economic Growth* (Cambridge, MA: Harvard University Press).

Soete, L.L.G. (1987): 'The impact of technological innovation on international trade patterns: the evidence reconsidered', *Research Policy*, 16, 101–30.

—— and S.M.E. Wyatt (1983): 'The use of foreign patenting as an internationally comparable science and technology output indicator', *Scientometrics*, 5, 31–54.

Index

Printed and bound by CPI Group (UK) Ltd, Croydon, CR0 4YY

23/04/2025

14661006-0005